CW00738849

Blood on the Marias

Blood on the Marias

The Baker Massacre

Paul R. Wylie

University of Oklahoma Press : Norman

Publication of this book is made possible by the generosity of Edith Kinney Gaylord.

Library of Congress Cataloging-in-Publication Data

Names: Wylie, Paul R., 1936– author.
Title: Blood on the Marias : the Baker Massacre / Paul R. Wylie.
Other titles: Baker Massacre
Description: Norman, OK : University of Oklahoma Press, [2016] | Includes bibliographical references and index.
Identifiers: LCCN 2015025347 | ISBN 9780806151571 (hardcover : alk. paper)
Subjects: LCSH: Marias Massacre, Mont., 1870. | Piegan Indians—Wars. | Piegan Indians—Government relations. | Baker, Eugene M. | Indians of North America—Wars—Montana. | Indians, Treatment of—Montana—History. | Montana—History—19th century.
Classification: LCC E83.866 .W95 2016 | DDC 978.6/02—dc23
LC record available at http://lccn.loc.gov/2015025347

The paper in this book meets the guidelines for permanence and durability of the Committee on Production Guidelines for Book Longevity of the Council on Library Resources, Inc. ∞

2 3 4 5 6 7 8 9 10

Contents

Illustrations

FIGURES

MAPS

Preface

On January 23, for a few years now, some faculty members and students from the Blackfeet Community College have gathered annually on the bluffs overlooking a spot on the Marias River in Montana known as the Big Bend. They come mostly from Browning on the Blackfeet Reservation in northwest Montana, just on the east side of Glacier National Park. Most of them are members of the historic Piegan tribe, now known as the Blackfeet. Observers might wonder what would bring this group sixty-five miles away from the reservation in the middle of winter, when the weather can sometimes be extremely cold and likely windy—particularly atop the bluffs overlooking the Marias. But nothing could be colder than January 23, 1870, when the temperatures were forty degrees below zero and the 2nd Cavalry under the command of an inebriated Major Eugene Baker arrived at the same location. They were in search of the renegade camp of Mountain Chief when they started firing through the icy air at the sleeping camp of Chief Heavy Runner.

As the group gathers in a circle to the sound of Indian drumming and singing, a twenty-one-shot salute is fired in honor of the 217 Piegan Indians, many of them women and children, who were massacred on that day in 1870. The 217 stones placed in the circle represent the count by the Indians, not the imprecise count of only 173 dead bodies made by the army, which refused to budge from that number even when evidence of more Indians killed came to its attention. To make the story more horrible, the village had smallpox.

Commemoration of Baker Massacre, January 23, 2008

Members of the Blackfeet tribe from Blackfeet Community College, some sixty-five miles away in Browning, Montana, leave the ceremonial site of the annual commemoration of the Baker Massacre. The site is near the massacre location, which lies beneath the bluffs along the Marias River. Courtesy Harry Palmer.

I became interested in this story in 2007, after I completed my work on a biography of the famous Irish patriot Thomas Francis Meagher, published by the University of Oklahoma Press as *The Irish General*. Meagher was a brigadier general in the Civil War who later served as acting governor of the new Montana Territory and died mysteriously in 1867. One of his first duties when he came to Montana in 1865 was to attend a treaty negotiation with the Blackfeet Indians to establish new boundaries for the Blackfeet Nation of tribes, including the historically prominent Piegans.

Looking for another topic for a book, I soon came upon scant information on the massacre and started researching for sources that would help in understanding the brutal Baker Massacre, as it came to be known. I read James Welch's *Fools Crow* and then followed it up by reading his *Killing Custer*. As a Blackfeet tribal

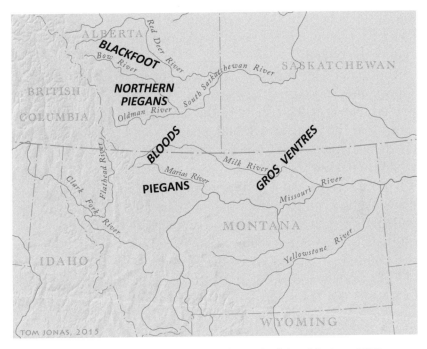

General location of the tribes of the Blackfeet Nation, 1870

This map shows the general locations of the five tribes of the Blackfeet Nation in about 1869–1870, using what are believed to be the most commonly accepted names. Because the tribes roamed, the locations could differ from year to year. Maps by Paul R. Wylie and Tom Jonas, copyright © 2016 by Paul R. Wylie. All rights reserved.

member, Welch had asked, "Why is the Massacre on the Marias known to so few people?"[1] He wondered, as I have, how to compare this incident with others more famous, such as George Armstrong Custer's battle at the Little Bighorn in 1876, where 263 white men and up to 100 Indians died. While both attacks had high fatalities, the event on the Little Bighorn is known to anyone with even the slightest interest in western history, while the Baker Massacre is known to relatively few and is somewhat obscure even to historians. My research led me to files in the Glenbow Archives assembled by the late Stan Gibson, an English professor at the University of Calgary. Stan had spent a good many years exploring the history of the massacre, and in his correspondence I found this statement: "This event, for a variety of reasons, has been incredibly obscure in histories of the West. In fact, by far the majority of our historians have no mention whatever of the tragedy."

The Baker Massacre did not start out in obscurity. In 1870, shortly after it occurred, it was nationally known and nationally reviled. News of the cruelty of the killings and the fact that the camp that the army struck had smallpox had reached the eastern newspapers. Chief among them was the *New York Times*, which remarked that "the slaughter of the Piegans in Montana is a more serious and a more shocking affair than the sacking of Black Kettle's camp on the Washita." The *Times* editors were appalled. Its March 30, 1870, edition noted that even Baker's "rude estimate admits of the killing of no less than fifty-three women and children." What incensed the *Times* most was Baker's report of "140 women and children captured and released." "Released to what?" the *Times* asked, and then answered: "To starvation and freezing to death."[2]

All historical nineteenth-century conflicts in the Montana Territory between the Indians and the U.S. Army have been overshadowed by Custer's battle on the Little Bighorn in 1876, which has spawned a huge number of books, most of which are still regularly reissued today. Perhaps that is because the site was preserved early on to mark the graves of U.S. soldiers and later became a national monument to which thousands flock every year.

Today, nearly 150 years after the Baker Massacre on the Marias, no monument or sign marks the exact location, with not even a passable road to get there. No physical element keeps it in people's minds. Consequently no detailed explanations of what happened there have been published. I expect that I know approximately where the massacre occurred, and certainly others do too. Yet I can't pinpoint it exactly. Certainly it is somewhere close to where the annual commemoration is held by the Blackfeet Community College. I understand it is a sacred place to the Blackfeet, and perhaps it is best not to go there regularly or stay long. That may explain why the nearest sign is a highway marker on Highway 2, around the town of Dunkirk, east of Shelby. The marker is probably some five miles from the Marias River, which can be reached via a two-track dirt road. While there has been discussion about seeking national recognition for the massacre site, doing so would open to the public what is hallowed ground for the Blackfeet.

The massacre on the Marias on January 23, 1870, did not occur spontaneously due to any sudden breakdown in relations between the Indians and the whites. It was the result of a six-decade history of contact between the Piegans and the whites who had gradually entered their traditional hunting territory. The whites came as trappers, fur traders, gold miners, and settlers and then as cavalrymen sent to protect the settlers from the Indians. Along the way, many alternatives failed, including treaties in 1851, 1855, 1865, and 1868 (a treaty that is hardly known in history).

This book takes a deep look at the major encounters between the Piegan tribe and the U.S. government, white settlers, and the U.S. Army over the years and in particular examines the role that the whiskey traders played in bringing about the massacre.

It also looks at the involvement of some major players in the detailed planning, execution, and cover-up of the event, in particular Eugene M. Baker, the commander of the army troops who had received brevet promotions to lieutenant colonel and colonel, but whose regular army grade was major (as used here), and Regis de Trobriand, the military commander in the Montana Territory, whose regular army grade was colonel even though he had received brevet promotions to lieutenant general.[3] The story is told in as few pages as possible, but in enough detail that the reader will understand how and why the events of the early and mid-nineteenth century set the stage for this brutal killing of a band of Piegan Indians.

Over my now lengthening years, my own eyes have witnessed some terrible things. These have been sad personal events, but nothing makes me sadder than to think about the killings of the innocent Indian people that January 23 on the Marias River in 1870.

Blood on the Marias

Prologue

A s the sun came up, the cold air full of ice crystals created a haze over the snowy winter landscape on the Marias. Immediately below the high, ravine-broken bluffs to the south stood a scattered grouping of Indian teepees with cut underbrush stacked around their bases for protection from the snow and wind, settled in among the stark and leafless cottonwoods, aspens, and willows on the river bottom. Most of them were on the south side of the frozen river, but some were to the north. In the early morning, Chief Heavy Runner and his tribe of Piegans, mainly women and children and old men, were still in their lodges; it was not their custom to rise early. Many of them were sick with smallpox, which was spreading through the band. The able-bodied men were away on a buffalo hunt. Even in the numbing below-zero weather they needed the meat for survival and the buffalo robes with their long winter fur to trade for white goods—including whiskey.

As cold as it was, and as remote as his camp was, Heavy Runner knew that the U.S. Army might be coming after the band of Mountain Chief, seeking revenge for the murder of Malcolm Clarke and the other crimes of the band's young braves. Heavy Runner did not fear the army. Only three weeks before he had gone to the agency on the Teton with all the other chiefs to meet General Alfred Sully. The whiskey traders had arrived in the Piegan country just before, and the chiefs who were not too inebriated to meet with General Sully were told that they would be protected if they brought in the murderers—dead or alive.

Although Heavy Runner promised to do this, not even Sully expected that they would. Because Heavy Runner had been peaceful, Sully gave him a document that would protect him from the soldiers—Heavy Runner did not know how. But he did know that the army would be after Mountain Chief, who had moved his band down the Marias the day before when the fur traders warned that the army was coming for him.

As Heavy Runner's village came slowly to life, a few smoldering fires were kindled. Smoke started to rise in the air. At first only a few Indians ventured outside. They were unaware that they were being watched. Had they looked to the top of the bluffs above them, they might have seen 2nd Lieutenant Gustavus Cheney Doane and his cavalry reining in their horses and dismounting to get a better look down from that height.

The soldiers had been on the trail for several days, traveling at night to avoid detection. Their commander, Major Eugene Baker, had become too inebriated to lead and would not believe it when his half-blood guides said that they were on the wrong trail. Baker ordered Doane and the others to continue on down the trail that he was sure would lead to Mountain Chief's camp, where it had been known to be a few days before. Doane's orders when he got there were to surprise the Indians and strike. The same instructions had been relayed a few days earlier in Lieutenant General Philip Sheridan's telegram: "Tell Baker to strike them hard." The order had to be obeyed.

When Doane reached the bluffs above Heavy Runner's camp his ride was at an end, for it appeared that he had found the village that he was looking for.

ONE

Lewis and Clark Meet
the Piegan Indians

I should resist to the last extremity preferring death to that
of being deprived of my papers instruments and gun.
MERIWETHER LEWIS, DIARY ENTRY FOR JULY 25, 1806

Captain Meriwether Lewis, a strong man over six feet tall and in superb condition, was terrified on July 25, 1806. He was contemplating a fight to the death. Lewis was on the banks far up the Marias River, in Piegan Indian country had he known it, in the most northern region of the unexplored Louisiana Purchase. With him were only three others from his command. Two of them were brothers, the sharpshooters Joseph and Reuben Fields. The other was a skilled hunter and linguist, George Drouillard (written "Drewyer" by Lewis), part French and part Indian, who had been hired by the expedition as an interpreter. He interpreted through sign language, and perhaps a few common words, because he did not know the languages of the tribes in the region.

Lewis's sole purpose in this remote location was to complete a key assignment given to him by President Thomas Jefferson in 1804 when the Corps of Discovery left to go up the Missouri River on the expedition. They were to "ascertain whether any branch of that river lies as far north as latd. 50," which would extend the northern boundary of the Louisiana Purchase to that point.[1] They had gone up Cut Bank Creek, the northern branch of the Marias. Time and again Lewis had tried to get a reading of latitude with his sextant, but the overcast and cloudy weather

Meriwether Lewis

Meriwether Lewis and three others encountered a small band
of Piegans at the headwaters of the Marias River in 1806. Artist unknown. Courtesy Library of Congress.

had frustrated him. The few days that he had allotted for the task
were at an end. The small group was now returning to the Missouri River, to rejoin the three others of Lewis's command who
were to meet them there. The plan was that they would then together navigate far downstream to meet Captain William Clark
at the mouth of the Yellowstone.

Lewis had jotted in his diary the day before that their resolve
was to leave their northern camp on Cut Bank Creek: he "had

the horses caught and we set out biding a lasting adieu to this place which I now call camp disappointment."[2] A frustrated Lewis was humbled by his failure to get the reading, but he took heart in knowing that they were getting nearer to the end of their long expedition, which had taken them up the Missouri, over the Rocky Mountains, and down the Columbia River to its mouth as it reached the Pacific Ocean. Passing the long winter there, they set out in the spring to come back up the Columbia and over the Rocky Mountains. By summer they had reached a place they called Travelers' Rest. Lewis wrote that on July 1, 1806, he and Clark had devised a plan that he would go "with a small party by the most direct rout to the falls of the Missouri." From there they would head out for the headwaters of the Marias. The volunteers for the expedition had been selected from the healthiest, strongest, and most skilled men available when Lewis and Clark set out on their transcontinental odyssey. Now from among these Lewis "called for the volunteers to accompany me on this rout, many turned out, from whom I selected Drewyer" and the "Feildses."[3]

Lewis had started out apprehensive on his trip to the Marias. As he noted in his diary on July 3, 1806: "I took leave of my worthy friend and companion Capt. Clark and the party that accompanied him. I could not avoid feeling much concern on this occasion although I hoped this separation was only momentary." Much of his worry came from the refusal of the friendly Indians that the corps had camped with at Travelers' Rest to serve as guides on the trail to the Marias. The Indians had said that "as the road was a well beaten track we could not now miss our way, and as they were afraid of meeting with their enemies the 'Minnetares,' they could not think of continuing with us any longer." So Lewis and his men were alone in Indian country on their unsuccessful journey.[4]

When the party members admitted failure and left Camp Disappointment, their ride toward the Missouri brought even more anxiety. They discovered "some Indian lodges which appeared to have been inhabited last winter" among the undergrowth of "rose honeysuckle and redberry bushes" in the cottonwood timbered bottomland of the Marias where the Two Medicine River joined. It was not long until they had their first encounter with the Piegans.

Lewis had brought his "spye glass" to his eye to scan the horizon and located some dark spots on the hills, which he soon made out to be "an assemblage of about 30 horses." He saw the Indians on an elevation above them and could not hold back the fear that swept over him. As the Indians drew near Lewis and his three men, the precariousness of their condition was apparent. They were the better part of 100 miles away from the other three men of Lewis's detail, who were on the Missouri and headed for a rendezvous with them at the mouth of the Marias. The other men of the corps were with Captain Clark, who had headed down the Yellowstone River, planning to reunite with Lewis at its confluence with the Missouri—hundreds of miles away in the vast high plains country.[5]

To the relief of all, it turned out that the Indians that Lewis had spotted were indeed a small party, far fewer than indicated by the number of horses, and were not hostile. Sergeant John Ordway, one of Lewis's men who had been left to come down the Missouri to the mouth of the Marias, reported that Drouillard told him later that the Indians "were armed with bows & arrows and 2 guns" and "at first appeared afraid but after a little rode up and shook hands with Cap Lewis & party and appeared friendly & they desired Cap' Lewis to go with them to their Nation which they said was . . . about 2 days march."[6]

Meriwether Lewis remained uneasy and "still supposed that there were others concealed as there were several other horses saddled." He had not determined the Indians' tribal identity and told the men with him: "I apprehended that these were the Minnetares of Fort de Prarie and from their known character I expected that we were to have some difficulty with them; that if they thought themselves sufficiently strong I was convinced they would attempt to rob us." If so, Lewis was prepared to "resist to the last extremity preferring death to that of being deprived of my papers instruments and gun."[7]

Lewis was wrong only in naming the tribe. As it would turn out, these Indians were in fact the Piegans of the Blackfeet confederation and not the "Minnetares" as he had imprecisely if not mistakenly noted. He was right in his assessment of what might happen. What Lewis seemed to appreciate was that in the Plains Indian culture, and particularly in the Piegan culture, horse stealing was not a crime but a way of existence taught to the young men as a skill in their quest for survival.[8] In Lewis's emotional seesaw struggle, he took comfort when he found that "the Indians were only eight in number" and concluded that "we could manage that number should they attempt any hostile measures." With his mind eased by this thought, Lewis wrote that "as it was growing late in the evening I proposed that we should remove to the nearest part of the river and camp together, I told them that I was glad to see them and had a great deal to say to them." The Indians responded and "formed a large semicircular camp of dressed buffalo skins and invited us to partake of their shelter which Dreweyer and myself accepted and the Fieldses lay near the fire in front of the shelter."[9]

Communication had been established. Lewis was able to note in his diary: "I had much conversation with these people in the course of the evening," but of course he meant through the assistance of Drouillard's sign language.[10] Lewis "learned from them that they were a part of a large band which lay encamped at present near the foot of the rocky mountains on the main branch of Maria's river" and that they were only "one ½ days march" away from their current camp. Lewis showed no hint of surprise when he recorded in his journal that the Indians had told him that "there was a whiteman with their band." Of course, Lewis's men knew little at that time about the existence of the fur trade in the area. A few white trappers and fur traders had been making lonely incursions into the region since the mid-1700s as they came down from the Hudson's Bay Company's and North West Fur Company's rival outposts, far to the north.

As the evening wore on, the Indians told Lewis, Drouillard, and the Fields brothers much about Piegan life on the plains. They learned that another large band of their nation was hunting buffalo near the "broken mountains" and, like Lewis and his party, was on its way to the mouth of the Marias River. It would

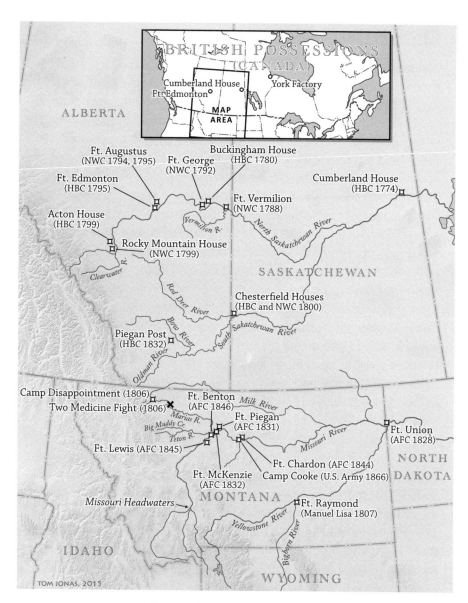

Fur trade map, 1790s to 1866

This map shows some of the principal fur trading forts of the Hudson's Bay Company (HBC), North West Company (NWC), and American Fur Company (AFC) as well as Manuel Lisa's fort, the U.S. Army's Camp Cooke, Meriwether Lewis's Camp Disappointment, and the site of Lewis's Two Medicine River fight with the Piegans. It also shows the location of the Missouri headwaters, where Drouillard was killed, and the Hudson's Bay Company headquarters at York Factory on the bay. Maps by Paul R. Wylie and Tom Jonas, copyright © 2016 by Paul R. Wylie. All rights reserved.

probably arrive in the course of just a few days. The Indians then intended to continue on "to the establishment where they trade on the Suskasawan river," which was "only 6 days easy march, or such as they usually travel with their women and children, which may be estimated at about 150 m." Lewis also learned "from these traders" that the Indians would "obtain arm[s], ammunition, speritous liquor, blankets &c, in exchange for wolves and some beaver skins." What had just been described to Lewis was the model of the basic Indian fur trading commerce on the upper Missouri river and to the north in the British possessions. The key participants were Indian hunters and white traders. One of the key items of the trade was alcohol.

When it became Lewis's turn to speak that evening, the reasons that he gave the Indians for his being there were not entirely factual. Lewis said that he "had come in search of them in order to prevail on them to be at peace with their neighbors particularly those on the Westside of the mountains and to engage them to come and trade with me when the establishment is made at the entrance of this river." He reported that "they readily gave their assent and declared it to be their wish to be at peace with the Tushepahs whom they said had killed a number of their relations lately and pointed to several of those present who had cut their hair" as a sign of mourning. In reality Lewis would have preferred not to see the Indians at all and certainly had not "come in search of them."

Later in the evening Lewis found the Indians "extremely fond of smoking and plied them with the pipe until late at night." He became curious about the white man who was with the main body of their tribe and toward the end of the evening asked some of the young Indians to go to their band "with an invitation to their chiefs and warriors to bring the white man with them and come down and council." But Lewis was not about to delay his return any longer and was "anxious now to meet my men," having been gone for some time. He promised the Indians that if they would go with him "I would give them 10 horses and some tobacco," but "to this proposition they made no reply."[11]

Soon the Indians "were all asleep." Lewis, who had taken the first watch, wrote that he "roused up Fields and laid down myself." He told Joseph Fields to watch the Indians and to awaken them if any Indians left the camp "as I apprehended they would attempt to steal our horses." He then "fell into a profound sleep and did not wake until the noise of the men and Indians awoke" him "a little after light in the morning."[12]

Dawn found the peaceful evening gone, and the hostilities started. Trouble might have been avoided if Joseph Fields had not "carelessly laid his gun down behind him near where his brother was sleeping." Seizing the opportunity, one of the Piegans simply "slipped behind him and took his gun and that of his brother." Lewis said that at that "same instant two others advanced and seized the guns of Drewyer and myself." When Joseph turned to look for his gun, he saw it in the hands of an Indian, who was "running off with her [the gun] and his brother's." Joseph called to his brother Reuben, who "instantly jumped up and pursued the Indians with him whom they overtook at the distance of 50 or 60 paces from the camp." Reuben Fields, no doubt panicked by the thought that they would either die at the hands of the Indians or be abandoned on the prairie without guns or horses, drew his knife. He ran after the Indian. As he later told Sergeant John Ordway, he "overhauled him . . . caught hold of the 2 guns had his knife drawn & as he snatched away the guns pierced his knife into the Indian's heart he drew out one breath the wind of his breath followed the knife & he fell dead." The Fields brothers "took one of the Indians' guns and all their bows & arrows and their shields which they were on their backs at war" and ran back to camp.[13]

Things also were not going well at the camp. Lewis had been jolted awake by the commotion. He said that he "then drew a pistol from my holster and turning myself about saw the Indian making off with my gun, I ran at him with my pistol and bid him lay down my gun which he was in the act of doing." Just then "the Fieldses returned and drew up their guns to shoot him which I forbid as he did not appear to be about to make any resistance or commit any offensive act." The Indian had "dropped the gun and walked slowly off" when Drouillard asked Lewis "if he might not kill the fellow," but Lewis stopped him, "as the Indian did not appear to wish to kill us." Then the Indians began to drive off all the horses. Lewis yelled to the men "to fire on them" as they pursued the main party, who were driving the horses up the river.

Lewis pursued the man who had taken his gun, "who with another was driving off a part of the horses which were to the left of the camp." Exhaustion was starting to overcome him: "Being nearly out of breath I could pursue no further, I called to them as I had done several times before that I would shoot them if they did not give me my horse and raised my gun." One of the Indians "jumped behind a rock and spoke to the other who turned around and stopped at the distance of 30 steps from me and I shot him through the belly." When the man "fell to his knees and on his right elbow" Lewis saw him partly raise himself and fire at him. Turning himself about, Lewis crawled behind a rock that was a few feet from him. It was an overshot but barely. Lewis wrote that "being bearheaded I felt the wind of his bullet very distinctly."[14]

The four men of Lewis's small detachment then prepared for a hasty departure toward the mouth of the Marias. They knew that they would have to ride far and fast to outdistance any pursuing Indians, so they left one of their own horses "and took four of the best of those of the Indian's." Drouillard loaded the horses with the "four shields and two bows and quivers of arrows which had been left on the fire, with sundry other articles." Lewis had previously bestowed a flag and a medal on the Indians. Now he and his men also "retook the flagg but left the medal about the neck of the dead man that they might be informed who we were." They also "took some of their buffaloe meat and set out ascending the bluffs by the same rout we had descended last evening leaving the balance of nine of their horses which we did not want."[15]

Concern that they might not be able to make it back to the Missouri now motivated Lewis; "no time was therefore to be lost and we pushed our horses as hard as they would bear . . . we passed a large branch . . . which I called battle river," finally traveling by moonlight. They passed "immense herds of buffaloe all night as we had done in the latter part of the day." Lewis said: "[M]y Indian horse carried me very well in short much better than my own would have done and leaves me with but little reason to complain of the robbery."[16]

The next day, July 28, 1806, Lewis awoke "so soar from my ride yesterday that I could scarcely stand, and the men complained of being in a similar situation." They had ridden over eighty miles the day before. He still needed to impress upon his men the seriousness of their situation and recorded that he "encouraged them by telling them that our own lives as well as those of our friends and fellow travelers depended on our exertions at this moment." He also vowed to fight to the death if another attack occurred. "I now told them that it was my determination that if we were attacked in the plains on our way to the point that the bridles of the horses should be tied together and we would stand and defend them, or sell our lives as dear as we could." The cloud of anxiety is almost visible in Lewis's writings, but it was lifted at the sound of shots nearby: "being then within five miles of the grog spring we heard the report of several rifles very distinctly on the river to our right, we quickly repaired to this joyful sound." Just as they arrived on the bank of the Missouri, they "had the unspeakable satisfaction to see our canoes coming down," being paddled by the other three men in Lewis's command. Soon afterward the party was safely aboard the canoes and headed downriver on the broad Missouri, away from the Piegan threat.[17]

The Piegan memory of the encounter with the party differs from the one that Meriwether Lewis recorded in his diary, but not drastically so. To the Piegans, taking another tribe's firearms or horses was common and was not a criminal act. The affair on the Marias was not just about that. Indeed it was considered "a much more complicated tale of young boys stealing into an enemy camp in an ancient ritual that had little to do with thievery and much to do with courage, honor and coming-of-age." According to Blackfeet history, "those two boys were doing what they were supposed to," as a time-honored "way of gaining honor in battle." According to the late Darrell Robes Kipp, director of the Piegan Institute in Browning, oral tradition has it that one of the Indians who was killed, Calf Looking, was only thirteen. "These were boys who were horse herders," Kipp said. "They weren't warriors."[18]

The situation may have been even more complicated: according to Blackfeet oral tradition, the young boys had social contact with Lewis's men and "stayed with them and gambled with them." The next morning "they went to part company and the Indians took what they had won."[19] According to Blackfeet tradition, it was a serious affront when Lewis put a peace medal around the neck of one of the dead Indian boys. Modern Indian historians consider this similar to "counting coup on them" and add that it might also be "viewed as a form of scalping."[20]

The small band of Indians that Meriwether Lewis and his men encountered were members of the Piegan tribe, which has always been described as having an affiliation with a larger group of other tribes: the Bloods, the Blackfeet, and the Gros Ventres. The confederation generally has been called the "Blackfeet" in the United States and the "Blackfoot" in Canada, with some exceptions. The Piegans themselves were divided into Northern Piegans living mostly in the British possessions and the Southern Piegans, who encountered Meriwether Lewis on the Marias.

Alexander Henry, a Hudson's Bay Company trader and explorer, said early on: "The Blackfeet, Blood Indians and Piegans may be considered under one grand appellation of the Slave Indians." Henry also described their hunting grounds at the turn of the nineteenth century:

The tract of land which they call their own Country at present commences by a due south direction from Fort Vermillion to the south branch of the Saskatchewoine and up that stream to the foot of the Rocky Mountains, then in another direction along the mountain until it strikes upon the North Branch of the Saskatchewoine again and down that stream to the Vermillion River . . . The Piegans or Picaneux Indians dwell along the foot of the Mountains. These people in general are remarkable stout, tall and well proportioned men . . . their dress and manners nearly correspond with the natives of the Missourie.[21]

Henry's description did not include the lands of the Southern Piegans, which extended down to the Marias and the Missouri.

For a long time before Meriwether Lewis arrived on the Marias in 1806, Indians of the Blackfeet confederation had been in contact with white people as far back as the late 1600s. Henry Kelsey of the Hudson's Bay Company was credited as perhaps being the first early European explorer to be in contact with the Blackfeet in the late seventeenth century in the area of the Saskatchewan River.[22] At that time, the Blackfeet tribe had neither the horses nor the firearms that Lewis found them with on the Marias in 1806. These came later and from different directions.[23]

Legend has it that one day a mounted Kootenai came into the Piegan camp riding a horse: "none of them had ever seen anything like it." After staying in the camp for some time, the Kootenai left and came back with more horses. The chief named Dog who asked the Kootenai to bring in the horses was afterward called "Sits-in-the-Middle, and at last, Many Horses," according to one writer. He was said to have "so many horses he could not keep track of them all." This marked the beginning of the horse culture among the Piegans. The horses became known as "elk dogs." The long era of foot travel, known by the Piegans as the "dog days" when dogs pulled their travois, came to an end.[24]

It was recounted that Many Horses began to trade horses for animal skins, and "then he would send his relations in to the Hudson's Bay post to trade, but he would never go himself." Finally the white traders "went to his lodge and began to unpack their things—guns, clothing, knives and goods of all kinds." Many Horses then sent word for all the "principal men, young and old, to come together at his lodge." According to the story, the white men "began to distribute the guns, and with each gun they gave a bundle of powder and ball. At this same time, the young men received white blankets and the old men black coats." The traders also gave the Indians knives: "the white men showed us how to use the knives; to split down the legs and rip up the belly—to skin for trade."[25]

Saukamappee, an elderly Cree Indian who had been adopted by the Piegans, told David Thompson (an early fur trader of the

North West Company) the history of the tribal battles, the first horses, the introduction of guns, and the devastating 1781–1782 smallpox epidemic. When he was a boy, Saukamappee said, the Piegans had come to his father's Cree tribe for help against the Snakes. His "account . . . of former times went back to about 1730." According to Saukamappee, "the Piegans were always the frontier Tribe, upon whom the Snake Indians made their attacks—there were a few guns amongst us, but very little ammunition, and they were left to hunt for our families." The weapons that the Piegans used against the Snakes were "a lance, mostly pointed with iron, some few of stone, a bow and a quiver of arrows."[26]

The Piegans eventually had guns that came largely from the Cree Indians to the north and east. The French and English fur traders had initially traded the guns to the Crees for furs. The Crees used the guns to force their western expansion into the area of the Blackfeet, while at the same time trading the guns to them.[27] The horses had added range and speed to the Indians' constant movement across the plains. Meat from buffalo hunts could be carried back to the lodges faster, and it was easier to follow the buffalo herds. With guns and horses, the Blackfeet became formidable warriors.[28] During the winter months, the horses had to be fed and the Piegans and their related tribes sought shelter in the river valleys. The valley of the Marias River where Meriwether Lewis had found them in 1806 had become one of the Piegans' favorites.[29]

The Hudson's Bay Company, with headquarters at York Factory at the mouth of the Nelson River on Hudson's Bay, was the oldest commercial corporation in North America and one of the oldest in the world. The British monarch had given the company a royal charter in 1670. Its legal name was "The Governor and Company of Adventurers of England Trading into Hudson's Bay." The charter gave the company a trading monopoly in the whole Hudson's Bay watershed area, an immense territory named Rupert's Land after Prince Rupert of the Rhine, the company's first governor. The Hudson's Bay Company became the de facto government within its land holdings. At one time that had made it the largest landowner in the world, when Rupert's Land constituted over fifteen percent of North America.[30]

At first Hudson's Bay traders did not extend their fur-gathering activities to the land of the Blackfeet. In the 1750s the company cautiously sent out a man to spend the winter with them. He was Anthony Henday, a common laborer, who bravely proceeded west on foot to take up his winter residence with the tribe. Henday was surprised when he met "an aged man and a horse loaded with moose flesh" on the trail. It had been four years since Henday had left England, where he had last seen a horse. Later he saw a number of horses, which may have been only recently acquired by the Blackfeet.[31]

When Henday met with tribes of the Blackfeet Nation in 1754, he stayed in a Blood camp of 322 lodges near present-day Red Deer, Alberta, Canada. He tried to convince them as best he could to trade with his company, but they were not interested. The horses had given them new hunting ability, and the buffalo had been plentiful.[32] When Henday was asked to write reports on his findings, the Hudson's Bay Company's managers found them "incoherent and unintelligible." They needed to know more. In 1772 the company sent inland a more literate man named Matthew Cocking, who had risen from a bookkeeper to become second in command at York Factory. Cocking spent the winter with the Blackfeet. Like Henday before him, he tried to convince the Indians to come to York Factory to trade. The Blackfeet were still reluctant. Cocking found that he was up against established competition from the French traders headquartered in Montreal, who had already penetrated the area and were trading tobacco and whiskey for furs in the area where the Indians lived. Visiting one of the French trading forts, Cocking observed: "The Frenchman introduced the Natives unto his house, giving about 4 inches of tobacco. Afterwards they made a collection of furs by the bulk about 100 Beaver, presenting them to the Pedler, who in return presented them about 4 gallons liquor, Rum adulterated . . . I endeavored all in my power to prevent the Natives giving away their furs, but in vain; Liquor being above all persuasions with them."[33]

In 1780 the Hudson's Bay Company management decided that trade with the Blackfeet in their own territory was imperative and built its first permanent trading post, Buckingham House, on the Saskatchewan River. This gave its traders a point of access to the Blackfeet country, but they did not have the vast Blackfeet area all to themselves.[34] In the eighteenth century the French fur traders moved out from the East onto the plains along the South Saskatchewan River, increasingly contacting and trading with the Indians. Loss of the war with England in 1763 prevented the French from claiming an empire in North America, but it did not eliminate French people from the fur trade. They continued to be "pedlars," a demeaning name given to them by the English of Hudson's Bay Company. Soon they were integrated into the mostly English- and Scottish-controlled North West Company out of Montreal and entered into a contentious rivalry with the Hudson's Bay Company. By the start of the nineteenth century the North West Company was prospering. It established Rocky Mountain House and Hudson's Bay Company started Acton House at the same location in 1799. The posts opened and closed several times over the years. Only after the two companies merged in 1821 did the location on the North Saskatchewan River become known under a single name as Rocky Mountain House.[35]

At the time Meriwether Lewis and his small crew killed the two Piegans on the Marias in July 1806, both the Hudson's Bay Company and the North West Company had trading forts on the North Saskatchewan River were still operating. Less than a year later, word of the killings had spread to the Rocky Mountain House fort of the North West Company. David Thompson, who started on a trek from there for the Columbia River and the sea the next spring, noted in his journal on May 10, 1807: "The murder of two Piegan Indians by Captain Lewis of the United States drew the Piegans to the Missouri to avenge their deaths; and thus gave me an opportunity to cross the Mountains by the defiles of the Saskatchewan River."[36]

The Blackfeet had been brought into the fur trade by the early British and French explorers and traders headquartered in what became Canada, but Piegan history became inextricably bound to the events that shaped the development of the United States. Those events started as early as 1763, when France, then allied with Spain, lost the Seven Years War to Great Britain. That started a series of land ownership changes in America. The English ceded Cuba and the Philippines back to Spain, in exchange for Florida. France, having lost Canada and the eastern portion of its vast Louisiana province, ceded the western half of the Mississippi Valley to its ally Spain. The seat of the Spanish government was in New Orleans, with St. Louis as the Spanish center for the upper portion of the province, even though a bulk of the population was French. The principal industry there was the fur trade.[37]

Even before Lewis and Clark made their heroic expedition to the headwaters of the Missouri and on to the Pacific coast, the fur traders from St. Louis had attempted the ascent of the Missouri River but found that the effort was fraught with danger. Jean Baptiste Trudeau left St. Louis on June 7, 1794, and proceeded laboriously up the Missouri toward the Mandan nation in what are now the Dakotas, only to be detained and robbed of his goods by the Teton Sioux. Despite that, he and his men were able to construct a cabin for their stay.[38] When a few other French and Spanish traders succeeded in making it partway up the Missouri, they found that English fur traders of the Hudson's Bay Company were already in the territory. In the summer of 1796 the Spanish sent a man named John Evans out from St. Louis to take possession of an English fur trade fort that had been built among the Mandans by traders from the Assiniboine River. Ten days after hoisting the Spanish flag, Evans was confronted by English traders. After a few tense days he was able to drive them from the territory, sending with them a proclamation prohibiting them from encroaching upon his Catholic majesty's dominions.[39]

In 1802 the momentous event occurred that would open the way for American fur traders on the Missouri River. Delegates from the United States met with French diplomats and bought rights under French claims to the land that became known as the Louisiana Purchase. The French had controlled this huge area from 1699 until 1762, when the land was given to its ally Spain. It was returned to France in 1800, when there was hope of building an empire in North America under Napoleon Bonaparte. After the transaction with France, President Thomas Jefferson acknowledged that the United States still had to purchase the land titles of the "native proprietors" within the Louisiana Purchase and that the tribal occupancy rights had not been diminished. Jefferson understood that what the United States had purchased from France was the right of France, as the discovering nation, exclusively to acquire lands in the Louisiana Territory. It was partly in furtherance of these rights that Captains William Clark and Meriwether Lewis with their Corps of Discovery came up the Missouri River in 1805.[40]

George Drouillard's close escape from the run-in that he, Meriwether Lewis, and the Fields brothers had with the Piegans on the Marias in July 1806 had not scared him out of the area forever. As frightening as the event was to Drouillard, he still saw the area's great potential for furs. As compensation for his service with Lewis and Clark, the government gave him and others land warrants. He purchased from Privates Joseph Whitehouse and John Collins their future land warrant rights. It took him only about a year to sell the warrants at a good profit and to make plans to return to the upper rivers, this time with the first expedition of Manuel Lisa. On Lisa's first expedition, which departed St. Louis in April 1807, he and his company of forty-two men moved up the Missouri River until they reached the mouth of the Yellowstone River. After ascending the Yellowstone some 170 miles, on November 21 Lisa established at the mouth of the Bighorn River the first trading post in the upper Missouri region, called Fort Raymond.[41] Drouillard settled down for the winter of 1807–1808 there. He was working under Lisa's system of obtaining beaver pelts by having his own men do the trapping, rather than attempting to trade with the Indians. Most of his traveling and trapping was in the land occupied by the Crow Indians in the Big Horn Mountains. In the spring he discovered many beaver near the mountain streams. Drouillard also found the Crow

Indians to be friendly and was unmolested. By August 1808 he was back in St. Louis with a lucrative cargo of pelts.

Drouillard did not return until the spring of 1809, when he came again with Manuel Lisa and a large number of men of the Missouri Fur Company, of which Lisa was a partner. Intent on having a productive fur-trapping season, some of the men split off to go up the Yellowstone to Lisa's original camp on the Big Horn, but a majority continued up the Missouri, expecting to get to the Three Forks of the Missouri, where the Jefferson, Madison, and Gallatin Rivers converged to form its headwaters. They were in for a surprise. The Crows were friendly and let them trap unmolested, but the Blackfeet, who had moved in to hunt the area, stalked and killed the trappers when they found them vulnerable.[42]

As part of a group of trappers led by Lisa's partner, Thomas James, intrepid George Drouillard came with the group that had split off to the Missouri headwaters. One fateful day in 1810 Drouillard was out checking his beaver traps away from the trapper's fort. He failed to return. James found Drouillard dead and described with horror what he had seen. "Druyer and his horse lay dead, the former mangled in a horrible manner; his head was cut off, his entrails torn out, and his body hacked to pieces. We saw from the marks on the ground that he must have fought in a circle on horseback, and probably killed some of his enemies, being a brave man, and well armed with a rifle, pistol, knife and tomahawk." James could do nothing but quickly bury the ghastly remains in an unmarked grave. Manuel Lisa later inventoried Drouillard's pathetic estate and wrote on a single sheet of paper, in bad French, that it consisted of only "a few shirts, coarse sheets and a sleeveless sweater," all of which were "well-used and worn."[43]

TWO

Protection for the Traders, Death to the Trappers

If you will send Traders into our Country we will protect them & treat them well; but for Trappers—Never.
ATTRIBUTED TO A BLACKFOOT CHIEF BY MAJOR JOHN
F. A. SANFORD, AGENT FOR THE UPPER MISSOURI TRIBES

In 1831 a grizzled Thomas Forsyth, sixty years old, sat down in his study in St. Louis to write a letter to the secretary of war, Lewis Cass, about the beginnings of Indian fur trade. Forsyth was the perfect person to tell the story. By the time he was seventeen, he had become a successful fur trader in the north woods, living with the Ottawa Indians on Saginaw Bay. Since then he had been both a fur trader and an Indian agent and had been involved in the start of the American fur trade on the Missouri, which would eventually reach all the way up to the Piegan country. Cass was formulating an Indian policy for the government and was looking for a firsthand report on the history of the fur trade, which Forsyth was able to provide. "I visited this country as early as April, 1798," Forsyth wrote, "and in many conversations I had with the French people of this place, all that they could say on the subject of the Indian trade was that there were many Indian nations inhabiting the country bordering on the Missouri River who were exceedingly cruel to all the white people that went among them." Forsyth explained that early on "the highest point then known up the Missouri river was Cedar Island which is somewhere in the Arikara country."[1]

As the fur trade moved up the Missouri, the Americans found that they had competition. Forsyth was able to tell Cass that back in the early 1800s, the "Arikara, Mandan, Blackfeet, Crow, Arapahoe, Assiniboine, and other Indians were well known in those days to the Hudson Bay and North West companies." He reported that traders ("clerks" he called them) belonging to those companies and their men would visit the Missouri annually at different places.

The Corps of Discovery had set a milestone in America, particularly for the fur trade, and Forsyth reported that "after the arrival of Lewis and Clark from the Pacific" the first company was organized in St. Louis "for the purpose of trading with the Indians up the Missouri" with plans to go "to its forks and higher if necessary." This location, the Three Forks of the Missouri, was exactly the place where Drouillard had met his bloody end in 1810. Despite the early efforts of Manuel Lisa to establish the fur trade in the upper Missouri area, a damper had been put on the business. Forsyth reported that the War of 1812 had a disruptive effect: "our Indian trade almost ceased to exist, except where it was continued by some few hunters who got up among the Indians and would, in the spring season bring down a few furs." The war, however, had not deterred the traders from the British possessions, and "the Hudson Bay and the North West companies at the same time extended their trade, and sent hunting parties to different points on the Missouri river and also to the rocky mountains."[2] The British possession companies would soon find that they had to face a strong new American competition, not from Lisa and the traders out of St. Louis but from the new American Fur Company started by a German immigrant, John Jacob Astor.

In 1779 Astor had left his hometown of Waldorf, Germany. At the age of seventeen he went to London to work in his brother's musical instrument factory. Four years later he booked passage on a ship to America to join his other brother, Henry, who had become a prosperous butcher in New York City. Stepping out of steerage after his boat was frozen in on Chesapeake Bay, Astor walked across the ice to Baltimore and headed toward New York.

He had little money and only a small number of flutes, which he hoped to sell on consignment for his brother George in London.

Astor soon found out that his greatest asset in America was the knowledge that he had gained quite by chance, from over-hearing conversations of Hudson's Bay Company employees as they crossed the Atlantic. What Astor learned was that in America an abundance of furs could be had from the Indians for small amounts of trade goods—and whiskey. The furs could then be sold in New York and London at a large profit. Astor eventually opened his own fur trade shop in 1786. To supply his shop, he bravely commenced traveling through the wilderness alone to procure the furs that he needed from Indians.

By 1808 Astor could see the rising popularity of furs in the fashion trade. On April 8 of that year he incorporated the American Fur Company to supply the market. His business had become prosperous, and his plan was to establish trading posts on the Pacific coast and ship furs to New York and to China to trade for goods. In 1810 he founded the town of Astoria on the Oregon coast at the site of Fort Clatsop, which had been the winter quarters of the Corps of Discovery on the Pacific Ocean at the mouth of the Columbia River.[3]

Astor later turned his efforts inland and in the 1820s started to move up the Missouri toward the Rocky Mountains and ultimately the Piegans. By buying out its smaller American competitors, Astor's company gained almost a monopoly in the United States.

At about the same time when Astor was expanding his business up the Missouri, the North West Company and the Hudson's Bay Company merged. Each company had long coveted the trade with the Blackfeet south of the South Saskatchewan River and along the upper Missouri. They each had a presence there that they wished to expand. The North West Company out of Montreal had always lacked the ease of transportation that Hudson's Bay Company enjoyed, however, and neither company was in a position to keep competing. On March 21, 1821, instead of continuing to struggle against each other, the two companies joined forces under the Hudson's Bay Company name.[4]

Both companies had historically tried independently to domi-
nate the fur trade in the region hunted by the Piegans but failed.
The new Hudson's Bay Company closed many of the posts to
the south and continued to operate posts in the north. It was a
long distance for the Blackfeet to travel as far north as Rocky
Mountain House or Fort Edmonton on the North Saskatchewan
River if they wanted to trade for English goods. The Bloods, who
generally ranged even farther north than the Piegans, in particular resented having to travel farther to trade at Fort Edmonton.
It would take about a decade for the Hudson's Bay Company to
try to establish a fort to the south around the Bow River and to
extend trade toward the Piegans.[5]

Before the merger the North West Company managers brought
in a man that they thought could learn and improve the trade. He
was Kenneth McKenzie, a young Canadian who had been born
in Scotland in 1797 and first immigrated to the United States in
1817 before he moved to Canada.[6] The managers' error was in
not retaining McKenzie after the merger in 1821. When the tal-
ented young man found himself out of a job, he headed for St.
Louis to apply for United States citizenship. He soon joined the
fledgling Columbia Fur Company that traded on the upper Missouri and rose to control the firm by the mid-1820s.

Seeking the services of Kenneth McKenzie, the American Fur
Company spent some years negotiating with him. In 1828 it finally bought his Columbia Fur Company. McKenzie was the
prize in the purchase. He was sent to the upper Missouri but to
a location still far downriver from the Piegan country. In 1829 he
established what became the legendary Fort Union at the confluence of the Missouri and Yellowstone Rivers. From there he
oversaw the company's operations in the region. As bourgeois
(the name given to the head trader) he lived in comfort and married an Indian woman, with whom he had a son named Owen
McKenzie. He had achieved a reputation as a "kind-hearted and
high-minded Scotsman."[7]

During the time when Astor and the American Fur Company
were getting established to trade with the Indians on the upper
Missouri River, a plan was underfoot in St. Louis to eliminate

the Indians from the fur-gathering process altogether. It would seriously affect the Piegan fur trade. William Henry Ashley, who was serving as Missouri's lieutenant governor, and his partner, Andrew Henry of St. Louis, incorporated the Rocky Mountain Fur Company in 1822. They placed an advertisement in St. Louis seeking "One Hundred enterprising young men . . . to ascend the river Missouri to its source, there to be employed for one, two, or three years." These men became known as "Ashley's One Hundred." Ashley was not looking for fur traders but for fur trappers. They had to be strong, brave men who could survive in Indian country on their own. Some of the men he hired became legends. They included the likes of Jedediah Smith and Jim Bridger and a man named Thomas Fitzpatrick, who would later figure prominently in mapping out a Blackfeet reservation in the 1851 Fort Laramie Treaty.[8] Ashley sent these men deep into the dangerous Piegan country to trap, in competition with the Indians.

Ashley's manner of procuring furs did not require trading whiskey to the Indians. The evils of this practice were being recognized in Washington at the time he was forming his company, though not until July 1832 did Congress pass an act providing that "no ardent spirits shall hereafter . . . be introduced under any pretense, into the Indian country."[9] Under Ashley's plan, the trappers brought the pelts from the animals that they trapped to a rendezvous, to be held annually at different places east of the Rockies. After his operations started, Ashley's trappers fared poorly with the Blackfeet, who viewed them only as competitors to be eliminated.[10] Soon Ashley retreated from the upper waters of the Missouri to the safer Crow country along the Yellowstone.[11] For a time the ill feelings of the Blackfeet stifled even the fur trade being conducted by the American Fur Company, where the Indians were still doing the trapping and hunting. A fragile peace was brought about after that. In time a more conventional fur trade with the Piegans was started, with great reluctance on the part of the Indians.

Since the early 1800s, when the American fur traders began their relentless move up the Missouri toward the land of the Piegans, the government back east had become increasingly concerned with how the new country would be divided with the Indians. For centuries a European legal principle called the "doctrine of discovery" had given rights to land previously occupied only by Indians to the first discovering European nation. The doctrine had papal origins, going back to 1493, when Pope Alexander VI divided the world into spheres of "discovery" and influence for Portugal and Spain to engage in commerce, conquest, and religious conversion. The justification at that time was based on such things as the existence of different religions and customs of the native peoples in a territory and "wasteful" use of land. The principle of *terra nullius* held that land not used by the native peoples as it would be used by the Europeans was considered "empty" and could be taken. These same themes were later adopted into the developing English legal theories of land acquisition by discovery, formulated from the mid-1500s.[12]

In 1775 a man named Thomas Johnson and some other British citizens had purchased land in the Northwest Territory—then part of the Colony of Virginia—from members of the Piankeshaw tribe. Over forty years later, in 1818, William McIntosh purchased some of the same land from the United States. Johnson had died, so his heirs brought a case to have McIntosh removed from the land and prevailed in the trial court. The case was appealed to the U.S. Supreme Court and was heard under the vaulted ceilings of the old lamp–lit Supreme Court Chamber inside the U.S. Capitol in 1823. Arguments of the parties started on Saturday, February 15, and continued on Monday and Tuesday of the next week, until the lawyers for each side stood down from the podium. The seven Supreme Court justices decided the case in the next few days. The court's opinion, authored by Chief Justice John Marshall, was handed down on Friday, February 28.[13]

Marshall's opinion applied the European discovery doctrine and confirmed that nations have title to the lands that they discover and that the Indian tribes do not have absolute title to their lands. The ruling gave the Indians only a right of occupancy, with any transfer of land being illegal unless approved by the federal government. But the government was given the exclusive right to obtain Indian land title either "by purchase or by conquest." This historic Supreme Court decision, now generally known as *Johnson v. McIntosh*, also held that tribes did not retain full national sovereignty and that the government could pass laws to restrict Indian rights through the "discovery doctrine."[14]

Of course, at that time the Supreme Court's legal decision had no immediate application to the nearly inaccessible Piegan hunting lands in the vast upper watershed of the barely navigable Missouri River. No one was acquiring private land there. It was far too hard to reach. The trip up the river from St. Louis to the heart of the Piegan culture at the mouth of the Marias River was an arduous 2,000-mile climb. The watercourse had been described as "repulsive—a stream of flowing mud studded with dead tree trunks and broken by bars."[15] As daunting as the task was, a few of the early river voyagers in a collection of canoes, dugouts, and flatboats did manage to reach the Piegan territory. For heavy hauling they used mackinaws and keelboats carrying up to ten tons or more, which were rowed, poled, and dragged by many men walking along the banks of the river, pulling the boat by a "cordelle," sometimes helped by a small sail.

None of these craft were big enough or comfortable enough to bring up large loads of goods or entire families, so wives and children of fur traders and trappers were left behind. There was no safe place for them to go anyway. The early men of the fur trade were both brave and enterprising. Often they were corrupt, and they came to a country without laws. As they stayed in the area, many formed families with Indian women, with their offspring becoming leaders in the fur trade for years to come.[16]

The old fur trader and Indian agent Thomas Forsyth had sent his 1831 letter to secretary of war Lewis Cass at a time when Cass had just taken his post in Washington under President Andrew Jackson. He became a central figure in the Indian policy of the Jackson administration. That policy was to relocate Indian tribes living east of the Mississippi River to lands to the west and was being implemented under the Indian Removal Act signed into law by President Jackson on May 26, 1830.[17]

Cordelle boat

A cordelle boat being towed up the Missouri River. Steamboats generally replaced the cordelle boats with larger capacity and faster ascent up the Missouri
River. Courtesy Library of Congress.

The Indian removals, when they occurred, were a drastic measure. That was not the way George Washington and the founding
fathers had visualized things back in 1783. With the Revolution
over and the British out of the way, General Washington had
turned his thoughts to the Indians. He believed that not just
the Indians but also the whites had to be controlled. In 1783 he
wrote to revolutionary leader and Continental Congress member
James Duane of New York about his concerns. He was prescient
when he said that troubles were ahead with "Land Jobbers,
Speculators, and Monopolisers or even with scatter'd settlers"
overrunning the country. This would "aggrandize a few avari-
cious Men to the prejudice of many, and the embarrassment of
Government." At the time Washington wrote to Duane, the new
country that he was soon to lead extended only to the western

boundaries of the original colonies. The Indian tribes to which he referred had for the most part been in contact with whites for a considerable time, dating back to the European settlement of the eastern seaboard.[18]

George Washington's vision for Indian policy had not proved to be serviceable for the expansion-minded new country. When Andrew Jackson was elected president in 1829, the government attitude toward Indians turned less sympathetic. The removals in the 1830s were supposed to be voluntary, but they were implemented by putting great pressure on tribal leaders to sign removal treaties.[19] In September 1830, under the first such treaty, the Choctaws in Mississippi ceded land in exchange for payment and new land in the West, with the subsequent removal being described by a Choctaw chief as the "trail of tears and death."[20]

At the time of the Indian removals in the 1830s, new American fur traders were starting to arrive in the Piegan territory. But they were after pelts and not land, so there was never any thought of moving the tribes. The Indians were vital to the trade as harvesters of furs in the lands that they roamed. With Kenneth McKenzie at the helm of the American Fur Company on the upper Missouri, a more energized American trade with the Piegans started. But the bad feelings of the Indians, left over from the invasion of the American fur trappers, were still an obstacle. It took an old Hudson's Bay Company trader named Jacob Berger to get the regular fur trade going again. One day in 1830 Berger appeared at McKenzie's Fort Union and became employed there. He knew the Blackfeet and Piegans from his years with Hudson's Bay and spoke their language. The shrewd McKenzie saw that he could use Berger to penetrate the Piegan country and persuaded him to embark on a dangerous mission to visit the Indians and coax them to come in and trade. Four weeks later, at a large Piegan village on the Marias, Berger convinced a party of about forty of the Indians to return with him to Fort Union, arriving there near the end of 1831. McKenzie promised the Indians that they could collect the furs and trade them at posts that he was going to build higher up on the river. But the Blackfeet had seen enough of the American fur trappers out of St. Louis and wanted to be assured that trappers would not be working in their territory again. Their chiefs were reported to have said: "If you will send Traders into our Country we will protect them and treat them well; but for Trappers—Never."[21]

In time the fur trade of the early 1830s created an incentive for the use of steamboats as a mode of transportation on the giant, powerful Missouri, to replace some of the keelboats, mackinaws, bullboats, and canoes. These large crafts brought up trade items and returned more speedily through the swells and currents downriver, with a wealth of furs and buffalo robes. These robes gave a big incentive to steamboat navigation, because they were heavy and could not be handled well with smaller vessels. The large profits to be made encouraged the captains of paddle-wheel steamboats to brave the treacherous Missouri and push ever farther upstream. Starting in 1831, the steamboat *Yellow Stone* reached Fort Pierre in what is now South Dakota and the next year got to McKenzie's Fort Union.

At about the time when McKenzie was expanding operations up the river, a man named James Kipp was starting to make his usefulness known within the American Fur Company. Kipp was born in New York in 1788 but fled with his family of British loyalists to Nova Scotia and then Quebec. Before he was even twenty, he went west to the Red River and was employed there by the North West Company, later returning home to become a carpenter. When his wife died in 1821, Kipp left his daughters with his mother and headed west again to be a fur trader. This time it was on the Missouri River with Kenneth McKenzie, who was then with the North West Company. But Kipp, like McKenzie, was put out of work by the merger of the Hudson's Bay Company and the North West Company.[22]

Kipp stayed with McKenzie and became an employee of Astor's American Fur Company when the Columbia Fur Company that McKenzie headed was merged into its upper Missouri operations.[23] The new operation was officially called simply the "Upper Missouri Outfit," a designation that went into effect at the beginning of 1828 and remained in use for the next twenty years or so. But the name of the American Fur Company was still used prominently with the business.[24]

In August 1831 Kenneth McKenzie sent Kipp and a crew of about seventy-five men out of Fort Union to build a trading fort near the mouth of the Marias. Aboard a keelboat, they slowly fought their way up the low-running Missouri and over the sandbars into the heart of Piegan country. Relying again on Kipp's carpenter skills, they built a trading post aptly named Fort Piegan. Kipp remained at the post as bourgeois.[25] At last McKenzie and the American Fur Company had established a permanent location in the land of the Piegans. The completion of the fort that year was an event that should have signaled years of peaceful trade with the Indians. But when the traders departed downriver the next spring, the Piegans burned the fort down.[26]

In 1832, undaunted, McKenzie sent upriver another experienced trader, David Dawson Mitchell, then about thirty years old. With a crew of sixty men, Mitchell established a more secure fort on a narrow ridge of land separating the Teton and Missouri Rivers at a point just above their confluence. The post, called Fort McKenzie, was constructed so that the traders inside were protected by a more elaborate log structure than the plain board enclosures of the former Fort Piegan.[27] James Kipp, who had returned there to trade, treated the Piegans to a three-day party with 200 gallons of specially concocted whiskey as an initial welcome and to encourage them to trade. This resulted in an impressive haul of 6,450 pounds of beaver, from which the company realized $46,000 the next spring. Soon buffalo robes became the main trade: in 1841 over twenty thousand buffalo robes were being traded annually.[28]

The traders at Fort McKenzie in 1832 anxiously waited there in fear that the hostile attitude of the Indians toward some of the few American trappers who were still in the area would affect them. The danger was highest during trading, when the traders remained barricaded: trade exchanges were made through narrow wooden grates in the walls of the log fort. Furs were passed

David Dawson Mitchell

David Dawson Mitchell was an early fur trader on the upper Missouri who built Fort McKenzie in Piegan country in 1832 and later organized the Fort Laramie Treaty of 1851. Courtesy Missouri History Museum.

in, and trade goods were passed out. All of the traders used whiskey as part of their bargains, according to those familiar with the transactions.[29]

Soon after Fort McKenzie was completed in 1832, George Catlin, an adventurous and experienced artist, arrived at the fort and commenced painting portraits of the Piegans. His detailed work gave many Americans back east the first glimpse of the tribe and their way of life. Catlin was not the only artist to come. Following on his heels, Prince Maximilian of Wied, the German explorer, ethnologist, and naturalist, visited the Piegans and Fort McKenzie. He had with him Karl Bodmer, a Swiss artist. They had come all the way from Europe in 1833 to study the Indians of the plains. They spent from August 9 to September 14, 1833, at Fort McKenzie, where they had frequent meetings with the Piegans, who sat for Bodmer's portraits.[30]

The Hudson's Bay Company for a long time had been limited in the region to a trading post on the North Saskatchewan River at Fort Edmonton. Some of the furs that they collected came from the traps that they had given to the Indians, as trusted beaver hunters. But even this arrangement started to fail when the American Fur Company became more active on the Missouri. The perception was that the problem was the increased whiskey supply, which kept the Blackfeet trade farther south and away from the Hudson's Bay traders.

John Rowand, who was in charge of the post, complained to his chief factor that the Indians "who came from the Americans (are) all dressed up better than I ever saw Indians this way before . . . What they speak of most is about the presents the Indians receive from the Americans twice a year." An additional problem, Rowand said, was that "tribes get as much liquor as they like from the Americans and . . . feel not a little displeased with us because they cannot get liquor to take away with them, as with the Americans."[31] In a competitive battle to lure the Piegans back to trade, Hudson's Bay Company had tried to move much farther south and established a new trading fort on the Bow River in 1831, named Piegan Post or Old Bow Fort.[32] John Herriott, the chief trader there, expected success but was thwarted in part by the duplicity of one of the traders, a half-blood called Jemmy Jock Bird (real name James Bird Jr.), who was a practitioner of deception. He had lived with the Piegans, was married to the daughter of a Piegan chief, and was hired by Hudson's Bay Company to find the Piegan tribe and bring them in to trade. But, as

Portrait of a Piegan chief by George Catlin

George Catlin, an adventurous painter and illustrator, made this image of a
Piegan chief in 1833, when he visited the tribe at Fort McKenzie. Courtesy
Smithsonian American Art Museum, gift of Mrs. Joseph Harrison Jr.

apparently suspected by some, Bird also worked with the American Fur Company traders to help them establish trade with the
Piegans. John Rowand distrusted him with good reason and
wrote: "Master Bird would prefer [to] be an American than what
he is & I am almost sure he is working for them."[33] In any event,

Karl Bodmer scene of Piegan Indians
attacking Fort McKenzie in 1832

Karl Bodmer, with Prince Maxmilian of Wied, visited the Piegans on the upper
Missouri in 1833 and rendered this image of the Indians attacking Fort McKenzie. Courtesy Library of Congress

either because of Bird or just due to the flow of events, fortune
was turning against the return of the Piegan trade to the venerable Hudson's Bay Company. In 1834 the post on the Bow River
was abandoned.[34]

The use of whiskey in the fur trade had become a problem for
Kenneth McKenzie and his fellows as early as 1832. It became
known about that time that the federal government was going
to ban whiskey from the Indian country. The American fur traders put up a protest against the ban. Their best argument was
that American companies should be able to use whiskey if the
Hudson's Bay Company used it. But the argument did not sway
Congress, which again outlawed alcohol in 1834 for use in trade.
Fines and forfeitures were set out for any person who "shall sell,
exchange, or give, barter, or dispose of, any spirituous liquor or
wine to an Indian" or set up "any distillery for manufacturing
ardent spirits."[35] Even before the law was passed, government

agents had confiscated fifty kegs of McKenzie's whiskey down-river at Fort Leavenworth.

The whiskey traded to the Indians was not usually pure. It was likely to be a watered-down version, doctored with tobacco, pepper, molasses, and anything else that would give it a kick. Yet the basic ingredient was still alcohol. In the spring of 1833 McKenzie took the bold step of smuggling a distillery into Fort Union. In August of that year he proudly showed off his still to independent fur traders M. S. Cerré and Nathaniel J. Wyeth. They were outraged at the prices that McKenzie was charging for his goods and the fact that he would not sell them any liquor for their own trade. When the two reached Fort Leavenworth, they reported the illegal still. McKenzie was suspended from the fur trade. The American Fur Company's license was not suspended due to the efforts of Senator Thomas Hart Benton of Missouri. Along with company representatives he advanced the implausible excuse that the whole distillery business at Fort Union was a scientific experiment in the development of agricultural markets.[36]

The distillery debacle at Fort Union effectively ended the career of Kenneth McKenzie. He was fired after years of being the American Fur Company's best field trader. For a long period McKenzie left the area. When he returned to the upper Missouri in 1837, he was ineffective as a trader and in time moved to a wholesale wine and liquor business in St. Louis.[37] McKenzie, once called the "King of the Missouri," spent his last years in Affton, Missouri, as a farmer. He was buried in St. Louis after his death on April 26, 1861.[38]

It was not just the absence of Kenneth McKenzie that caused John Jacob Astor to take a critical look at his American Fur Company in 1834. Always the astute businessman, Astor sensed that the American Fur Company's remaining life as a company atop the business world would be short. A general decline of fur's popularity in fashion was already beginning. In 1834 Astor withdrew from the company and sold the upper Missouri division of American Fur to Pierre Chouteau Jr., who had been his St. Louis agent since 1827. Chouteau carried on the business. Its official legal name now was the Upper Missouri Outfit, the name that had been previously adopted for that portion of Astor's business, although the new company would continue to be referred to in the region for decades as the American Fur Company.[39]

One of the first things that Chouteau did was bring in Alexander Culbertson to become Kenneth McKenzie's successor at American Fur Company, as he continued to call it. As a young man in his mid-twenties, Culbertson's experience was far greater than expected of a man his age. After receiving the same quality preparatory education that sent his younger brother Thaddeus to Yale, he had left the home of his well-to-do family in Pennsylvania while in his teens to make his own way in the world. He ended up working for Pierre Chouteau and the American Fur Company on the Missouri River. He was immediately effective as McKenzie's replacement. Some believe that it was the young Alexander Culbertson who entered into a gentlemen's agreement with Hudson's Bay Company, with a mutual pledge to avoid direct competition.[40] Others say that the matter was handled on a high diplomatic level when overtures were made by the American government to the British government to eliminate liquor in the West. As a result the Hudson's Bay Company agreed to stay well away from the border. More likely the absence of Hudson's Bay Company was due to economic reasons. The company sought smaller, more valuable pelts such as beaver, otter, and mink, which were trapped out of the forests and streams. They were a conveniently light cargo to be taken by canoes and small boats sometimes called York boats over a complicated waterway system to arrive at York Factory on Hudson's Bay. The large bulky buffalo robes that were taken by the Piegans and traded to the American Fur Company were not as preferred by Hudson's Bay.[41] At about this time the demand for beaver pelts in the fashion industry was decreasing, as silk hats replaced beaver hats as fashion choices. The demand for buffalo robes in America was rising, however, as a source of the best leather available for drive belts in the new factories of the industrial age appearing in the East.

James Kipp, who had built Fort Piegan in 1831, stayed on with Chouteau, even though he married a white woman in Missouri in 1839 when he was fifty-one and later bought a farm there. But he stayed on the upper Missouri as a trader for most of the rest of his life. Kipp later married another Mandan woman. Their child, Joseph Kipp, was born in 1849. Twenty-one years later his life would be inextricably bound to the destiny of the Piegan Indians.[42]

The Piegan tribe's own written history of those early fur-trading times in the 1830s and beyond was kept in a "Winter Count," which used pictographs to record events for the year. These records show that in 1831 the Blackfeet suffered a smallpox epidemic that spread to the Sioux.[43] Destruction by disease was recorded again in 1836, when many children died of diphtheria, called "strangulation of the throat." And in 1837 another small-pox epidemic was recorded, which was brought to the Upper Missouri on the steamboat *St. Peters*. It killed nearly six thousand Blackfeet, about two-thirds of their total population. The small-pox epidemic was so prolonged that it was also recorded in 1838. A Blood winter count in 1834 noted the success of a horse steal-ing party against a Crow camp on the Yellowstone River, and the count in 1835 showed that an enemy raiding party chased two Piegans who jumped into the Marias River and were killed.[44] The Blackfeet persevered through all these tragic events and con-tinued to trade with the American Fur Company and others, al-though not always under peaceful conditions.

In the early 1840s Pierre Chouteau made a bad personnel judg-ment when he sent Francis A. Chardon, a mercurial Philadel-phian of French extraction, to take command of Fort McKenzie. Chardon's quick and destructive temper shattered what peace there was with the Blackfeet. He was a violent man and by the time he arrived at the fort had already left a trail of unrest and accusations of murder. When Indians killed one of Chardon's men in January 1844, he decided to retaliate and kill the very next group of Blackfeet to come to the fort. For this purpose he needed help: he enlisted Alexander Harvey, another employee of the American Fur Company. When an unsuspecting group of Blackfeet arrived, Harvey and Chardon fired at them with small arms and a cannon, killing at least six. Various commentators on the incident said that some of the Indians were scalped. When the Blackfeet refused to trade any longer at Fort McKenzie, Chardon abandoned the locality and moved the post ninety river-miles down the Missouri to the mouth of the Judith River. He flattered himself by calling it Fort Chardon, which only antagonized the suffering trade relationship. It became apparent to Pierre Chouteau that it was time to bring a peacemaker to the Piegan country.[45]

In 1845 Chouteau sent Alexander Culbertson to restore trading relationships with the Blackfeet. Culbertson's first task was to get Francis Chardon out of the region. He was soon dispatched down the Missouri. Culbertson then had a new fort built farther up the river from the site of the old Fort McKenzie and on the south bank. It was finished in January 1846 and named Fort Lewis, in honor of Meriwether Lewis. But it was on the wrong side of the Missouri, because most of the Piegan camps were on the north side, along the Teton and Marias Rivers. In the spring of 1847 Culbertson tore down the new fort and floated the materials down the Missouri to a new site on the north bank, called Fort Clay and then named Fort Benton on Christmas in 1850 in honor of Senator Benton, a strong political supporter of the American Fur Company and the Upper Missouri Outfit.[46]

The new trading fort fostered a village built up around it and thrived as a center of commerce for the region. The Indians and white fur traders exchanged their pelts and hides there for clothing, arms, illegal liquor, and other items.[47] Fort Benton, or Benton City as it was sometimes known, also became the head of navigation on the Missouri and the trade center for the vast region that included lands west of the mountains as well as the southern plains of the British possessions. The Fort Benton trading post was a site where the various tribes of the Blackfeet confederacy could reliably trade their furs.[48]

In the 1860s, with a fur-trading community now firmly in place at Fort Benton, paddlewheel steamboats gradually began to appear at its riverbank. The vast profits to be obtained from hauling passengers and trade goods up and furs down encouraged steamboat captains (many of whom owned their own boats) to risk the treacherous waters. The steam vessels first used on the Missouri had been used on the Mississippi River, where they had the luxury of deep channels and could draw water up to six feet or more. These deep-draft boats turned out to be not well adapted to the Missouri's shallow channels, which grounded many of them. Nor did these boats have the power required to battle against the strong Missouri current. Eventually it became necessary to design a new steamboat, with a broader beam and a shallow draft (about two and a half feet). The stern paddlewheel was operated by more powerful steam engines, whose wood-fired boilers required huge quantities of timber and brush that had to be harvested from the shores almost daily as the boats powered up the river against the current.[49]

Christian missionaries arrived in the Piegan country to convert the Indians in the 1840s. The first were Wesleyan Methodist missionaries in 1840 and Episcopal missionaries in 1841, who performed the first baptism of a Blackfeet Indian on Christmas day. Belgian-born Jesuit Father Pierre-Jean De Smet and his priests had also been in the northwest region since 1841, first bringing Catholicism to the Flatheads.[50] In 1846 De Smet met with the Blackfeet. He and Father Nicholas Point conducted the first Catholic mass among them at the new Fort Lewis on the south side of the Missouri, where thirty-three Blackfeet, largely children, were baptized.[51]

Father Point spent the winter of 1846–1847 among the Blackfeet and Gros Ventres. He was an accomplished painter and like Catlin and Bodmer before him left portraits of the Indians. To his artistic eye, the Blackfeet territory appeared to be "an immense expanse of rolling prairies, with scarcely any timber. It has but a few insignificant clusters of mountains . . . Here and there can be seen detached elevations rising abruptly from the general level of surrounding plains. These straggling mounds or isolated elevations of different form and shape—some oblong, some round and others square . . . are natural curiosities, and a puzzle to geologists." Father Point described the Blackfeet as a

Pierre-Jean De Smet

Father De Smet in 1863–1864. Photograph by G. Sohon's
Photographic and Ambrotype Gallery, San Francisco,
California. Courtesy Montana Historical Society Research
Center Photograph Archives, Helena, Catalog #941–955.

nation "composed of three principal groups or families having
different names, but all speaking the same language": the Blackfeet proper, "named in their tongue Siksikana; The Piegans or
Pidani [sic], and the Bloods, whose Indian name is Kaenna."[52] It
was at this time that the border between Canada and the United

States was established as the 49th parallel in the 1846 Oregon Treaty, dividing the traditional hunting ranges of these tribes between two countries.

Many of the Blackfeet tribes and bands that had traditionally roamed farther north than the upper Missouri and the Marias found themselves on British soil, where they remained. On the American side of the border were the Pikanis or Piegans. Father Point had both good things and bad things to say about them. The good thing was that they were "the most civilized." The bad thing was that they were "the most noted thieves." According to Point, "If they can rob adroitly and in large value from an enemy of their nation they never fail to do so. Not seldom, even friendly tribes were the victims of the thieving propensities of these Indians."[53] The Piegan methods of survival clearly did not fit with Point's Christian morality.

In the meantime intertribal warfare continued for the Piegans on the plains, who included battles and events in the Winter Counts. In 1841 Walking Crow was killed by a Crow war party. It was also noted the Small Robes Band of Piegans was massacred by Crow Indians in 1846. That same year a war party of Crows crept into a Blood camp and took the best horses picketed in front of their owner's lodge. In 1847 a Blood Indian named Not a Favorite Child was killed by Assiniboines on the Milk River. In 1849 a war party of eight hundred Blackfeet attacked Assiniboine horse raiders and killed fifty-two, while the Blackfeet lost twenty-five. In 1850 the Crees killed Eagle Calf, also known as Boy, near the Sweetgrass Hills.[54]

As far back as 1843 James Bridger, a trapper and guide, had founded Fort Bridger in present-day southwest Wyoming. Its purpose was to trade with the immigrants as they crossed the Oregon Trail. Located at Black's ford of the Green River, just west of South Pass where the immigrant road crossed over the Continental Divide, the fort had a business of outfitting immigrant trains after their difficult journeys and exchanging healthy, well-fed horses and cattle for the footsore animals that came across the plains with them. These animals were herded the long distance to the grassy valleys in the mountains of Montana, to be fattened up and then returned for trade. A few of the settlers engaged in this business ended up as farmers and ranchers; but it was the fur trade that brought most of the residents who became permanent.

Some of the new arrivals were violent men. One of these, who arrived on the upper Missouri in the 1840s, went by the name of Malcolm Clarke. His real name was Egbert Malcolm Clark (without the "e" that he had added to the spelling of his family name). In time it became known that he committed at least two murders in the region, attempted another one, and had a history of trouble in his early life. Having been raised in a military family in Wisconsin, Clarke entered the Military Academy at West Point in 1834. It was the year of his seventeenth birthday, and he already had a mean streak. He almost immediately assaulted a classmate who refused to duel him. The academy dismissed him for the act, but President Andrew Jackson intervened, only to have Clarke attack another classmate and face a court-martial that caused him to be expelled from the academy after only a few months there.[55]

After spending several years in the Texas Army, where he had more trouble, Clarke accepted employment with the American Fur Company on the upper Missouri. He was soon partnered with Alexander Harvey, who had helped Francis Chardon fire a cannon that killed six Blackfeet and generally had a bad reputation among them. The Blackfeet even had a cryptic record of the event in their winter count in 1843, with a notation that translates "1844. Alexander Harvey killed 30 trading Piegans."[56]

A short time later Malcolm Clarke and Alexander Harvey lived up to their reputations. For unknown reasons, they pursued and overtook Kah-ta-Nah, a mixed Gros Ventre and Blood, and killed him.[57] Several years later Clarke and Harvey had a falling out. It was serious enough that Clarke planned to kill Harvey with his accomplices. Jacob Berger—the man who had opened trade with the Piegans in 1830—and a trader named James Lee also had scores to settle with Harvey and were enlisted by Clarke to help him kill Harvey. On August 16, 1845, Harvey boarded a keelboat on the Missouri to find that Clarke and his companions

Malcolm Clarke (1817–1869)

Clarke was murdered by members of the Piegan tribe, ultimately setting off the military attack on the Marias River. Photograph by G. W. Floyd Studio, Minneapolis, Minnesota, no date. Courtesy Montana Historical Society Research Center Photograph Archives, Helena, Catalog #941–761.

were waiting for him. Clarke refused Harvey's proffered handshake and instead swung a tomahawk that hit him on the head. With Harvey's head cracked open, Berger hit him with his rifle butt. As Harvey tried to wrestle Clarke overboard, Lee pounded the butt of his pistol on Harvey's grasping hand.

The attempted murder was thwarted when Alexander Culbertson intervened and convinced the "badly wounded" Harvey to take a canoe downstream to Fort Pierre. But Harvey instead got to shore and went to the trading post where Charles Larpenteur and another fur trader, Edwin Denig, were sitting on the porch. They saw "Harvey walking up to the house with his rifle across his arm." Harvey cautiously stopped "at a little distance" and asked: "Am I among friends or enemies here?" Harvey told them that he "came very near being killed . . . By Malcolm Clark, Jim Lee, and old man Berger; but the d——d cowards could not do it." His credibility was soon verified when he "pulled off his hat, showing the mark of Clark's tomahawk" and his damaged hand, "where Lee had struck him with a pistol." That was not the end of the affair, as Harvey threatened retaliation. In April 1846 a grand jury indicted Clarke and his accomplices for their assault on Harvey, and the three were ordered "out of the Indian country" by the superintendent of Indian Affairs.[58] But they did not leave. Later Harvey collected his pay from Culbertson and boarded a small canoe to leave the area. Before he left, however, he said: "You will see old Harvey bobbing about here again; they think they have got me out of the country; but they are damnably mistaken. I'll come across Clark again."[59]

In later years Clarke was somehow able to build a better reputation along the Missouri, even with the facts of his attack on Harvey known. He was aided by his almost entirely false claim that he had attended West Point, which the locals treated with great respect. According to Charles Larpenteur, respected trader, "This Mr. Clark had been educated at West Point, and was extremely punctilious." When Alexander Culbertson's Yale-educated younger half-brother Thaddeus Culbertson paid an unusual visit to the upper Missouri in 1850, he was introduced to Clarke and found him "to be very informative." The younger Culbertson, who had been trained in biology, was one of the few who were not there to participate in the fur trade. His mission was to make natural history observations and collect fossils for the Smithsonian. He came away from his meeting with Clarke with some strange insights into both Clarke and the Indians. He found that Clarke did not have a high opinion of the Blackfeet. With some disdain, Clarke described the Blackfeet custom of leaving the dead and their possessions in lodges. Wolves invariably got to the bodies. Thaddeus Culbertson also reported that Clarke took a dim view of the treatment that errant wives received from husbands or from their own brothers if the husband failed to revenge an indiscretion. Cutting off a woman's nose could punish adultery.[60]

Thaddeus Culbertson had difficulty in distinguishing between the tribes on the plains and was not the first or last white man with that problem. He believed that the Blackfeet were broken down into the northern Blackfeet, who traded with the Hudson's Bay Company, and the southern Blackfeet, who traded with the American Fur Company. He had other distinctions for the subtribes but thought that all together the Gens du Large, as he called them, numbered ninety-six hundred.[61] It was indeed a hard number for whites to estimate. It was also difficult for them to comprehend the sometimes baffling customs and languages of the Indians, all of which intrigued white scholars for decades to come, as they struggled for an understanding of the Piegans.

THREE

The Government Comes
with the Treaties

The Blackfoot has always been regarded as a treacherous,
bloodthirsty savage; this is a mistake, growing out of
ignorance of his true character.
DAVID DAWSON MITCHELL TO H. R. SCHOOLCRAFT,
JANUARY 26, 1854

In 1851 at Fort Laramie two men of great experience on the
western plains sat down together to face the difficult task of
organizing a treaty conference that was to include all the Indian
tribes in the vast region. They were Thomas Fitzpatrick, fifty-
two, and David Dawson Mitchell, forty-five. Fitzpatrick was described as having "a spare, bony figure, a face full of expression,
and white hair; his whole demeanor reveals strong passions."
He had been one of "Ashley's One Hundred," hired in 1822 in
St. Louis to go into the Indian country to trap furs and cut the Indians out of the fur trade. During his sojourns he discovered the
South Pass through the Rocky Mountains, over which he guided
settlers on their way to the Oregon Territory. In 1841 he guided
Jesuits Pierre-Jean De Smet and Nicholas Point to their mission
to the Indians west of the Rocky Mountains. He later served as
an Indian agent, having already gained the respect of many of
the tribes. The Indians called him "Broken Hand" after an acci-
dent left him missing two fingers.[1]

David Dawson Mitchell was then a superintendent for the
western Indians. He was a veteran of the fur trade in the West:

Thomas (Broken Hand) Fitzpatrick

Thomas Fitzpatrick was an early fur trapper and guide in the
West. Along with David Dawson Mitchell he organized the
Fort Laramie Treaty signing in 1851. Portrait of Thomas Fitz-
patrick by Charles Waldo Love, h. 6130.27 (scan #10027099).
Courtesy History Colorado, Denver.

the same man that Kenneth McKenzie of the American Fur Company had sent up the river in 1832 to build Fort McKenzie on
the north side of the Missouri in the Piegan territory.[2] Since that
time Mitchell had risen to become a partner in the company. He
was later the government superintendent of the western Indians
from 1841 until he entered the Mexican War in 1846 as a lieutenant colonel with the Missouri volunteers. When the war ended in
1851, he returned to his job with the Indians.[3]

The need for the treaty conference that Mitchell and Fitzpatrick were organizing indirectly had been brought on by the discovery of gold. It had first been found in California in 1848, which was followed by California statehood in 1850, furthering the interest to unite the country as thousands of immigrants and miners from the East joined the gold rush to seek their fortunes. Only three routes led to California: sea travel all the way around Cape Horn; travel by boat to Panama and then across the isthmus to board another boat; or overland across the plains and over the mountains. The last route was full of danger. Hostile Indian tribes attacked immigrant wagon trains and frequently attacked each other over hunting rights.[4]

The best the government could do to make travel across the plains safer was to use treaties to try to create peace among the Indian tribes and whites. This would allow passage of immigrants and give the various tribes hunting rights to lands that would not then be open to other tribes. To accomplish this, Congress passed an appropriation of $100,000 "for expenses of holding treaties with the wild tribes of the prairie, and for bringing delegates to the seat of government."[5] Getting representatives from all the tribes gathered for the conference was the biggest problem for Mitchell and Fitzpatrick, because it was to include all the "Indian nations, residing south of the Missouri River, east of the Rocky Mountains, and north of the lines of Texas and New Mexico."[6]

When a date for the treaty conference was decided upon, Mitchell and Fitzpatrick sent out messengers to bring in the tribes. Fitzgerald knew Father Pierre-Jean De Smet well from their travels ten years earlier, and he and Dawson prevailed on De Smet to convince the northern tribes to come in. That would include the Piegans or more broadly the Blackfeet. When all the tribes were assembled, roughly ten thousand Indians were camping together along the Platte River at Horse Creek, where there was pasture and forage for their horses. It was about thirty-six miles downstream from Fort Laramie. A small military force of only around two hundred troops was present to maintain peace. The troops were not sufficient to be effective if trouble broke out, but the council was orderly. Conspicuously absent were the

Piegans or any of the tribes of the Blackfeet Nation except the Gros Ventres. Even if they had wanted to come, they were not informed in time.[7]

Mitchell (as superintendent of Indian Affairs for the area) and Fitzpatrick (as Indian agent for some of the western Indian tribes) were there officially as commissioners "specially appointed and authorized by the President of the United States." The Indians were represented by the "the chiefs, headmen, and braves" of the "Indian nations, residing south of the Missouri River, east of the Rocky Mountains, and north of the lines of Texas and New Mexico." The tribes there were the "Sioux or Dahcotahs, Cheyennes, Arrapahoes, Crows, Assinaboines, Gros-Ventre, Mandans, and Arrickaras."[8]

The ever-present fur traders were the voices of the Indian tribes that they traded with. They represented tribes, witnessed signatures, and served as interpreters. Top fur trade leaders were there, including Edmond Chouteau, now the leader of the Upper Missouri Outfit acquired by his family from John Jacob Astor's American Fur Company. Chouteau had traveled to Fort Laramie with Father De Smet. They were staying together at nearby Fort John, a trading post consisting only of "a blacksmith shop and several cabins besides a number of Indian tents and a fine spring."[9] The only representative of any tribe of the Blackfeet Confederation was the fur trader Alexander Culbertson, the lead trader on the upper Missouri for the American Fur Company. He served as official interpreter and signed his name for the Assiniboines and Gros Ventres, but he had also been there representing the Crows. Culbertson, who traded with the Blackfeet, had not succeeded in his task of informing them of the treaty, which drew a boundary between their future hunting lands and those of the Crows along the Musselshell River. He was unable to locate the Blackfeet in time to attend the signing, so they were not present. As to the Indians who were there, the *Missouri Republican* reported that it was "Mr. Culbertson who had induced them to attend the treaty. He has long been at the head of the principal trading post on the headwaters of the Missouri, and the Indians regard him with great respect and consideration."[10]

Alexander Culbertson

Alexander Culbertson ca 1865, taken in Peoria, Illinois. Photographer unidentified. Courtesy Montana Historical Society Research Center Photograph Archives, Helena, Catalog #941–817.

While the Piegans had hunted south of the Missouri, and even wintered there in recent years, their main territory traditionally was north and west of the river. No one should have known that better than Mitchell, who in 1832 had built Fort McKenzie on the land north of the Missouri to make it more convenient for the Blackfeet to trade there. Others may have had another view of where the Piegans roamed, however, because Father De Smet had conducted the first Catholic mass and baptisms among them in 1846 at Fort Lewis on the south bank of the Missouri.[11]

After the treaty was concluded, Father De Smet returned to St. Louis and had a map made, on which he wrote "Respectfully Presented to Col. D. D. Mitchell." The map showed the territories for the various tribes that had supposedly been agreed on at the council. Land marked as "Blackfoot Territory" was south and east of the Missouri, extending to present-day Yellowstone Park and the Yellowstone River.[12] The map also showed that the Crows shared the eastern boundary of the Blackfeet territory, the Flathead and other tribes shared the boundary to the west, and the territory designated for the Flatheads included the Piegans' traditional buffalo hunting range north and west of the Missouri, along the Sun, Teton, and Marias Rivers.[13] It would not be likely that the Blackfeet would respect these boundaries, if informed of them.[14]

For reasons that appear to be obvious, the Fort Laramie Treaty did not work. First, the boundaries set for the various tribes may not have been realistic and certainly were not realistic for the Blackfeet. Second, the treaty failed politically because it promised annuities to the Indians for fifty years, but the U.S. Senate reduced the period of annuities to ten years. That began a process to obtain tribal approval of the change. In 1854 Alfred J. Vaughn, Indian agent of the Upper Missouri Agency, said he had obtained approval from the tribes. But confusion as to whether this had actually been done resulted in the treaty never being proclaimed by the president. Annuities were paid anyway, but only for fifteen years.[15]

After the 1851 Fort Laramie Treaty the Indians continued to war against each other as well as attack some of the settlers moving through the country. This hazard, along with natural fatalities from disease and exhaustion brought on by the slowness of the wagon trips, prompted the government to consider a safer and faster method of travel across the plains. Railroads were looked to as the solution.

1851 Fort Laramie Treaty map

1851 Fort Laramie Treaty map done by Father Pierre-Jean De Smet, S.J., who attended the treaty council and presented the map to David Dawson Mitchell. Courtesy Montana Historical Society Research Center Photograph Archives, Helena, Catalog #B 1100.

In the spring of 1853 secretary of war Jefferson Davis appointed Isaac Ingles Stevens to lead a party to survey a railroad north of the Missouri, with its route going through Piegan country. The diminutive and aggressive Stevens had graduated first in his 1839 West Point class and had become a military engineer. He had supported Franklin Pierce for president, and Pierce appointed him governor and Indian superintendent of the new Washington Territory. Stevens was on his way to Olympia to take his post, but first he had to map out a route for a railroad. His surveying party came up the Missouri River to start work on the route, but first Stevens tried to secure peace among the tribes.

Stevens had met with Alexander Culbertson at Fort Union and gave him a message for the Blackfeet: "Do not make war upon your neighbors. Remain at peace, and the Great Father will see that you do not lose his [good graces]." On September 21, 1853, Stevens arrived in Fort Benton, which was then part of the Washington Territory. He met with thirty chiefs of the local Indian tribes. Lacking any knowledge of the Indians he was dealing with, and being short on diplomacy, Stevens decreed in forceful terms that the government wanted the Indians' horse raiding and hostilities with other tribes to stop. He left immediately to take his post in Olympia.[16]

Isaac Stevens had not waited long enough in Fort Benton to see the results of his decree, but he left his secretary, young James Doty, at Fort Benton to observe the Indians and report to him. During the winter of 1853–1854, Doty used his time in Fort Benton making weather observations and exploring. He was not bored, because he was inquisitive about the Piegans and how they lived. It was not until he made a trip up the Marias River that he realized "how the People divided themselves." According to Doty's best estimates: "Two hundred lodges of Piegans, or about 1800 persons, were subject to the United States. Another ninety Piegan lodges, including about 270 men or 500 souls, living north of the line, had no authority other than the Hudson's Bay Company." One of his observations was that the tribes were warlike, and the winter seemed to bring on increased hostilities among them. Doty guessed that more than five hundred Piegan or Blackfeet warriors went out against the Flatheads, Shoshones, and Crows in that winter. The passage of "forty-eight outward bound and returning war parties" was reported that same year at Fort Benton. In fact Stevens's son, Hazard Stevens, later noted in his father's biography: "War was their sole business, the only means by which the young braves acquired influence, gained wealth, and found favor in the eyes of the maidens."[17]

Much of the Piegans' trouble with other Indians came from tribes on the west side of the mountains, where the Flatheads, Nez Perces, and others had roamed for years and made frequent buffalo hunting trips to the east through the mountain passes. They were considered trespassers by all the Blackfeet tribes. The Piegans, who usually ranged farthest to the west of all the tribes of the Blackfeet confederacy, bore the brunt of these incursions. The resulting battles were violent enough to make any thought of a railroad through their country unrealistic.

As James Doty was whiling away the winter of 1853–1854 in the Piegan country, he started looking for something positive to report on how peace among the Indians might be obtained, but all he could find was their sometimes peaceful relationship with whites. According to Doty, the Indians "present disposition towards the whites is unquestionably friendly." But whites would still be at risk in the region: the "danger would be that the Indians might take them for Indian enemies and rush upon them in the night" and "horses might be stolen." Doty's idealistic solution was that this risk could be avoided "under the protection of a chief or an influential white man, one who is friendly and well known to them." This man of course would have to come from either the fur traders or the priests (who were the only professions intrepid enough to venture into the hostile land), most likely from the fur traders.

Mitchell, who had built Fort McKenzie in 1832 and staged the Fort Laramie Treaty in 1851, had his own view of the friendliness of the Piegans toward whites. In 1854 he concurred with Doty's assessment that the Blackfeet were friendly, but he had an important caveat: "The Blackfoot has always been regarded as a treacherous, bloodthirsty savage; this is a mistake, growing out of ignorance of his true character. It is true, they killed and scalped a great many of the mountain trappers; but it must be considered, that they were under no treaty obligations, so far as the United States were concerned. They found strangers trespassing on their hunting grounds, and killing off the game upon which they relied for subsistence; any other tribe, or even civilized nation, would have done the same with less provocation."[18]

The young James Doty took special notice of the methods of the American fur trade that winter. He found that the infamous Alexander Harvey was somehow back in the good graces of the Indians and had set up what was known as an "opposition company" to compete with the Upper Missouri Outfit still known at that time as the American Fur Company. Doty described the "traders and employees at the American Fur Company's post, Fort Benton, and at Mr. Harvey's or the opposition fort" as being "on friendly terms with the Indians": "traders with large quantities of goods" went to remote locations, where they were "permitted to go and come without molestation, but are treated with much kindness and hospitality at the camps."[19]

Doty also learned that even though American fur traders had been present on the upper Missouri for some years now the Indians still did some trade in the British possessions. "So far as has been ascertained, their present relations with the Hudson's Bay company are simply those of a limited trade, which is entirely confined to a portion of the Blackfeet and Blood bands." Like Meriwether Lewis long before him, Doty learned that "these Indians procure in the northern part of their territory a considerable number of small peltries, and the summer at which season they go farthest north—trade them at one of the Hudson's Bay Company's posts on the Saskatchewan river—'Chesterfield House,' I think." Doty had concluded that the reason they traded there was because they were paid "a higher price for their small peltries than is given by American traders." He had also found that the Indians could "procure at that post an abundance of whiskey; and it is undoubtedly this latter consideration that induces them to go."[20]

By 1855 Isaac Stevens, now established as the Washington territorial governor and Indian superintendent, decided that it was time to put treaties in front of the tribes on the west side of the Rocky Mountains: the Flatheads, Kootenais, and Upper Pend d'Oreilles. They met there in a treaty council held in the Bitter Root Valley on July 16, 1855, in what became known as the Treaty of Hellgate.[21] Stevens wrongly assumed that all the tribes there were Salish and would "constitute a nation," even though the Kootenais did not speak Salish and did not have a peaceful relationship with the Flatheads. Plowing ahead with his wrong assumption, Stevens appointed "Victor, the head chief of the Flathead tribe, as the head chief of the said nation," only to have him refuse to sign the treaty until it included provisions for a separate reservation for his people in the Bitterroot Valley. When dissension erupted, Stevens heatedly called Victor "an old woman and a dog." Victor taciturnly replied: "I sit quiet and before me you give my land away." Chief Alexander of the Pend d'Oreilles, a convert, favored the treaty and signed it (because it would give his people an opportunity to learn more about Christianity). After the treaty was concluded, Stevens told Moses (one of the Indians), that he was taking a Nez Perce chief with him to the Blackfeet council, to which Moses replied: "They will get his hair. The Blackfeet are not like these people. They are all drunk."[22]

Believing—or perhaps just hoping—that with the Hellgate Treaty he had obtained peace on the west side of the mountains, Stevens and his party moved on to the east side to deal with the Blackfeet Nation. A major goal was to allow the Indians west of the Rockies to hunt buffalo peaceably in the Blackfeet territory on the eastern side. The council was convened in the fall of 1855 at the mouth of the Judith River on the Missouri in what was then the Nebraska Territory, even though the original plan was to have it at Fort Benton (which at that time was in the Washington Territory). It became known as the Lame Bull Treaty, named after one of the principal Blackfeet chiefs.

Lame Bull Treaty signing, 1855

The 1855 Lame Bull Treaty was signed on the Missouri River at the mouth of the Judith River. *Blackfoot Council—1855* (drawing by Gustavus Sohon). This treaty significantly modified the land granted to the Blackfeet in the 1851 Fort Laramie Treaty. Courtesy Washington State Historical Society, Tacoma.

The Blackfeet territory had not been realistically defined in the 1851 Fort Laramie Treaty. This time an attempt was made to set out the Blackfeet lands more accurately. The boundaries started with a line from "the Hell Gate or Medicine Rock Passes, in an easterly direction, to the nearest source of the Muscle Shell River, thence down said river to its mouth," which defined the southern boundary of the Blackfeet territory. Instead of going up the river toward the Missouri's three forks, the line then ran down the Missouri "to the mouth of Milk River" and "thence due north to the forty-ninth parallel" and "thence due west on said parallel to the main range of the Rocky Mountains." The border then ran south "along said range to the place of beginning" at Hell Gate or Medicine Rock Pass. The treaty had restored the natural hunting grounds along the Sun, Teton, and Marias Rivers to the Blackfeet, as well as the plains that lay to the east. All the lands were north of the Missouri.[23]

In the Lame Bull Treaty, the "Blackfoot Nation" agreed that some of the land recognized just four years before in the Fort Laramie Treaty of 1851 as "Blackfoot" territory would be given up as a "common hunting ground . . . where all the nations, tribes and bands of Indians . . . may enjoy equal and uninterrupted privileges of hunting, fishing and gathering fruit, grazing animals, curing meat and dressing robes." The treaty provided that the Blackfeet were prohibited from establishing villages or exercising exclusive rights within ten miles of the northern line of the common hunting ground. Other tribes were given the right to hunt on the southern line of the Blackfeet territory and north, "within ten miles thereof" in the newly defined Blackfeet territory. The council resulted in a written peace treaty between the tribes present and made peace with "the Crees, Assiniboines, the Crows and all neighboring tribes," but those tribes were not in attendance.[24]

Isaac Stevens and Alfred Cummings, the Indian superintendent for the Nebraska territory, were there at the signing of the treaty representing the U.S. government. Also present were Henry A. Kennerly, an assistant to Cummings, along with Alfred J. Vaughan Jr., a special Indian agent for the Upper Missouri Region; Major Edwin A. C. Hatch, agent to the Blackfeet Indians; Major Alexander Culbertson, general supervisor for the American Fur Company on the upper Missouri; and Charles P. Chouteau, son of Pierre Chouteau Jr. and now the director of his father's varied American Fur Company Interests. The group had come up the Missouri on the American Fur Company's steamer *Saint Mary*, piloted by Captains Joseph and John LaBorche (LaBarge), as far as Fort Union. From there the party proceeded overland to Fort Benton. Importantly, they had come to the meeting together with "Little Dog, then accepted to be the head Chief of the Blackfeet, Baptiste Champine [Champaign], and a number of others." Two of the others were fur traders Benjamin Deroche as an interpreter for the Blackfeet and Charles Schucette, whose tribal connection was not stated.[25]

After the group had been at Fort Benton a short time, Henry Kennerly was given the job "to go out in search of the Bloods,

Blackfeet, and Piegan Indians, who were known at the time to be some 150 to 200 miles north of Fort Benton and far into the British territory, but their exact location was not known." Kennerly reported: "With Baptiste Champine as my guide and interpreter, we started out on our mission to make a search for the people in question . . . and after a reconnaissance and examination of signs by Baptiste that the Indians upon whose trail we were traveling were none other than the Piegans, and after three or four days traveling we overtook the camp above the confluence of the Kootenai and the Billy [Belly] Rivers in Canada."[26]

The 1855 Lame Bull Treaty required the government to establish an agency located at Fort Benton, with Edwin A. C. Hatch appointed Blackfeet agent on March 3, 1855. Alfred J. Vaughn succeeded Hatch in May 1857. Part of the government plan for the Piegans was to introduce them to farming. In September 1858 Vaughan, along with the Flathead agent, Major John Owen, who had some experience in crops, selected a site for a government farm on the Sun River, which operated for a short time before the experiment was abandoned. Luther Pease, who was appointed April 22, 1861, succeeded Vaughn, followed by Henry W. Reed on April 4, 1862, and then Gad Ely Upson on October 13, 1863.[27]

In the meantime the Jesuits were seeking a place for a permanent mission for the Piegans. Fathers Nicholas Congiato and Christian Hoecken wanted to establish it at the location of the Blackfeet Agency, but that site was not safe enough. Father Hoecken took over the search and ran into the dangers that existed even for missionaries in the Piegan country. Hoecken's first site choice was about seventy-five miles from Fort Benton on the Teton River, where some small cabins were constructed. Father Camillus Imoda joined Hoecken there in October, but the site lacked wood. The mission site was changed in the spring of 1860 to the Sun River, close to the planned government farm and about eight miles above where Fort Shaw was later placed. When Father Hoecken was reassigned to the east, the site was quickly abandoned. The priests moved on to the old Fort Campbell trading post on the Marias River, where Father Joseph Menetrey joined them in October 1861.

With all these moves, the Jesuits still had not found the right place and did not have the accoutrements for a formal mission. When Father De Smet left St. Louis by steamboat bound for Fort Benton in May 1862, he had with him religious ornaments, sacred vessels, and other items necessary for a permanent mission. Father Joseph Giorda and Father Imoda met him at Fort Benton, where he delivered his materials, said a mass, and then departed on July 6 downriver to St. Louis. With the necessary religious items, the two priests decided to locate the new mission on the Marias at a place known as Willow Rounds, at the confluence of Two Medicine River and Cut Bank Creek where the headwaters of the Marias are formed. Disturbances between the Blackfeet and Crows changed their minds. Several of the Indian chiefs objected and insisted that the mission be established elsewhere. The reason seemed to be that the Marias was a fine buffalo ground: the Indians did not want it taken over by the whites that they thought would soon be arriving in numbers once the priests were there.[28]

Searching again, the Jesuits moved a safe distance away from any troubled areas to a place far to the south, on the north bank of the Missouri River "some six miles above the mouth of the Sun River." Log cabins were soon constructed, and the mission opened in February 1863 as St. Peter's. Peace there was short lived. A new priest, Father Francis Xavier Kuppens, subsequently noted that the Indians "had suddenly become strangely reticent and sulky." At one point an Indian who was trying to steal Kuppens's horse struck him with an arrow shot.[29]

Kuppens soon found out that whites near Sun River Crossing had hanged four Indians and thrown their bodies into the river. One of the suspected perpetrators had fled for safety to the mission. In retaliation the Indians killed the mission's herder and some of the livestock. Apprehensive again, the fathers finally moved the mission to Bird Tail Rock (south of the Sun River), where a building was already under construction, the mission's fourth location.[30]

Since the end of the 1850s the Piegans had started to see incursions of white settlers into their hunting grounds. Most of it was for fur trapping and trading, but in 1859 the Piegans were given a taste of the white thirst for gold when rumors prevailed about rich strikes in the Indian territory along the Teton, Marias, Old-man, and Bow Rivers. Numerous prospecting parties came, but they found nothing of great value. The British too had an interest in their adjacent lands for possible business expansion and sent out John Palliser in 1859 to make a study of their potential and report back to Parliament. The members of Palliser's expedition found the region inhospitable and nearly mutinied when they learned of the approach of Blackfoot Indians.[31]

As Fort Benton became more important as a fur-trading and commercial center, it was the goal of river captains on the Missouri to reach it with their large steamboats. In 1859 Captain John LaBarge, accompanied by Charles Chouteau of the American Fur Company, attempted to reach Fort Benton but had to unload his boat, the *Chippewa*, short of this goal, at the site of old Fort McKenzie about twelve miles downstream. The following year LaBarge was successful: on July 2, 1860, he reached Fort Benton with the *Chippewa*. He was soon followed by the *Key West*, and together they established that existing boats could navigate the Missouri River. This started an era of steamboat travel and increased immigration into the upper Missouri and the Piegan hunting grounds. It also brought an increase in the insidious whiskey trade, when white fur traders brought larger quantities of whiskey up on boats to trade with the Indians on a regular basis.

In 1862, just as steamboat transportation was being firmly established at Fort Benton, gold was discovered some two hundred miles away at Grasshopper Creek, a small stream east of the mountains in what was then the Idaho Territory and is now in southwest Montana. The gold mining camp of Bannack sprang up there, and the next year gold miners hit pay dirt just fifty miles away in Alder Gulch, where Virginia City was established. In 1864 gold was discovered about seventy miles away from Virginia City in Last Chance Gulch, which became the home of Helena. The region had become a focal point for fortune seekers who flooded in, swelling the population from only a few to a hard-to-count white population of around 20,000. The area to the north, around the Marias, at that time had an even harder-to-count Blackfeet population of a few thousand Indians, who made frequent migrations across what they called the "Medicine Line" into the British possessions.[32]

The principal transportation route to Bannack and the new gold fields was by wagon road from the Oregon Trail north, starting at Corinne in the Utah Territory. In 1863 John Bozeman, a Georgian who had come west in the previous year in search of gold, teamed with wagon train guide John Jacobs to scout a new and shorter route to the gold fields that was called the Bozeman Trail. It cut off from the Oregon Trail in Nebraska Territory and angled northwest over the plains into Montana. The trail was a good route but passed through the traditional hunting grounds of the Shoshone, Arapaho, and Lakota tribes. The first large group of settlers came over the trail in 1864, but the presence of Indians posed a major threat. The army established Fort Reno, Fort Phil Kearny, and Fort C. F. Smith along the route to quell the Indian raids that had daunted settlers since its beginning, but the trail was always difficult to defend.[33]

Meanwhile the tribes of the Blackfeet Nation in the more northern extremes of the Montana Territory were having ongoing trouble with the whites. A number of white trappers were still in the area, and the fur-trading tribes wanted them out of their territory. Also upsetting to the Indians was the appearance of wagon trains of settlers. James Liberty Fisk had established a new immigrant trail from Minnesota to Fort Benton. The wagon trains were bothersome because they ran through Indian country from the mouth of Milk River to Fort Benton.[34]

The Blackfeet tribe proper, the Gros Ventres, and Piegans all remained at peace at that time. The Bloods were of a different mind. Trouble started in December 1864, when a band of fourteen Bloods stole the horses of twenty white trappers who were hunting near the Little Rocky Mountains, a small range north of the Missouri. Nine of the trappers overtook the Bloods at daylight, killed two of them, and recovered the stolen horses. In April 1865 the Bloods stole forty horses from Fort Benton. On May 10 they stole all the horses and mules from the government farm on the Sun River that had been set up by agent Alfred Vaughn to instruct the Indians on farming. On May 22 a party of drunken white men at Fort Benton retaliated by attacking a party of Bloods there and killed three of them. Three days later a large party of Bloods attacked ten white men, who were cutting logs on the Marias River, and killed them all. According to Lieutenant James H. Bradley of the army, who gathered accounts of historical events in his journals, the "real trouble began when a party of Blood Indians destroyed a party of nine white men and one negro at the mouth of the Marias on May 25, 1865." These hostilities were all confined to a small group of Bloods, whose homes were properly in British America.[35]

Gad E. Upson, was forty years old when he was sent in 1863 to the Montana Territory to take up his position as Blackfeet agent. He had soldiered in Mexico and then as part of a mercenary filibustering expedition against Cuba. After working for a time in the Department of the Interior, he was sent to Montana as Blackfeet Indian agent. Once there, he added other side-line interests and acquired gold mining claims in the Virginia City area (two hundred miles away) and formed the Upson and Clark Mining Company to process ore. He had also run in the 1865 election for the single seat as Montana territorial delegate to Congress on the Unionist ticket, only to suffer defeat at the hands of the Democratic incumbent, Samuel McLean.[36]

Gad Upson did not think highly of the Indians that he supervised. He believed that encounters with white settlers "had a tendency to create in their ignorant minds a jealousy and prejudice against the whites, amounting in several instances to open hostilities, and resulting in bloodshed to both parties." Citing intertribal wars, disease, and moral decay, Upson predicted that "but a few years will elapse before all but a remnant of what they once were will have passed to their last 'hunting lands,' to return no more forever."[37]

On March 28, 1865, Upson was back east on his way to a meeting with William P. Dole, the commissioner of Indian Affairs, who was his superior in the Interior Department. The government in Washington had been taking a look at more protection for white settlers in Montana and chose to move the Blackfeet onto a prescribed reservation. On March 3, 1865, just before Upson's planned meeting with Dole, Congress had appropriated $15,000: "To enable the Secretary of the Interior to negotiate a treaty with the Blackfoot and other tribes of Indians to relinquish so much of their reservation as lies south of the Missouri River."[38]

When Upson arrived for his meeting with Dole, the commissioner laid out the treaty that he wanted Upson to put before the Blackfeet. It provided for ceding the lands south of both the Missouri and Teton Rivers to the United States and for the Indians to move from the ceded lands to the north of those rivers. A special provision gave half-bloods the right to select a quarter section of land for their own, and the commissioner gave instructions for "special provision to be made for granting one section of land to each of certain parties long resident among the Indians in consideration of long and faithful service in keeping the peace between the government and the Indians." These "certain parties" turned out to be fur traders and may already have been selected, based on the wording. But they would be named in the treaty only at the time of negotiation.[39]

Dole advised Upson that by "opening a large district of country to settlement by the whites, it will secure an object well worthy of your utmost efforts." But he was quick to acknowledge that the new lands were far away from civilization and that "it is doubtful whether this is practicable." Commissioner Dole directed Upson to involve the superintendent of Indian Affairs of Montana and to "report the result of your negotiations through him."[40] With that, Dole sent Upson back west. On July 12, 1865, Upson reported from Fort Benton that the Piegans and the Gros Ventres were peaceful, but the Bloods and now the Blackfeet proper were hostile. He hoped that "no time will be lost in sending troops to this point; the necessity for so doing must be apparent."[41] In the meantime Dole was replaced by Dennis Cooley as Indian commissioner.

The year 1865 was proving to be a time of increasing white intrusions into the lives of the Piegan Indians, some welcome and some not. The fur trading industry now had more free traders bringing their whiskey and trade goods directly to the camps of the Indians. Many of these traders came out of Fort Benton and Sun River.[42] Transactions in those days proceeded quickly. One example was in the spring of the year when James Boyd Hubbell and Alpheus F. Hawley formed the Northwestern Fur Company—not to be confused with the earlier North West Company—and bought the upper Missouri posts of Chouteau and Company. Pierre Chouteau had sold the posts to Hubbell when they met in Washington, DC, and then Hubbell sold a half-interest to Hawley. They took in Francis Bates and J. A. Smith as partners, with a four-year contract. At the end of the year the arrangement was not working, however, and they all agreed to dissolve the new company. By 1869 they had sold the posts below Fort Union to Elias Durfee and Campbell Peck (doing business as Durfee and Peck trading company) and retired from the upper river.

Gold miners were starting to populate the new small communities to the south (Bozeman City, Deer Lodge City, and Helena) and Bannack, where gold had first been found, which had already given way to Virginia City as the seat of government, such as it was. The U.S. Army was also taking more interest in the Montana Territory, spurred on by the reports of Indian depredations in the fledgling newspapers, which were just being established there. Gold found in Alder Gulch had brought forth the thriving new town of Virginia City and with it the territory's first regular newspaper, the *Montana Post*. On May 28, 1865, the editor published a letter written by an unknown author only two days earlier from the new town of Ophir on the Missouri River, close to the mouth of the Marias, who reported that "here to-day, to my horror and amazement I learned the melancholy fact that H. W. Burris, Frank Angevine, Abraham Lott, John Allen, John

Andrews, Henry Martin, James H. Lyon, and a 'colored man' named James Prince were massacred by the Indians yesterday morning on the Marias, about three miles from here."[43] These were the killings noted by James Bradley.

By this time Lieutenant General William Tecumseh Sherman, now in charge of the army in the West, had already sent Brevet Major General Delos Bennett Sackett up the Missouri River to scout a site for the first military post in the territory.[44]

Sackett and his party explored during the spring and into the summer of 1865 and went all the way up past the mouth of the Marias to Fort Benton before finally recommending that a post be placed on the Missouri above the mouth of the Musselshell River near either Cow Island or the mouth of the Judith River. Fort Benton was a more logical site, but Sackett believed that the shortage of wood in the vicinity would make it too hard for the post to be built and maintained. Sackett's further recommendation was that in time a second post should also be built near the Sun River and close to St. Peter's Mission on the main wagon road from Fort Benton to Helena and Virginia City.[45] It was actually a misfortune when Sackett's location was approved, because it turned out to be almost inaccessible except by the Missouri River during high water. The troops ultimately stationed there were of no value either as a deployed force or as a deterrent to Indian depredations.

FOUR

Montana's First Indian War

General Sherman vs. General Meagher

This conflict of authority will exist as long as the Indians exist, for their ways are different from our ways, and either they or we must be masters on the Plains.
    WILLIAM TECUMSEH SHERMAN TO THOMAS
    FRANCIS MEAGHER, FEBRUARY 16, 1866

I believe you are stampeded until I hear of some fight in which you whip the Indians or they whip you. I won't believe it is anything more than a stampede.
    TELEGRAM FROM WILLIAM TECUMSEH SHERMAN
    TO THOMAS FRANCIS MEAGHER, MAY 9, 1866

In September 1865 a well-known Irishman stepped off a stage-coach in Bannack, Montana, to take up his duties as territorial secretary. Brigadier General Thomas Francis Meagher had never been in Indian country before, and his life up to then had given him no experience or skill on the frontier in dealing with Indian tribes like the Piegans. He was an Irish exile who had been educated in a Jesuit college in England and had introduced the Irish national tricolor to his homeland in 1847 on his way to becoming a famous revolutionary. He had been sentenced to death by hanging, for treason against the British. Meagher dodged execution when his sentence was changed to exile for life in Tasmania. Escaping from there to New York in 1852, he became in turn a nationally known orator, newspaper publisher and editor, attorney,

Central America explorer, and leader of the famous Irish Brigade in the Civil War. There he received his rank as brigadier general and served at the front lines in the bloody battles of Antietam and Fredericksburg. Meagher survived these battles, but during his Civil War career not only Confederate cannon but frequent charges of intoxication were leveled at him.

After the war, along with most of the volunteer generals, Meagher was mustered out of the service. A few months later President Andrew Johnson appointed him secretary of the Montana Territory. At the time he was in St. Paul, planning to accompany James Liberty Fisk's third immigrant train to the territory on the Fisk Wagon Route that cut north of the Missouri through Piegan lands, a venture for which Meagher had already been denied a requested military escort.[1]

Instead of going with Fisk, Meagher traveled across the plains to his new duties on a safer southern stagecoach route, arriving on September 5, 1865. He had been in Montana only a few days when Sidney Edgerton, the territorial governor, left with his family for the east, leaving Meagher as both acting governor and acting Indian superintendent. He had learned from Fisk in St. Paul that the Indians posed a threat to white settlement. His additional concern since being in Montana compelled him to write Brevet Major General Frank Wheaton, commander of the Military District of Nebraska stationed at Fort Laramie, warning him that "the circumstances of this Territory require the permanent presence, within it, of a very efficient military force." Meagher went on to request that "not less than five hundred cavalry should be the strength of the force." Wheaton handed down Meagher's letter to Brigadier General R. E. Conner, attached to the Division of the Missouri headquarters in Omaha. Conner in turn refused his request "at this time." An always sanguine Meagher embellished the denial by saying that Conner "was compelled to pronounce it unadvisable to march troops into our Territory, at this time, the weather being to[o] broken and inclement. He assures me, however, that we will have them with the opening of Spring."[2]

In the meantime Blackfeet Indian agent Gad Upson was back in Montana and going ahead with his instructions from Indian

Thomas Francis Meagher

Brigadier General Thomas Francis Meagher was
the leader of the Irish Brigade in the Civil War before he was appointed secretary of the Montana
Territory and then became acting governor and
acting Indian superintendent. He clashed with
General William Tecumseh Sherman both during
the Civil War and when he was in Montana. Courtesy Library of Congress.

commissioner William Dole to have a treaty council in Fort Benton with the Blackfeet. Dole had told him to include Sidney Edgerton, who was the Indian superintendent as well as governor.
Edgerton was gone, however, so Upson invited Meagher to go
in his place. Meagher of course accepted the new adventure.[3] A

party of interested people in the territory selected by Meagher and Upson also accompanied them, including federal territorial Judge Lyman E. Munson, a prominent Unionist Republican with whom Meagher would later have incendiary disputes. During the 130-mile journey on horseback, Meagher and Munson, two of the best-educated men in Montana, would find that they had nothing in common but their forensic abilities to level political charges at each other. By the trip's end, their mutual disrespect foreshadowed Meagher's divisive relationships with the territory's judiciary and the entire Unionist Republican faction in the territory.[4]

Malcolm Clarke, a known murderer, was also with the group headed to Fort Benton. He brought along his years of experience in trading with the Indians and his new hard-won respectability in the Helena community, which masked his violent background. If Meagher had known of Clarke's spotty past, including his murder of Indians and attempted murder of fur trader Alexander Harvey, he might have thought it unwise to bring him. But his only recorded thoughts were that he viewed Clarke as a fellow Catholic who was "a sincere and active friend of the Jesuit Fathers."[5]

After leaving Helena in early November, the members of Meagher's party fought early cold weather and snowfall all the way to Fort Benton. They were stranded in the snow and out of provisions several times and were rescued by the Jesuit priests, who gave them food and shelter. The group finally arrived in Fort Benton, where several thousand Indians dressed in tribal regalia and sporting painted faces reportedly had assembled for the "negotiation."

As a correspondent in the blossoming newspaper trade noted, the weather had changed to "a bright, bracing day." The meeting started when "to the Council House, about noon, went forty-three chiefs and head-men, with their wild retinues, delegates being present from the Piegans, Gros-Ventres, Bloods and Black Feet [sic], all embraced under the general name of the Blackfoot Nation." In a colorful moment the Gros Ventres "came into the place in fine style, the chiefs prancing along at the head of quite a troop of young warriors, drawn out in line, who chanted a song of peace as they advanced." The article reported that "the hostile band by whom the murder of the eleven whites was perpetrated last spring, on the Marias river was not represented, these savages, ever since the murder having outlawed themselves beyond the British line."[6]

On November 16, 1865, after passing out gifts and goods brought up the Missouri River for the various tribes, Gad Upson got the Indian leaders to mark crosses next to their names on the treaty that was put before them. Over forty Indians made their marks. Conspicuous were the signature marks of Mountain Chief and Heavy Runner of the Piegans. Upson signed as special commissioner and Meagher signed as both acting governor and acting superintendent of Indian Affairs.[7]

Under the treaty the principal Indian chiefs were to receive $500 a year so long as they kept the peace, with peace between the various tribes being an important point. The Blackfeet ceded to the United States all of their lands south of the Missouri River and lands south of the Teton River to the point where it joined the Marias and then south of the Marias River for a short distance before it joined the Missouri River. These ceded lands had previously been granted by Governor Stevens's 1855 Lame Bull Treaty and before that by the 1851 Fort Laramie Treaty. The remaining land extending north from these rivers to the boundary with British America was to be an Indian reservation where no whites would be permitted to reside, although roads for whites could be constructed. Because the new reservation came only as far south as the Teton River and mouth of the Marias River on the Missouri, it left Fort Benton well south of the boundary and off the reservation.[8]

Malcolm Clarke had been along on the trip as an interpreter, but his interest in the affair was much more than just serving that function. He was actually a beneficiary under the treaty, which gave him an entire square mile of land. The other interpreters, who received the same amount of land, were fur traders Benjamin Deroche, Charles Schucette, Baptiste Champagne, and John Steele. The 640-acre parcels were to be selected anywhere except in the mining districts and would be granted in fee simple. As the *Montana Post* reported on December 9: "The interpreters, and other whites having influence among the natives," were seated at the negotiation.[9]

With the treaty done, Meagher and his party left to return home. Almost immediately trouble broke out in Fort Benton between two of the tribes. When the news caught up with Meagher, he decided to return to Fort Benton. After commandeering a small cannon along the way from an emigrant train, Meagher was back in Fort Benton the next morning. He threatened to fire the cannon unless the some four hundred warriors dispersed, which they did before nightfall.

Thomas Francis Meagher had his own thoughts on the treaty. He felt that the Indian chiefs had been bribed and that the Indians were not fairly represented at Fort Benton. In a letter to Indian commissioner Dennis N. Cooley on December 14, he let his views be known in Washington. When he got back to Virginia City, Meagher addressed Madison County's Democratic convention and told the crowd that he was not in favor of the treaty and had only signed it to dignify the occasion. Meagher then attacked the government's distribution of food and trinkets to the Indians to get them to sign a document that they never intended to honor, if they even understood the terms.[10]

Meagher's almost two-month trip to Fort Benton had brought home to him the difficulty of a single Indian superintendent covering the hundreds of miles of the Montana Territory on horseback. He proposed that the responsibility of Indian superintendent be separated from the responsibilities of territorial governor and that the Montana Territory be divided along the Rocky Mountains into separate eastern and western divisions, each with its own federally appointed Indian superintendent. Meagher also made a request to the secretary of state to obtain from the War Department a competent cavalry (Meagher's second request for troops in the few months he had been in Montana).[11]

The signed treaty was left with agent Gad Upson, who made no immediate effort to send it to Washington. He was becoming ill with tuberculosis and was bedridden by mid-January 1866.

Determined to get to the east coast for treatment and personally deliver the treaty to Washington, Upson left for California in February, after getting rid of his mining claims in Virginia City. His plan was to board a ship there to Panama and another ship on the east side of the isthmus to Washington. Sadly, he died in California on March 28, 1866, at the age of forty-three. When his body was discovered, the treaty was found near him in his baggage. It was forwarded to the Interior Department, but William P. Dole, the Indian commissioner who had wanted the treaty made, was no longer there. On April 12, 1866, Dennis Cooley, the new Indian commissioner, forwarded it to James Harlan, secretary of the Interior, with his recommendation that it not be ratified. By that time it had become clear to officials in the Interior Department that neither whites nor Indians planned on respecting the boundaries laid out by the treaty, so the document was never presented to the Senate for ratification. The signing of the treaty had done nothing at all to solve the Indian problems. Misunderstandings in Montana regarding its legal status would only cause problems for both Meagher and the Piegans.[12]

Even though the 1865 treaty required peace among the tribes whose chiefs had signed it, they did not have a moment's peace. Gad Upson, who left Fort Benton on January 9, 1866, for his life's final trek, had left Hiram D. Upham, a clerk, in charge of the Blackfeet agency. Upham wrote to Upson on that same day and again on February 2, saying that the Indians were killing whites and stealing horses, sometimes from each other. There was other bad news. Upham told Upson that white men in Fort Benton had organized a vigilance committee for self-protection against both Indians and whites. As he observed, "for two weeks . . . there was not a day but that war parties of Piegans were passing here."[13]

Upham had only partly described the situation around Fort Benton, which had become hostile. Indians were killing whites, only to be faced with retaliation by individuals and the organized vigilante groups, who were also killing Indians. One such Fort Benton group wrote a letter on January 10, 1866, expressing indignation at the activities of the Indians even at the time when the treaty negotiation was going on in 1865. They announced that some of the citizens of the area had "put themselves on a war footing" for mutual protection and that by the next summer they hoped to make it safe for any white person traveling or living on the prairie. The letter also announced the group's motto: "wipe from existence the name of P[i]egan, Blood and Blackfoot." The vigilante justice that had been at work a few years before in the mining camps of Bannack and Virginia City was now active again in Montana, this time around Fort Benton, against the Indians.[14]

On February 17, 1866, Major General William Tecumseh Sherman, commander of the United States Army forces in the western United States, was troubled by the latest request that Meagher had made to put troops in Montana. This time Meagher had asked that regular army cavalry troops be sent, of which Sherman had precious few. Territorial governors were under the State Department, so Meagher had followed the right protocol when he requested the secretary, William H. Seward, to obtain from the War Department a competent cavalry. The request had come through channels from Seward, so Sherman felt compelled to give a reasoned response, even though he had no respect for Meagher.[15]

Any military effort in Montana that involved Thomas Francis Meagher and William Tecumseh Sherman was doomed from the start. As fate would have it, back in 1861 when the Civil War began, Meagher had been a militia captain of the volunteer Irish New York 69th. His volunteer troops had been called into the first Battle of Bull Run under Sherman. After the battle, Meagher believed that the volunteers' term of enlistment was up and told Sherman that he was returning to New York. Sherman had a different view on the term of enlistment: threatening to pull a gun, he told Meagher that if he left "without orders, it will be mutiny, and I will shoot you like a dog." When Meagher finally got back to New York he sealed his fate by charging Sherman with mistreatment of the Irish and calling him an "envenomed martinet" in the press.[16]

General William Tecumseh Sherman

Sherman was the head of the army in the West as lieutenant general and then general of the army after Ulysses S. Grant was elected president. He was involved with General Philip Sheridan in issuing orders for the expedition to the Marias and for the cover-up after the campaign failed. Courtesy Library of Congress.

Setting aside his dislike for Meagher for the moment, Sherman went to some lengths to try to explain that he had only "one Regiment of Regular Cavalry, the 2nd, for all of Montana, Dacotah, Nebraska, Colorado, Kansas, and New Mexico." He added: "It is idle to expect all my Cavalry in one remote Territory." The army at that time was still involved in Reconstruction in the South after the Civil War. Sherman told Meagher that "a still more important question is now under debate, whether to the Hostile Indians, we are to add all the white people of the South as permanent enemies to be watched and kept in subjection by Military Force." He did offer some hope: as soon as the number of troops available for the West "are determined, we can arrive at the approximate estimate of what troops can be shared for Montana." In the meantime, he told Meagher, "Your people may safely count on the Missouri River and Platte Route to Laramie Fort Reno &c. to Montana, and that is about all we can attempt now. We cannot for months, if this year, promise to place any cavalry in Montana." Sherman's assessment emphasized that only the immigration routes to Montana had any semblance of protection from Indian attack. It went unsaid that once the settlers arrived they had to fend for themselves.[17]

Sherman had been in an unusually appeasing mood when he took time to try to educate Meagher on some of his philosophy. As he said, "this conflict of authority will exist as long as the Indians exist, for their ways are different from our ways, and either they or we must be masters on the Plains." His view, put simply, was that the Indians and whites could not live peaceably together and that "both races cannot use this country in common, and one or the other must withdraw."[18]

Meagher was not one to accept no for an answer, even if it came from Sherman. He doggedly kept up his pressure on Washington for troops. On April 20, 1866, in total frustration, Meagher wrote to the Indian commissioner, complaining about the lack of military forces. This time his letter may have had some effect, because in the spring of 1866 Brigadier General Philip St. George Cooke, the commander of the army's new Department of the Platte in Omaha, directed the Thirteenth Infantry to proceed to Montana under the command of Major William Clinton. These troops were neither the cavalry that Meagher had hoped for nor stationed anywhere near Virginia City or the Bozeman Trail as it ran through the small settlements in the Gallatin Valley. Instead the post was going to be placed at a remote location on the Missouri improvidently selected the previous summer by Colonel Delos Sackett and General Sherman.[19] It was to be called Camp Cooke and sat on the banks of the Missouri at the mouth of the Judith, about a hundred miles downriver from Fort Benton. The location was isolated from all transportation except for the Missouri itself, which was frozen over during the winter months and was not navigable by steamboats for an even longer period.[20] In all, the eight companies of the 13th Infantry stationed there consisted of around 680 officers and enlisted men. A minimum number of small buildings were put up, fitting for a military camp, which was not intended to have the permanence of a fort.[21] The closest civilization was a minor community and trading post at the mouth of the Musselshell River some eighty-five miles away.[22]

From its location on the Missouri River, Camp Cooke was not even situated to provide good protection for the little-used Minnesota-Montana wagon road, sometimes called the Fisk Wagon Road after its original use by James Liberty Fisk of Minnesota in 1862. The road was rugged and slow and turned out to have had only a total of eight emigrant trains crossing it from 1862 to 1867. The path of this road proceeded along the Missouri River, but only until it reached the mouth of the Milk River. It went up that stream, to the north of the Little Rocky Mountains and Bearpaw Mountains, and then south to Fort Benton. The road completely bypassed Camp Cooke. As one traveler said, two hundred miles of the trip could be saved, "could we have kept [to] the Missouri Bottoms." This the wagon trains "could not do on account of the abrupt and broken features of the country, nor could we cross the Missouri and cut off the great northern bend on account of the supposed hostile feeling and intentions of the 'noble red fellers' that are supposed to reside in that secluded and romantic clime."[23]

If there was any justification at all for placing so many valuable troops at Camp Cooke, it would have been to protect the ever-increasing river traffic as steamboats brought people and supplies to the gold fields and returned downriver with gold, furs, and passengers. The cargos were rich. In 1866 just one of the boats, the *Luella* captained by Grant Marsh, pointed downstream from Fort Benton with a shipment of two and a half tons of Confederate Gulch gold dust. Valued at $1,250,000, it was one of the richest cargoes ever to go down the Missouri.

Soon after its establishment, acting governor Meagher visited Camp Cooke, making the long trip of several days from Virginia City on horseback. He spent three days there in late July. The trip appears to have been not so much to visit the camp commander, Major Clinton, as to spend time visiting with Lieutenant Martin Hogan in his tent. When Meagher was in Ireland, his activities on behalf of the freedom of Ireland from the British had resulted in his being sentenced to death by hanging and instead being exiled to Tasmania for life. He still supported the cause of Irish freedom, and he and Hogan had mutual friends in the Irish Fenian cause. Hogan later became involved with the secret Fenian organization in Helena.[24]

Camp Cooke was also a target for unprovoked Indian attacks. One morning Lieutenants E. F. Wenekebach and W. J. Reedy and some troops had to proceed cautiously out of the post to gather the bodies of four soldiers who had been killed (presumably by Piegans) while they were on a mail route to Fort Benton. The lieutenants were under orders from Major Clinton to be on the lookout for "any straggling bands of Indians" and to "detain any without a justifiable reason for being in the area."[25] On December 1, 1866, the *Montana Post* reported the event and noted that Camp Cooke had "turned out for the soldiers to be a dangerous place to serve."[26] An even more interesting related incident came to light a few days after Christmas, when the *Post* reported the killing of a Piegan "Chief" named Strangling Wolf. The *Post* included a December 10 letter from Fort Benton's Chouteau County sheriff, Bill S. Hamilton, reporting that the chief's body "was conveyed back to Camp Cooke, with the four soldiers, and buried." According to the Camp Cooke Mortuary Record, his headboard was inscribed "In Memory of Pitanista Chief of the Piegan Tribe Killed on 30 Nov. 1866."[27]

In the meantime business in Fort Benton from both the gold rush and the fur trade was booming. Almost as exciting as the steamboats was the overland transportation industry from Fort Benton farther inland to Helena and Virginia City. Stage lines, bull trains, and mule trains were available for the commodities and passengers destined for points beyond Fort Benton. "All trails lead out of Fort Benton" was a familiar statement. The community was also the anchor of the Mullan Wagon Road, a military route to Fort Walla Walla in the Washington Territory.

To the Montana gold miners in faraway Virginia City who were clamoring for protection, the location of so many troops at distant Camp Cooke did not make sense. The *Montana Post* soon harangued: "The magnificent force will be rendered useless and totally unemployed, except in the scientific starvation of horses of the command by a winter's course of 'cottonwood bark and willow tops.'"[28]

The presence of troops at Camp Cooke appears to have had no effect at all on Indian attacks. In the summer of 1866 the peace treaty that Meagher, Upson, and the Indian chiefs had signed the previous fall completely unraveled. Hiram Upham, the clerk that Gad Upson had left in charge at Fort Benton, wrote to the Indian commissioner about repeated attacks by the Bloods, Blackfeet, and a portion of the Piegans on white settlers and upon each other. Upham described these tribes as being all one nation, speaking the common Blackfeet language, and intermarrying. According to him, the Blackfeet, Bloods, and the Northern Piegans lived mostly in Canada, crossing the border only to travel to Fort Benton to receive their annuity goods. Only the Gros Ventres, who were of a different origin, had lived up to the bargain. They had kept their part of the treaty but were at war with the Blackfeet, Bloods, and Piegans because they had to fight their way through each other's territory to come to Fort Benton for their government annuity goods. The only solution that Upham could see was the creation of separate agency for the Gros Ventres and the Crows, who were friendly to each other. That did not happen.[29]

George B. Wright was appointed in April 1866 to replace Gad Upson as the Blackfeet agent. He suffered from a lack of judgment and a quarrelsome disposition. Even before he arrived at his post, he had antagonized three out of four members of the Indian Peace Commission who were on the Missouri River. Members of the commission had even signed a "report to protest" against Wright's appointment as Blackfeet agent. Clearly out of the mainstream, Wright saw it as his duty to protect the Indians from the excesses of the white settlers and railed against those who supported the use of force to subdue the tribes. "This government is too humane to annihilate those who, from wrongs inflicted upon them, justly punished the white aggressor," Wright wrote.[30]

Wright's perspective was far removed from acting Indian superintendent Meagher's. His manner was so difficult that he had no influence on Meagher whatsoever. In fact the two developed such an antipathy that Wilbur Fisk Sanders (a Montana politician) later suspected, although without stated evidence, that Wright had something to do with Meagher's untimely death. But George Wright would not have to deal with Meagher much longer that year.

Green Clay Smith, at the age of forty, came to Montana in October 1866 to take over as territorial governor and Indian superintendent, having been appointed by President Johnson to replace Sidney Edgerton, who had been gone for over a year. Smith brought with him a wealth of experience that included serving as a brigadier general of Kentucky volunteers in the Civil War until 1862, when he resigned his army commission to enter Congress. He stayed there until he resigned in 1866 to accept his post in Montana. Curiously, he had been brevetted major general of volunteers for meritorious service during the war even though he served only a short time. As it turned out, Smith was a man of contradictions, although the full battles of his life were not fully played out until after he left the territory in 1869. Toward the end of his tenure he would be accused of intoxication and gambling away government funds, for which he did not have a good

Green Clay Smith

Smith was appointed governor of Montana in 1866 but took
an absence from the territory in 1867 when acting governor Thomas Francis Meagher formed a militia to fight the
Indians. After Smith returned, he increased the size of the
militia and ran up additional expenses, all of which were
blamed on Meagher. Courtesy Library of Congress.

answer. Nevertheless, when he left Montana he became a Baptist
minister and then a presidential candidate for the National Prohibition Party in 1876.[31]

Smith's presence in the territory in 1866 temporarily took Meagher out of the picture, to the delight of some.[32] The new editor

Henry N. Blake

Henry N. Blake was the editor of the *Montana Post* in Virginia City and did much toward creating the climate of fear in Montana. Courtesy Montana Historical Society Photograph Archives, Helena, Catalog #941-161.

of the *Montana Post*, Henry Blake, scornfully noted that "General Meagher, who has brought disgrace upon himself, his race, the Territory and country generally, has been superseded." Meagher was still territorial secretary. Although he got along well with Smith, he realized that he had no future in Montana and sought to resign. When President Andrew Johnson nominated John P. Bruce to fill the position, the Senate refused to confirm him. Meagher continued to serve as secretary.[33] This was just as well, because Governor Smith left early in 1867 to go back east after being in the territory only a few months, leaving Meagher once again as acting governor and acting Indian superintendent to face the escalating Indian controversies.

On November 2, 1866, shortly after Smith had arrived, an important event occurred in the Montana Territory: the arrival of the telegraph. Although not historically remarkable, it marked a breakthrough for the citizens of Montana and more dramatically for the military forces that would come there. For the first time in Montana's short history, dispatches could be sent on a daily basis and replies received by return telegraph. "Montana is no longer an unknown Territory," said Henry Blake in the *Montana Post*, and would not be "hidden from the view of the country and the world by the Rocky and Wind River Mountains, but is united with civilization."[34] Of course the telegraph lines never reached Camp Cooke on its remote stretch of the Missouri River, further reducing the potential of Major Clinton and his infantry there.

In 1866 a series of concerted Indian attacks along the Bozeman Trail caused great concern. News had reached Montana of attacks by the Sioux on the trail, leaving at least twenty-four civilian travelers and soldiers dead.[35] As the *Helena Herald* said, the "roadways and trails of the unoffending pioneer and emigrant were continuously marked by more fresh-made graves—the victims of the tomahawk and scalping knife in the hands of merciless savages."[36]

On November 3, 1866, Henry Blake lashed out in the *Montana Post* at the army in Montana for not using troops at Camp Cooke to provide protection. He proclaimed that the soldiers were worthless in Montana and that in the "observations of the Sheriff of the county of Chouteau, . . . the settlers in the vicinity of Fort Benton would be obliged to look out for the safety of the cavalry, because they could not defend themselves." Sarcastic humor aside, Blake said there would "be no permanent peace between the settlers and any tribe that is now upon the warpath, until the suitable chastisement has been inflicted." He called outright for "slaughter of a large number of braves." Blake

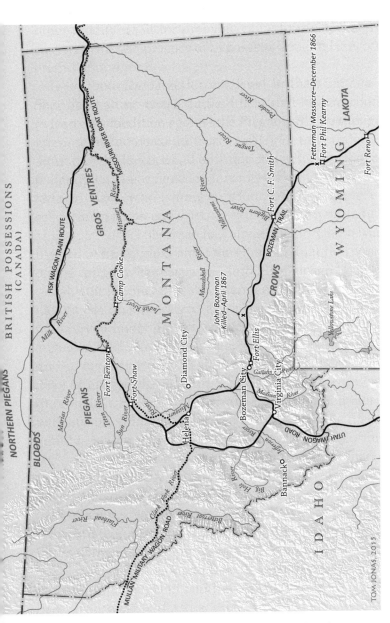

Immigrant and trade routes into Montana in the 1860s

The immigrant routes into Montana in the 1860s included the Utah Wagon Road, the Bozeman Trail, and the Fisk Wagon Train route. The route to the west on the Mullan Military Road to Walla Walla was not used frequently as an immigrant trail. The map also shows the locations of Bannack, the first capital of the Montana Territory, and Diamond City, which became prominent toward the end of the decade, as well as Camp Cooke on the Missouri River. Maps by Paul R. Wylie and Tom Jonas, copyright © 2016 by Paul R. Wylie. All rights reserved.

also predicted that "no acts of violence will be perpetrated by the regular soldiers under the present officers."[37] An officer who would perpetrate acts of violence would come to Montana in a little over a year: Major Eugene M. Baker.

The grim picture became even worse after news reached Montana in early 1867 that late in December 1866 Sioux warriors had killed ninety men of Captain William Fetterman's command along the Bozeman Trail at Fort Phil Kearny. As even more anxiety gripped the white settlers in Montana, Captain Nathaniel C. Kinney, commander of Fort F. C. Smith on the Bozeman Trail, sent a letter to "His Excellency the Governor of Montana," which Meagher received in Green Clay Smith's absence. He learned from it that a possible uprising was brewing among the Crows as well.[38]

In the meantime Governor Smith was back east, still acting in his official capacity but not communicating with Meagher, whom he had again left to serve as acting governor in the Montana Territory. Smith, like Meagher, was concerned about Indian attacks and presented a case in person to General Ulysses S. Grant, then commander of the army. He pointed out to Grant that Montana desperately needed troops to hold off the Indians. But the army had no more troops to send, and instead all he would get were arms to equip a militia. After listening carefully to Smith, Grant sent a telegram around noon on February 20, 1867, to Lieutenant General William Tecumseh Sherman, asking for his opinion: "What do you think of giving to the Governor of Montana 2500 stand arms to enable him to organize Citizens for defense against Indians?" Sherman responded that evening: "I think very well of your proposition to let the governor of Montana have twenty five hundred 2500 stand of arms to arm the Militia of the Territory. There is a good class of people in Montana & if they can protect themselves it relieves us to that extent."[39]

This might have been a good time for either Grant or Sherman to order the activation of the idle and unused troops at Camp Cooke, so they would be of some use. They remained at Camp Cooke, however, and Sherman could only promise on April 2 that two additional companies of the 13th Infantry and some recruits would be on their way up the Missouri to Montana as soon as the river opened, destined for Camp Cooke. Two days later Sherman telegraphed more good news to Smith, who by that time was in Lexington, Kentucky. Sherman had received orders from Grant to send the arms and ammunition to Montana and was only awaiting assignment of a boat that carried troops to bring the supplies upriver. All of this was going on without any information (which could easily have been sent by telegraph) being given to Meagher, the acting governor in the territory, who had to deal with the intense demands of the citizens for protection.[40]

Matters had gotten worse in Montana when John Bozeman, founder of the trail bearing his name, wrote to Meagher from Bozeman City in the Gallatin Valley, on March 25: "We have reliable reports here that we are in imminent danger of hostile Indians, and if there is not something done to protect this valley soon, there will be but a few men and no families left." When Henry Blake, the editor of the *Montana Post* in Virginia City, became aware of Bozeman's panic, he reacted with equal and immediate alarm in his paper. His words were not calming: he proclaimed the Indians must be stopped in the Gallatin; otherwise "it uncovers both our cities and we would probably have to fight the savages on our own door sills . . . Let [the Indians] once be successful, and all the fiends will inspire them to massacre and rapine."[41]

John Bozeman himself was killed in Crow Indian country on April 18, 1867. Almost a month after he had written his letter to Meagher, Bozeman and his companion Tom Cover were on Bozeman's trail in Crow Country. But it was not the Crows who were blamed for Bozeman's death. Montana citizens were treated to reports that members of the Piegan tribe under Mountain Chief had killed him. This story was confirmed by George Reed Davis, a Crow interpreter, who claimed that "Mountain Chief and three sons, one of whom was named Bull," were with a party of Crows "when they met two white men traveling up the river" (Bozeman and Cover). "Not wishing to harm the whites or to be

John Bozeman

John Bozeman established the Bozeman Trail, leading immigrants to the gold fields. His unsolved murder in April 1867 was blamed on Mountain Chief
of the Piegans and set off a fear of Indian attacks in
Montana. Courtesy Montana Historical Society Photograph Archives, Helena, Catalog #941-362.

harmed by them the Crows passed on but the Piegans shortly
disappeared from among them which fact was not discovered
for some time. The latter not putting in an appearance for some
time, the Crows started back to hunt them up and found that
they had killed Bozeman while away." The same Piegans were
later "recognized by the Crows as the sons of Mountain Chief
who had killed Bozeman."[42]

As the news spread, so did the bad reputation of Mountain Chief, who was reported to be head chief of the Piegans in a May 16 edition of the *Montana Post*. That same edition declared in an unrelated article that Heavy Runner "is one of the very best Indians in the Piegan camp."[43]

In June 1866 the *Montana Post*, then under editor Thomas Dimsdale, had reported the death of Little Dog, head chief of the Piegans, at the hands of "a party of drunken Indians of his own tribe." None of the Indian perpetrators were named.[44] A year later, in July 1867, new editor Henry Blake reported that "Mountain Chief, his two sons and two nephews, renegades from the Blackfeet . . . were expelled from their tribe for killing Little Dog."[45]

These articles in the *Post* would be the settlers' initial acquaintance with these two Piegan chiefs, whose names would go down together in history. Heavy Runner would meet his fate at the Marias River on January 23, 1870, when he was killed by troops looking for Mountain Chief.

The killing of John Bozeman evoked a flood of correspondence and opinion on the telegraph and in the newspapers, mainly the *Montana Post*. Meagher, federal judge Hezekiah Hosmer, Virginia City mayor James Castner, and Henry Blake sent requests back east calling for troops. But no promise of help for the territory was heard. Finally Meagher directly asked Major Clinton to send his unused troops from Camp Cooke. Clinton, responding in a disinterested manner, said that the area of the Gallatin was out of his official command and control: "even had I the will, I do not have the authority." At a war meeting in Virginia City citizens listened to this reply being read "with profound disgust."[46]

On May 3, 1867, General Sherman finally realized that real trouble might be brewing. He knew that Governor Smith was not yet back in the territory, so he reluctantly telegraphed Meagher that "General Augur [Christopher C. Augur of the Army of the Platte] will soon be among the Sioux and Crows on the Yellowstone, prepared to punish them." Sherman also belatedly told Meagher that "boats with twenty five hundred (2500) muskets and ammunition" were on their way to Montana.[47]

With the only help from the U.S. Army being the shipment of muskets, Meagher pressed on with an urgent new request. This time he wanted cavalry to be sent from Utah and warned that "no time should be lost." On May 9 Sherman responded angrily: "I cannot and will not order cavalry, arms and equipments from Utah." His old antagonism against Meagher had been revitalized. He then mocked Meagher: "If the danger is so great that not an hour is to be lost, how can you wait for saddles from Utah?" He challenged Meagher to provide evidence of the necessity of raising a militia: "I believe you are stampeded until I hear of some fight in which you whip the Indians or they whip you. I won't believe it is anything more than a stampede." Finally, a frustrated and spiteful Sherman, possibly remembering when Meagher had once publicly criticized him in the New York press, turned to downright pettiness when he told Meagher: "I expect you to pay for dispatches at your end of the line."[48] Meagher and the citizens in Virginia City set about raising their own militia, which was enthusiastically subscribed to and soon assembled.

Even with a militia being raised in Montana, it was apparent to Sherman that he and the army would lose face if they did not at least look into the matter, so he sent Major W. H. Lewis from Utah to investigate and report.[49] When Lewis arrived in Virginia City by stage around May 19, he had special army intelligence and a belief that an Indian "campaign under General Augur was to take place by troops going north from Platte river." He feared that the campaign "would force the Indians into Gallatin Valley and that troops would be necessary to protect the settlers in that valley." Lewis soon reported back to both Sherman and Augur that "troops should be mustered in, and it was my intention to muster in a battalion of not to exceed four hundred men." Sherman responded by a telegram sent to Virginia City on May 24, with unmistakable orders. Lewis was to muster in "a battalion of eight hundred (800) men at once, at the cost of the United States for three months." As to arms and their mounts, Sherman instructed: "Equip them as best you can till the arms *en route* reach Fort Benton . . . Let the men furnish their own horses and arms, at forty cents per day, and be rationed by contract . . .

When the service is rendered I will order payment by the regular paymaster."[50]

This was a seemingly undeniable order to raise, arm, and equip troops in Montana at the expense of the government, and Sherman's telegram was circulated to the people of Virginia City. It was clear to them that authorization of troops had been given and that the troops would be paid for by the government. Lewis even looked for volunteers to serve under him but had a problem finding them, primarily because Meagher had already enlisted many of the willing men for the Montana militia. In desperation Lewis requested that Sherman authorize him to move Major Clinton's forces of the regular army from their encampment at Camp Cooke into the Gallatin Valley. Sherman, for reasons he never explained, refused to order Clinton to act and instead almost apathetically authorized Lewis to communicate directly with Clinton to ask for a portion of his troops. Clinton was steadfast in his refusal to be involved, so troops were never sent.[51]

The only movement that the army at Camp Cooke made could be characterized as a token act. In May a small number of the troops were deployed by Clinton to serve as a deterrent on the Benton Road between Helena and Fort Benton. The *Virginia City Tri-Weekly Post* of May 30, 1867, reported that "Majo. Horr is at the Dearborn, with 67 men, and will guard the route between Kennedy's and Sun River. Lieut. Hogan is stationed at Sun River, with another detachment, and will guard the road between that point and Benton. Ten men will be posted at each station and no danger need be apprehended."[52]

Sherman, no doubt grudgingly, decided that the convenient thing to do would be to put Lewis in charge of the militia that Meagher had already assembled.[53] On May 27, while still puzzling over the matter, Sherman wrote twice to Grant. He admitted that the troops at Camp Cooke were too far away and that "Maj Lewis has reached Virginia City from Salt Lake & reports a great scarcity, I have authorized him to Employ for two (2) months a Battalion of Eight hundred (800) men to drive out of Montana the Sioux and open communication with Ft Benton. This will give time for the arrival of the arms for Governor Smith to reach his post & for Genl Augurs expedition to the Yellow Stone to produce its effect." By mid-June that situation was changed by a Cheyenne attack on white settlements along the Pawnee River in Kansas, so Sherman had to cancel his plan to have General Augur advance against the Sioux—the maneuver that Lewis had feared would drive them into the Gallatin Valley.[54]

Lewis never did take over the militia, which was in the field under Meagher. No battles were fought, but a large expense was being run up. The citizens who volunteered and supplied the army with goods and services believed that it would be paid for by the government.[55]

Throughout the West, the call by settlers and local politicians for military support against Indian attacks came pouring in. Finally it became apparent that the resources available to fight the Indians and calm the settlers were simply not available. Sherman, Grant, and secretary of war Edwin M. Stanton found it necessary to issue a formal policy circular on June 21—well after the Montana Militia had already been formed and its expense authorized—explaining when and how such militias could be authorized. The policy was inconsistent with Sherman's previous orders. "It must be clearly understood," the circular stated, "that it will require an appropriation by Congress to make the actual payment of everything, except rations, forage, and supplies." That was the bad news for the Montana militia. There was no good news, other than the hope given that "Congress will so appropriate, there is little doubt, provided the necessity for the call be manifest, as evidenced by the judgment of the department commander, ratified by myself and the General-in-Chief."[56]

Even before the official circular came out Sherman had begun an after-the-fact implementation of the new policy. This required him to do an immediate about-face on the government's commitment to make payment. On June 8, 1867, he telegraphed Grant: "Major Lewis who was sent to Montana reports 'that all the excitement here was founded on the murder of Boseman' [sic] I will not therefore accept any volunteers." On June 27, around noon, Grant telegraphed Sherman: "I do not think it advisable to call any Volunteers into service except such assistance becomes necessary for preservation of existing settlements and lines of travel." Sherman dutifully responded: "Your conclusion is exactly right and I have called for no Volunteers at all." At best Sherman was displaying a convenient memory. At worst he was showing a blatant disregard for his previous authorizations communicated not only to Meagher but also to Judge Hosmer, to Mayor Castner, and to his own officer, Lewis, as well as a disregard for Lewis's previous report that the territory needed troops.[57]

What Sherman failed to realize—or perhaps chose to ignore—was that many Montana citizens, entirely independently of Meagher, believed the risk of Indian attack was great and that the United States government had agreed to come to their defense. One of them was Davis Willson of the Gallatin Valley, who had just welcomed back home his brother Lester, a Civil War brevet brigadier general. Lester Willson had ridden up to Virginia City from Corinne, Utah, in the same stagecoach with Wilbur F. Sanders—a Meagher antagonist—and Major Lewis. Lester Willson had heard much from Lewis during the trip, which he then reported to his brother. When Davis Willson wrote a letter to his relatives back east, he wrote that Major Lewis had told him that "the United States government was now interested in the Indian troubles in Montana and would do something about it." In the same letter he also reported rumors that some members of the army doubted the severity of the problem. "We did not know how our Indian troubles were regarded by those in authority—but find that many are in doubt about it and are inclined to think it was got up for the purpose of making money." However, Lester Willson's recent encounter with Lewis had reassured him. "We are made to feel easy about this however from the fact that Gen. Sherman has taken interest enough in us to send us a man to inquire into the actual state of things, and are assured now that we will get the required support." Based on this intelligence, Davis Willson decided to remain in the Gallatin Valley instead of moving back east.[58]

It is true that most of the concern in Virginia City and in the Gallatin Valley was based on fear of an attack from the tribes to the east (the Sioux, Cheyennes, and Crows). But the citizens also feared an all-out attack by the Blackfeet and the Piegan tribe. The venerable Granville Stuart, one of the territory's earliest pioneers, pronounced that "the news of recent murders together with the report from a Bannack chief that the Bloods, Blackfeet, and Piegans had sent their squaws and children across the British line and were prepared to attack the Gallatin valley created the wildest excitement."[59]

General William Tecumseh Sherman had a convenient explanation of the situation. He simply placed the entire blame on Meagher for wanting the troops for his own personal gain. As Sherman said of the Indians: "They take no prisoners and always scalp the dead. It is this that enrages the People" who "are clamorous for extermination which is easier said than done. . . . Like Meagher in Montana, and Hunt in Colorado they must use events of this kind as means to secure local popularity."[60]

The flaw in Sherman's assessment was his failure to realize that Meagher was really not that interested in being a politician. In 1848 he had lost an election to one of the Irish seats in the British House of Commons. He had not run for office since then. At this late date in 1867 Meagher was unequivocal in his desire to leave the Montana Territory and leave government service altogether. In a letter to his brother-in-law, Samuel Latham Mitchell Barlow, written on June 15, 1867, Meagher explained his predicament: "Governor Smith has not as yet relieved me. He is on the river, however, and expected at Fort Benton in another week or so. On his arrival, I shall be free—and right glad it will make me to be so, for I am downright sick of serving the Government in a civil capacity." Nor did Meagher have any political aspirations to be a territorial delegate or a senator should Montana achieve early statehood. As he told Barlow: "I have been urged by many of the party to accept the nomination, but have obstinately declined. Not being rich enough, as yet, to support the grand responsibilities of the position." Physically ill and financially troubled, Meagher wanted only to move on—he was not completely sure where—in search of a better turn of luck and a better life.[61]

Sherman was wrong about Meagher but was right about the extreme excitement in Montana. It turned out to be hollow, and the war was both bloodless and a bit of a fiasco. Meagher's troops did not engage in battles and spent their time riding through the passes and valleys of the territory. The Jesuit missionary Father Francis Xavier Kuppens, who had asked Meagher to order his troops not to fire the first shot, offered one opinion on why there were no battles. He believed that Meagher had in fact issued such orders.[62]

Meagher's own personal view was that the militia had achieved its aim and that the patrols had deterred Indians from making an attack. In his letter of June 15 to his father, Thomas Francis Meagher Sr., in Ireland, he wrote that "for the last six weeks" he had "been constantly on horseback, and taking long rides . . . to distant points of our Territory—it having become necessary to adopt precautions and defensive measures against the Indians on the line of our Eastern settlements." The reason was that the Indians "have for some months displayed a very hostile spirit, and serious apprehensions were entertained early in April, that Montana would be threatened by them in formidable force." He added: "But I am satisfied, that having acted promptly, . . . no mischief will accrue to the Territory from the spirit that animates the savages on our borders."[63]

Two weeks later Sherman would no longer have to worry about his Montana antagonist. Meagher was dead. He had drowned in the Missouri River after falling—or some say being pushed—off a steamboat docked at Fort Benton. Meagher was staying aboard the boat, waiting to go downriver to pick up the arms that had been sent by General Sherman. They had been put off at Camp Cooke. Once again the troops there proved to be of no help and did not take it upon themselves to bring the arms to Fort Benton. Meagher's death remains a mystery to this day.[64]

FIVE

Trouble Back East

The War Department vs. the Interior Department

The policy being carried out by Gen. Sherman I believe to be the only one by which a permanent peace can be secured with these Indians, and recommend that he be allowed to execute his plans without restrictions.
GENERAL ULYSSES S. GRANT, JANUARY 21, 1867

W hen Confederate general Robert E. Lee entered the room at Appomattox to surrender his army to Union general Ulysses S. Grant, he was introduced to each member of Grant's staff and shook hands with each of them in a courteous and affable manner, until he was introduced to Colonel Ely Parker, Grant's military secretary. Lee was taken aback by Parker's swarthy features. He soon realized that Parker was an Indian. The story is told that Lee quickly shook hands with him, saying, "I am glad to see one real American here," to which Parker responded, "We are all Americans." Parker in the end wound up as the commissioner of Indian Affairs in the Interior Department. During Grant's presidency, both men had to straddle the competing philosophies of the War Department to wage campaigns against Indians of the plains, such as the Piegans in Montana, and the policy of the Interior Department to place them safely on reservations.[1]

Parker was from the Seneca tribe on the Tonawanda Reservation in western New York. He had two other names: Ha-sa-no-an-da as a child and Do-ne-ho-ga-wa after he became a sachem in the Iroquois Confederacy in 1851. He used his English name, Ely S. Parker, as he entered the white culture. He studied law but was not admitted to the bar because he was not considered a citizen, so he then became an accomplished civil engineer. By chance he formed a friendship with Ulysses S. Grant and served on his staff from Vicksburg to Appomattox, where he copied the terms of surrender.[2]

After their meeting with General Lee, Grant and Parker steamed to Washington on the *Mary Martin*. The president soon invited Grant to the White House. On the next day Parker met with Lincoln, which gave him an opportunity to express gratitude for a medal he had received. Later that same day Lincoln left his office to go to Ford's Theater and his destiny with the assassin John Wilkes Booth. A few weeks afterward Parker commented, "You white men are Christians, and may forgive the murder. I am of a race which never forgives the murder of a friend."[3]

When the war was over, Colonel Parker stayed on in Washington with Grant. Secretary of war Edwin Stanton soon recognized Parker in his own right as a "highly educated and accomplished Indian." It took little time for President Andrew Johnson to ask Parker to accompany the newly appointed commissioner of Indian Affairs, Dennis Cooley, to Fort Smith, Arkansas, to meet with the Indians of the Southwest who had supported the Confederacy. Twelve Indian tribes came to the meeting held on September 5, 1865. Some of them had slaves of their own and as Confederate supporters had lost their rights under treaties with the United States. Nine of the tribes agreed to abolish slavery and pledged renewed allegiance to the United States, as Cooley and Parker had required them to do.[4]

It had become apparent in Washington that Parker with his Indian heritage could be useful handling high-level Indian affairs. In early 1866 Grant directed Parker again to give Commissioner Cooley assistance with a delicate situation, when delegations from the Seminoles, Creeks, Cherokees, Choctaws, and Chickasaws came to Washington seeking peaceful relations with the government. Parker signed treaties with them as a representative

Ely Samuel Parker

Parker (the large man seated second from the left) is shown here with Lieutenant General Ulysses S. Grant and his staff during the Civil War. Courtesy Library of Congress.

of the government and from then on became a fixture in Washington in the making of Indian policy. As he told his brother Nic, "hardly any thing affecting the N. Y. Indians is acted upon without my being first consulted about it & whatever I say determines the matter. But this you need not repeat to any Indian, as they are too ignorant to comprehend how I can obtain such influence."[5]

General Grant's long association with Parker led him to rely on his aide for policy advice. When the governor of Texas demanded troops to stop Indian depredations, Grant asked Parker if it was necessary. This was Parker's opportunity to advocate for peaceful resolution to Indian problems, so he told Grant that he favored a peace conference with the Indians. He wanted to assure the Texas Indians—who had fled to Mexico before the war after they had been expelled from their reservations by the Texans for refusing to support the Confederacy—that the government would extend its goodwill and escort the Indians to new lands west of Arkansas. There, according to Parker, the army could watch them while they were supported by the Interior Department.

Grant liked what he heard of Parker's views on peace so much that he asked him to outline a permanent solution to the Indian problems. In January 1867—about the same time that the fear of an Indian war was at its highest in the Montana Territory—Parker submitted an optimistic plan "for the establishment of a permanent and perpetual peace and for settling all matters of differences between the United States and the various Indian tribes." It had four points. First, the control of Indian affairs was to be returned to the War Department. Second, the Indians would have their own reservations. Third, an agency would be created in the War Department to oversee Indian agencies and "see that every cent due the Indians is paid to them." And fourth, a permanent Indian commission with both whites and educated Indians would "hold talks" to convince the Indians of the benefits of abandoning their nomadic lives and becoming farmers.[6]

Grant cautiously concurred only generally in the views submitted by Parker and forwarded them on to Edwin Stanton. Parker's plan had not provided for military action. The timing was unfortunate, for it was exactly at this time that the army's wrath was raised to its highest by the Sioux ambush along the Bozeman Trail at Fort Phil Kearny when on December 21, 1866, the Indians killed all eighty-one soldiers that had been led out of the fort by Captain William Fetterman. It was the largest killing by Indians in the West at that time and incited fears among the settlers in the Montana Territory that pitted the will of General Sherman against that of acting governor Meagher.[7] In the meantime Grant's influence was increasing: on July 25, 1866, Congress established a new rank of general for Grant, making him the first four-star general in U.S. history.

President Andrew Johnson had appointed Orville H. Browning to be secretary of the interior in September 1866. He was a man of broad experience that included fighting Indians in the Black Hawk War, but he too now clearly favored peace. On January 15, 1867, Browning sent Stanton an ill-timed suggestion by Dennis Cooley, who had been Indian commissioner since July

1865. Under the circumstances at the time Cooley's suggestion could only have been considered ill advised, because he proposed sending a commission to make a treaty with the same Sioux Indians who had just massacred Fetterman and his entire command. As good as Cooley's proposal might have been, it was the wrong time to give it to Grant, who as head of the army was offended by the idea. He endorsed Browning's papers on January 21 with the notation: "I dissent entirely from the views of the Commissioner of Indian Affairs!" At that same time Grant had been considering a more militant plan from General Sherman. He noted that "the policy being carried out by Gen. Sherman I believe to be the only one by which a permanent peace can be secured with these Indians, and recommend that he be allowed to execute his plans without restrictions."[8]

Sherman's plan was simple. He wanted to put the Indians on reservations where they would be safe and punish them if they were off the reservations. In a letter to Stanton on June 17, 1867, he made it clear that "if fifty Indians are allowed to remain between the Arkansas and Platte we will have to guard every stage station, every train, and all railroad working parties. In other words, fifty hostile Indians will checkmate three thousand soldiers." Sherman wanted the Indians out of the frontier and on reservations and coldly said that "it makes little difference whether they be coaxed out by Indian commissioners or killed." In his annual report for 1868, Sherman remarked on this policy as a "double process of peace within their reservations and war without." He further intended to "prosecute the war with vindictive earnestness against all hostile Indians, till they are obliterated or beg for mercy; and therefore all who want peace must get out of the theatre of war."[9]

The issue that faced the decision makers—Grant, Parker, Browning, Stanton, Sherman, Cooley, and all the others making Indian policy—was which department of government should be in charge of dealing with Indian strife in the West. Parker himself had favored placing the office of the commissioner of Indian Affairs in the War Department but also believed that the Indians should be on reservations. The struggle was evident in Washington and resulted in talk of forming a Peace Commission that would include members of the military as well as others. By May 19 President Grant had yielded to the new ideas, among them those of his old friend Parker. He told Sherman that such a commission "may accomplish a great deal of good, beside that of collecting the Indians on reservations." But Grant still had military tactics in mind and said that the Peace Commission had the possibility of "attracting the attention of the Indians during the season practicable for making war" as well as getting the attention "of our white people, who seem never to be satisfied without hostilities with them." This, according to Grant, would also make it "much better to support a campaign against Indians." Grant did not mean "to insinuate that real and lasting good" would not also come from the labors of the Peace Commission, but, as he said, "the incidental good is a compensation."[10]

On June 20, 1867, Congress formally authorized a Peace Commission, providing for a board of commissioners "to proceed to the Indian country" and deal peaceably with the tribes. The members of the commission first assembled at the Southern Hotel in St. Louis on August 6, where they engaged in their work immediately, appointing Nathaniel G. Taylor, commissioner of Indian Affairs in the Department of the Interior, as president. In the words of General Sherman, who had been appointed to the commission, they were "to take in charge the whole question." Pending the action of the commission, Sherman gave orders to the army that "made all military movements purely defensive, and subordinate to their plans and purposes." According to him, Indian hostilities in "the departments bordering on the Platte and Missouri . . . have in a measure ceased since the board has been at work." In Sherman's view, however, it was not "equally practicable to restrain the people who live in contact with the Indians, and who have less faith in their sincerity as to peace." These words were not taken as peaceful, and Sherman was recalled to Washington when he openly disagreed with the policies of peace.[11]

After observing the tumultuous winter and spring of 1867 in the Montana Territory, which had seen the raising of a large militia under the acting governor Thomas Francis Meagher, General Sherman was not leaving matters up to the Peace Commission alone. In July 1867, just after Meagher's death, he assessed the situation and predicted that things would go better for the military in Montana. As he scornfully said: "Meagher is no longer there, and Governor Smith has reached his Post, I feel satisfied matters in that remote territory will be less threatening."[12] But even Sherman could not avoid the reality that it was not all Meagher's fault. After a year of a large number of regular army troops wasting their time at Camp Cooke, and not even being visible as a deterrent, it was apparent to all that the army deployment in Montana was flawed and that Camp Cooke was in its dying days. As an army officer said later of the troops stationed there: "Hid away at the mouth of the Judith, in a pocket as it were, they were practically wasted and out of the zone of any influence whatever, except as holding a point on the Missouri, fifteen miles from the worst rapids on it."[13]

On August 1, 1867, under orders from Sherman, Brigadier General Alfred Terry, fifty years old and an experienced military man, rode into Helena, Montana Territory. He had with him "an escort of one hundred and twenty-five mounted men." Sometime prior to June 7, the date Terry left Fort Leavenworth, Sherman had given him "verbal instructions" as to what he wanted accomplished in Montana. Based on what followed, he had clearly empowered Terry to use his judgment and act decisively on matters for which Sherman did not give official orders. Instead Terry had "received official information" from Sherman on the problem that Meagher's militia had raised in Montana and "of the instructions and authority given to Colonel Lewis." Terry had been "directed to examine into the matter" and, as he said, "if I should find that volunteers had been called out, to retain them, or dispense with them."[14]

Terry met "the honorable Green Clay Smith, the governor of the Territory, on the 4th of August, and conferred with him upon the matter." The meeting produced the results that Sherman

General Alfred Terry

General Alfred Terry, as commander of the Department of the Missouri,
came to Montana in the summer of 1867 to disband the Montana militia
and establish Fort Ellis and Fort Shaw. Courtesy Library of Congress.

wanted to hear. Terry reported he "found that Brevet Colonel
Lewis had not mustered any volunteers or militia into service."
Next the blame was laid on Thomas Francis Meagher, who, Terry
reported, as "secretary and acting governor of the Territory had
in the spring and early summer, during the absence of Governor

Smith, called into service a battalion of militia, and that it was still in the field" as a force of "five or six hundred men." It was true the militia was still in the field. It was definitely not true that Meagher had called in all of them in Smith's absence. In fact Smith himself had called in many, perhaps even a majority, of the troops in the field after his return to the territory, after Meagher was dead. Had he lived, Meagher would certainly have had something to say about it. But as it was Terry had only Governor Green Clay Smith to rely on, and the report he submitted was what Sherman wanted to hear. When he inquired as to the necessity of the militia, Terry "found great differences of opinion among" the people of Montana, "some believing that there had been, and still was such a necessity; others, that it had been necessary, but that the emergency had passed; and still others, expressing the opinion that the alarm had been groundless, and that the troops never should have been put in the field." It confounded Terry that after the militia buildup "none of these troops had then met hostile Indians!"

As Terry rode into the Gallatin Valley after his meetings in Helena, he observed that "the mountain range lying east of this valley is an Indian frontier line, which should be guarded by a military post." The second thing he reported was the presence of early farmers in the valley, for which "such a post is demanded and justified by the importance of the productions of the valley, and by the fact that its inhabitants being agriculturists, living dispersed on farms, and having their families with them, are far less capable of protecting themselves than are the inhabitants of the mining regions." The scope of Terry's authority from Sherman had apparently been very broad. Without waiting for further orders, he decisively issued his own order on August 7 for "the construction of this post, and the movement of the troops to garrison it." This was the start of Fort Ellis. By this time Terry had been in Montana long enough to see that the militia, now under Governor Smith, was not needed. Smith, however, had other ideas. When Terry "wrote to Smith expressing the opinion that his troops should be mustered out," Smith refused to accede to Terry's prompting. Subsequently "the militia were pushed down the Yellowstone into the Indian country, where they met and fought with a party of Indians." A vexed Terry could only report to Sherman that he did not know "by whose order this movement was made" but that he had "strongly remonstrated with Governor Smith against it, and similar movements."[15]

Governor Smith wanted his militia kept together, even if it became part of the regular army. Terry said: "I have received repeated and urgent applications from Governor Smith to receive his militia into the United States service, under the authority vested in me by the lieutenant general commanding." Terry refused to accept Smith's men and reported to Sherman on September 27 that the "latest intelligence from the governor is that he is mustering his troops out of the territorial service." Sherman was now unhappy with Smith, who had "brought about a conflict with the Crows and other Indians outside of the settled limits of the Territory, when he knew that the government desired very much to retain peaceful relations with them."[16]

In late summer of 1867, before he left Montana, General Terry had one last thing to do. Perhaps with some satisfaction he closed the miserable, nearly inaccessible Camp Cooke on the Missouri River. Terry noted that a large number of officers were "at posts where they did not properly belong." One of Terry's early victims was Major Clinton, the commanding officer at Camp Cooke, who had been reliable only in his consistent refusals to respond to requests for troops. Terry reported that "the district of the Upper Missouri" was now "commanded by Colonel L. V. D. Reeve, thirteenth United States infantry." Terry had put the 13th Infantry into movement and ordered most of the companies, "on the opening of navigation . . . to proceed to their proper station . . . as fast as practicable."[17]

By September 27 Terry was back at his headquarters in St. Paul and reported to Sherman that he was sending more troops to the new posts, which now included Fort Shaw, in Montana and that "new companies, I and K of the thirteenth infantry . . . were at Fort Leavenworth, Kansas, awaiting the opening of the Missouri river to join their regiments." Terry proposed that at a time "prior to the beginning of the year . . . the construction of several new posts and the enlargement and rebuilding of others, with a view to the better protection of the two routes of travel from the States to Montana which lie within this department, viz, the Missouri river, and the overland route from Minnesota." Terry made no mention of protection for either the Bozeman Trail, which was likely to be closed, or the alternate wagon route to Virginia City from Corinne, Utah, which had been used over the early years as the principal route to the gold fields of Bannack, with little problem from the Indians.[18]

Until the point when General Terry came to Montana, Governor Green Clay Smith had enjoyed a good public reputation there, at least as far as the leading newspaper, the *Montana Post*, was concerned. That all changed in October 1867, when its editor Henry Blake reported that he had discovered that corruption was the motivator for gathering the large number of troops in Montana. He stated without reluctance that Smith was at the heart of the corruption. In the past Blake had been a detractor of Thomas Francis Meagher. But when the Indian matters arose, he himself had accepted a militia commission from Meagher. In his attack on Smith, Blake said that the Indian threat had been real and that the militia was needed. Nevertheless, he was convinced of wrongdoing in maintaining the militia.

Blake did not limit his attack to his editorials. He wrote U.S. senator Henry Wilson of his home state of Massachusetts to tell him the details. "An attempt will be made by certain parties to procure the passage of a bill by Congress appropriating money to defray the expenses," Blake said. This called for "a thorough investigation . . . by an upright commission duly authorized by Congress to scrutinize every item of alleged expenditure," but he warned that "Gov. G. Clay Smith and most of our Territorial officials' should not be named to the commission." According to Blake, "I have the best of reasons for saying that Smith and others are implicated in the rascality connected with the movement, and will profit enormously, if the vouchers are paid by the National Government." Blake may have been effective in his protest. It took several years, but in the end Congress authorized only the payment of $513,343 against a total of $980,311 claimed.[19]

By the fall of 1867 General Sherman was getting a clearer view of the problems of carrying out his policies against the Piegan tribe and the other members of the Blackfeet Nation in the Montana Territory. He could see that in the tracts assigned to the Piegans and the other tribes by treaties "public lands have been surveyed and sold, railroads and stage roads located, and telegraph lines, with their necessary offices and stations, established in a country where the Indian title is clearly recognized; and all parties interested turn to the military, the only visible national authority, to give force and effect to their titles or to their rights." The only legal grounds that Sherman knew of that might give him authority to control the situation at that time was "the Indian intercourse law of 1834," which he said was "utterly inapplicable to the case, for by that law we may at any moment be called on to eject by force the white population of these Territories, which embrace more or less . . . Indian lands." But the Intercourse Act had not stopped the settlers, miners, and fur traders from coming. Sherman pointed to the example of the Dakota Territory, where "towns and settlements are daily 'occurring' in western Dakota without any civil government, and the seat of the civil authority is at Yancton [Yankton], on the Missouri river, too distant and inaccessible to be regarded. Murders and robberies are of frequent occurrence, with no practicable means of punishment or prevention."[20]

Sherman wanted to see the military have the authority to police crimes in the Montana Territory and invited the War Department to "lay the subject before the Congress." It was his hope that they would "provide an efficient civil government, or empower the military to exercise such authority where the civil authority is manifestly inadequate." But Congress took no action, and Sherman continued to move military forces into the troubled Montana Territory, without the legal means to control the white settlers' crimes.[21]

Fort Shaw, the military compound that General Terry had ordered constructed in the Piegan hunting lands, had its official opening in the fall of 1867, but it was not garrisoned fully at that time because the buildings had yet to be constructed. The first troop movement from Camp Cooke involved just a part of the 13th Infantry, and the men had to be housed in tents. It took hard labor that fall for the command to erect "one-half of each set of company quarters, a small part of the post hospital, a temporary wooden store-house, and three sets of officers' quarters."[22] The location itself was on the Sun River, a "stream of moderate size during the greater part of the year," running "in a succession of short curves" and "scarcely more than twenty yards wide, and is fordable anywhere except toward its mouth." It cut through "simply an extensive depression in the elevated plains of the country," where "on the south are three isolated buttes." Fort Shaw was still under construction when four companies of the 13th Infantry (A, C, D, and F) were permanently detached from Camp Cooke and moved there in June 1868. Two companies of the 13th (I and K) had still not arrived up the Missouri at that time. Later Company I came up and was moved to Fort Shaw. K Company, when it arrived, was left at Camp Cooke to "guard the stores in transit for Fort Shaw on Sun river."[23]

Construction had also begun on Fort Ellis in the Gallatin Valley in the early fall of 1867, and the commissary, quartermaster storehouses, and stables were completed by November. Final construction took until October and November of 1868, when the fort was completed with the erection of additional officers' quarters and a stockade.

The military was now firmly established in Montana, with permanent buildings at Fort Shaw and Fort Ellis. The former, an infantry post, was located in the Piegan lands. Fort Ellis was later converted from an infantry to a cavalry post, to give the soldiers a greater tactical range in quelling Indian troubles.[24] When Lieutenant Colonel Samuel B. Holabird, chief quartermaster of the Department of Dakota, reported on his 1869 reconnaissance to Montana Territory, he thought that Fort Ellis was appropriately located, because it was "placed with the view of closing at least two" of the three passes through the mountains to the east and "affecting as far as may be the third and last one."[25]

As soon as the troops of the U.S. Army became settled in their new forts in the Montana Territory, they were deluged with citizens' complaints and petitions requesting military action. These generally related to Indian depredations and the illegal supply of whiskey by the fur traders. Even the presence of troops at Fort Shaw on the road between Fort Benton and Helena and at Fort Ellis in the Gallatin Valley seemed to do little to deter clashes between the Indians and whites. Reports of troubles started to mount. With Fort Shaw now up and running, the focus of the reports was on the Blackfeet. Problems with the Crow and other Indians on the Bozeman Trail began to slip into the background.

The Piegans—or the Blackfeet as the newspapers seemed to prefer—had now taken center stage. Under the screaming headline "Indian Massacre," the *Montana Post* of February 15, 1868, reported that a Wells Fargo and Benton coach had "brought in from Dearborn Station the body of a man named Charles R. Scott who was murdered by Indians Sunday night last."[26]

Many stories of depredations by the Indians like this were published. Sometimes the stories were wrong, but they all contributed to the climate of fear. The *Montana Post* reported under the headline "The Indians—Protection for the Road" that "the rumor brought to town on Saturday night to the effect that Kennedy's ranch [near Wolf Creek] had been attacked and burned, and the inmates either killed or prisoners in the hands of the Indians, happily turned out to be without foundation." According to the same paper, 1st Lieutenant J. L. Stafford at Fort Shaw had written R. T. Gillespie, the agent for Wells Fargo in Helena, to tell him that "Major Clinton, Commanding officer of this post has ordered the mounted company (seventy men), which I command, to patrol the road between those points. We will be on the road every day, a portion going up and the other going down, so that I hope we may prevent any further depredations."[27]

The presence of Stafford's mounted infantry did not stop the problem or quell the fears, and it was not long until the citizens of Little Prickly Pear Valley and the neighboring Trinity Gulch petitioned Governor Smith for arms and ammunition to "protect our lives and property." The governor responded by authorizing Colonel W. F. Scribner, aide-de-camp of what remained of the Montana Militia in Helena, to "investigate personally" and if necessary "go to the threatened locality and furnish the citizens of Little Prickly Pear Valley with one hundred stand of arms and sufficient ammunition."[28]

On May 2, 1868, the *Post* carried news of the murder of Nathaniel Crabtree, "one of the few daring spirits who thought it advisable to penetrate the hostile country occupied by the Blackfeet Indians." He "was attacked by a large party of Blackfeet Indians, and shot six or seven times with arrows." The *Post* went on to report that while "this 'murder' was going on, a portion of the same band," who reportedly numbered between 200 and 800, went to Camp Cooke "and in full sight of 400 soldiers, well armed and equipped, proceeded to quietly appropriate 23 head of government horses and nine head of mules." As to the horses and mules, the *Post* sarcastically speculated that the Indians "will probably return them when called upon." Under the headline "Indian Rumors," the *Post* reported that three prospectors were attacked by Indians near the Benton Road in the vicinity of Lincoln gulch. A party of "well mounted and armed miners are now in search," the newspaper said.[29]

On May 29 the *Weekly Montana Democrat* printed a copy of an article from the *Post* under the headline "Indians Captured," describing "an Indian thievery expedition." It reported the actions of "twenty-one Blackfeet," who "made their appearance at the station of Wells Fargo & Co. at the Leaving of Sun River, on the Benton Road." The Indians were on foot, "well armed and provided with a rope."[30] Jim Makins, a freighter, was reported to have been wounded in the hip by a Piegan bullet near Fort Benton. The bullet was left in his hip, and he died from it.[31] Many more stories of attacks were published.

George Wright, the erratic Blackfeet agent, was in the middle of some of these troubles. He reported that he was "constantly besieged by the Indians for food and clothing" and fed them "when they called on a friendly visit to see me." He said he "found amongst them many who were suffering from diseased eyes, ulcers and arrow wounds," which he thought, "as an act of duty and justice, should be cured." The Piegans afflicted were treated by "Dr. H. M. Lehman, former surgeon 13th United States infantry, who attended to them kindly and attentively, and they were recently considered cured." Among them was Mountain Chief.[32]

Amid these constant attacks and problems with the members of the Blackfeet and Piegan tribes, it was questionable whether the tribes were receiving promised services and goods from Wright. He was miraculously still on the job after having been appointed in April 1866 and had a habit of annoying anyone who might be the territorial governor at the time with his constant bickering. In time the antagonism reached career-ending heights for him. On June 11, 1868, Wright wrote a disastrous letter to Nathaniel G. Taylor, commissioner of Indian Affairs, claiming that he had been given only $1,000 of a requisition of funds for his agency and that Governor Smith had lost the balance of $1,645 gambling. Wright said with great certitude: "When I last saw him in Virginia City . . . I had to actually wait upon him until he made a winning of $500 at a Faro Bank, which winning he gave me." This was something that Wright would have to prove. The letter went all the way up to Orville H. Browning, secretary of the interior, who turned it over to Seward, secretary of state. A short time later, on July 10, 1868, the State Department sent Smith a letter, informing him that "charges have been proffered against you" for "conduct unbecoming a public officer," for failing to pay over "the amount of $1645, the balance of the sum entrusted to you . . . having lost it at the gaming table." But Smith was not in Montana to receive the letter. He had already left for Washington.[33]

The accuser Wright was himself not above suspicion. According to one source, he had supplied annuity goods that were intended for the Indians to local stores in Fort Benton to pay off his personal debt.[34] When he wrote to Nathaniel Taylor about Smith, he included a requisition and a bizarre personal plea. As to the requisition, he shamelessly wrote: "Please don't reduce it, for it is a just one, and if I misappropriate the money after receiving it—surely my bonds are sufficient security." Realizing that he was about to be fired, he admitted that he was in "embarrassing surroundings" and would resign if requested. On June 15 Wright realized that he had blundered in his accusation against Governor Smith and tried to make a retraction—an *"amende honorable"* he called it—saying that his accusation against Smith was false and trying to claim that it was not his fault because people that he had considered gentlemen "informed me of the Governors having lost that money" but that they turned out to be "personal and political enemies and misled me into the erroneous report."[35]

It took until August 10 for Browning to forward Wright's retraction to Seward. By that time Wright was on his way out. On August 25, 1868, Green Clay Smith finally responded to the charges against him from Washington. He had not seen Wright's letter but had heard about his retraction. "This being the fact I don't think it is necessary to raise any defense—but I will say I never in all my life lost or won at any game of chance or otherwise . . . so much as fifteen hundred dollars. Whatever I have done in that line has been of my own means, not that of trust from the Gov't or others."[36]

Wright's last act as Blackfeet agent was to send in his annual report dated July 1, 1868. He had much to say about the alcohol traded to the Indians and wrote dramatically: "It was during last winter, occupying some five months, that king alcohol continually held high carnival while his admirers were masked in buffalo robes. It was indeed a painful sight to witness the debauchery of the Indians, made so by liquor given them by whites in exchange for their peltries." Wright claimed that he had tried to stop this practice by obtaining military assistance "but failed in it as Colonel I. V. D. Reeve, commanding 13th United States infantry at Fort Shaw, stated . . . that he had no authority to establish new military posts, should he send a squad of soldiers to this place to remain until the legitimate Indian trading was closed, it would be establishing a military post." This was the very problem that Sherman and the army had foreseen when they tried to get Congress to enact a law giving them some authority to enforce laws in the territory. Failing to get action from the military, Wright had written to Neil Howie, United States marshal at Helena, and then to Governor Green Clay Smith for assistance, but he received no reply. According to Wright, his efforts succeeded only in that "some person or persons" alleged that he himself "was with the whiskey ring and thereby benefiting." Wright soon left the agency for good, leaving his brother, W. C. Wright, in charge. He was quickly relieved by Nathaniel Pope, who was appointed as a "Special United States Indian Agent."[37]

Governor Smith's record shows that he had done little in the first six months of 1868 other than granting pardons and signing extradition orders. One lengthy proclamation was issued on March 25, where he came down hard on the continued violations of the 1834 Trade and Intercourse Act for providing liquor to the Indians. Although the unratified 1865 treaty with the Blackfeet had made Fort Benton outside the reservation, Smith wanted the liquor trading in Fort Benton to stop. He believed that a violation occurred at any location where Indians who were under the control of an agent or superintendent were given liquor. Smith called "upon all officers and citizens of Montana, to take immediate and energetic measure to suppress the liquor traffic with the Indians . . . especially at and about Fort Benton."[38]

In March 1868 Grant was still the commanding general of the army and wrote to secretary of war Stanton: "The line of Military posts known as Forts Fetterman, Reno, Phil Kearny and C. F. Smith, intended originally to cover an emigrant road to Montana, are found to pass through a country so desirable to the Indians for its game that no use can be made of the road covered, except the traveler is protected by an escort." As to the forts, Grant proposed to "abandon them this Spring or Summer" and had already "instructed Gen. Sherman accordingly." He also recommended carrying out Sherman's suggestion that the fort buildings "be disposed of to the Indian Bureau."[39] On April 29, 1868, General Sherman and the Peace Commission obtained signatures on a treaty with the Sioux and closed the forts. This was the very treaty that the army had refused to consider in early 1867. According to the treaty, the establishment of the forts "was one of the principal causes of" the Indians' "late hostilities . . . and the Indians are now satisfied on that point." This treaty was ratified on February 16, 1869, and proclaimed on February 24.[40]

From that point on the Peace Commission's treaty-making process in the upper Missouri region was substantially reduced in importance. Most of the treaties that were made were not being ratified by the Senate. So little importance did the commissioners put on the further treaty-making process that when they sought a treaty with the Piegan Indians and the other tribes of the Blackfeet Confederacy they sent only Major W. J. Cullen of the U.S. Army instead of the usual impressive cadre of peace commissioners.

Cullen was appointed as special agent "by authority of the President" and "was instructed to visit the different tribes in Montana Territory to effect such treaty arrangements as might be best for the interests of the Indians and the citizens of that Territory." The orders did not specify what the treaties should cover, almost as if the peace commissioners knew that the treaties would ultimately have no effect and would not be ratified. For Cullen, however, it was a challenging assignment, and he arose to the occasion. When Cullen first arrived in the Montana Territory, in the summer of 1868, he went to the west side of the mountains and found that things were going well with the tribes there. Coming back to the east side in Piegan country, he learned that everything was in disarray, with deceits and conspiracies and the ever-present effects of the liquor used in the fur trade. After several delays Cullen was able to meet on July 3 in Fort Benton with "a delegation of 160 Blood and Blackfeet Indians, and concluded a treaty with them." He had "sent for these Indians three times," but he had problems. As he saw it, "through superstitions and prejudicial ideas impressed upon their minds by designing men, it was with difficulty I succeeded in inducing them to meet me." Cullen said that the Hudson's Bay Company traders had "informed them that the Americans put poison in the provisions and sickness in the goods issued to them."[41]

The Indians had a more legitimate reason for not meeting with Cullen: the failure of the treaty that they had signed a few years earlier at Fort Benton. "Major Upson made a treaty with them in 1865," Cullen said, "which the United States has disregarded, and they think their Great Father has forgotten them." Cullen also blamed the "illicit whiskey traders," who would prefer not to have "Indians located permanently on reservations," where "the intercourse law will be enforced . . . thereby ending their trade." Even with these distractions, he had succeeded in making the treaty. To complete it he was required to meet in Fort Benton with the Bloods on September 1, the date assigned to the treaty. When it was signed, the treaty did not change the boundaries of the 1865 treaty.[42]

A few years after the signing of the 1868 treaty (whenever, wherever, and possibly even with whomever it was done) Henry Kennerly, a fur trader of Fort Benton, had an interesting observation. It came to light when Kennerly made what was said to be a sworn statement, claiming that Commissioner Cullen tried to assemble the Blackfeet at Fort Benton to sign a treaty. The Indians had conflicts with the whites of the area, however, and would not come in to meet Cullen. Kennerly swore under oath that he observed the camp almost daily and never saw any Blackfeet. He was sure that the Indians would have come to his house if they came to the fort, but none did. On one of Kennerly's visits to the camp he found Commissioner Cullen, lawman Francis X. Beidler, and trader Alexander Culbertson all drunk. When Cullen asked Kennerly to sign the treaty as a witness, he would not do it, because he had not personally seen any Indians signing the treaty. Culbertson, whom Kennerly called "Old Man," broke out in laughter and said: "By God we can make treaties without Indians."[43]

Despite these suspected irregularities, the treaty that Cullen finally carried back to Washington did have signatures, whether genuine or not, and among them were the marks of the Piegan chiefs Heavy Runner (Exsaquiamacan) and Mountain Chief (Nina-is-take Puquges).

Trouble erupted after the first of the "negotiations" with the Piegans in Fort Benton on July 3. That was when Cullen said that "'the Mountain Chief,' an old man and principal chief of their tribe, was without cause struck and shot at by two white men." Nathaniel Pope, the new Blackfeet Indian agent, claimed that the affray started "immediately after the treaty" when "Mountain

Chief, while visiting this place was insulted and abused in an outrageous manner by some whites." It appeared that "the only reason for their conduct was the fact" that Mountain Chief, "in council, had asked the commissioner to have certain men sent out of the Indian country." Pope did not give the men's names, but he did say firmly that "all good citizens agree that these men are not fit to be in an Indian country." Commissioner Cullen was appalled by the treatment of Mountain Chief and tried to have a warrant issued for the arrest of his attackers, but "rather than have a white man punished for assaulting an Indian, the justice of the peace and sheriff resigned their offices."[44]

It was beyond Cullen's authority as a special agent of the Peace Commission and an army officer to serve as a law enforcement officer, but he did. He tried to deal with the lawlessness in Fort Benton and "caused the seizure of 10 bales of buffalo robes which had been bought with whiskey." Cullen's case against the whiskey traders failed when the deputy United States marshal placed the main witness on a horse and started him toward Helena to give testimony. Cullen said the man "was pursued, and caught a few miles from this place, a rope put around his neck and hung until nearly dead; whereupon he promised to quit the country, and was then released." Cullen also arrested eighteen Piegans who were believed to have stolen horses and was holding them at Fort Shaw, but he said that they "will be released upon the delivery at the fort of the horses stolen from the whites." In his short time in Piegan country, Cullen found that "most of the whiskey trade is done in winter," which would have been when the tribes were in their permanent winter locations and buffalo robes were rich with heavy fur. "There is no possible way to prevent it," he said, "unless the Indians were given settlements of their own, away from the white settlements."[45]

After the Blackfeet negotiations in Fort Benton, Cullen moved as quickly as a boat could take him downstream to Fort Hawley, a trading post established on the south side of the Missouri about twenty miles above the Musselshell River. Accompanied only by a mixed group of fur traders and interpreters, he was able to get marks on a treaty document with the Gros Ventres on July 15 and on a separate treaty with the River Crows on that same day. Moving on by horseback to Virginia City, Cullen completed another treaty with the mixed tribes of Shoshones, Bannocks, and Sheepeaters.[46]

Nathaniel Taylor, commissioner of Indian Affairs, reported in November that Cullen had reached Washington and handed to him "treaties made by him with the Blood, Piegan, and Blackfeet Indians, Gros Ventres, Missouri River Crows, and the Bannocks and Shoshones." The "treaties provide for the extinguishment of the title of the Indians to a large extent of country." This was what Taylor was after, and he thought it would go a long way to stop the criticism that was being leveled at the Indian Peace Commission, of which he had been elected president. He had responded to these criticisms by saying, "Its mission and its labors have been pre-eminently successful; for wherever the commission has been enabled to carry out its plans, and fulfill its promises, its efforts for peace and settlement of these Indian troubles have succeeded, and . . . none of the Indians have disappointed them."[47]

If Taylor had been in Montana he could have seen that "peace and settlement of these Indian troubles" had not succeeded there. Cullen sadly reported to Taylor that the "Piegans have recently stolen from the settlers at Diamond City and other places about 80 horses." When "a number of citizens started in pursuit," they had to quit the chase so as not to "venture into the Indian camps."[48]

During the summer of 1868, while the treaty councils were going on, Governor Smith was in Washington on his second extended absence from his post in Montana. Smith cared little about being in the territory he governed and had now left territorial secretary James Tufts as its second acting governor. Thomas Francis Meagher had served two times in that capacity, so this was the third time an acting governor was in charge in the territory's short history.

On September 25, 1868, Tufts as acting governor took it upon himself to issue a public proclamation announcing Cullen's treaty with the Blackfeet and Piegans. With no warning that the treaty still had to be ratified to be effective, Tufts announced that

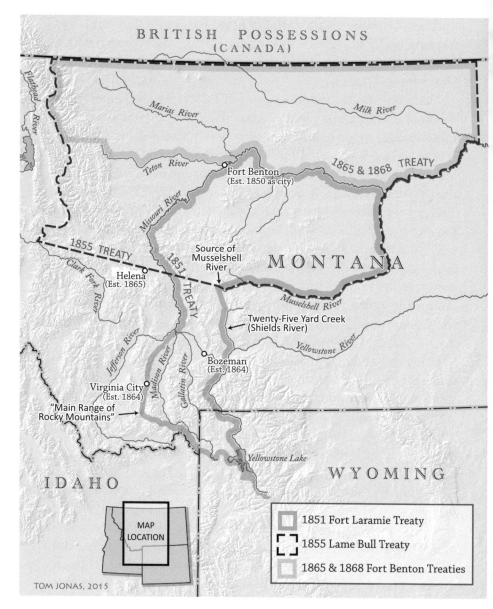

Blackfeet treaty lands

This map shows the boundaries of lands granted to the Blackfeet in the 1851 Fort Laramie Treaty, the 1855 Lame Bull Treaty, and the 1865 and 1868 Fort Benton Treaties. Maps by Paul R. Wylie and Tom Jonas, copyright © 2016 by Paul R. Wylie. All rights reserved.

boundaries under the treaty had been drawn around the "Gros Ventres and Blackfoot nations." In his haste to publicize the new boundaries, either Tufts or the press made an obvious error in the description by saying that the 49th parallel was south of the 48th.[49] No mention was made that the boundaries were exactly the same as in the 1865 treaty, which had never been ratified.

Nevertheless, the people of Montana and General Sherman and his army had been given new grounds for saying that they could attack the Indians if they were not within those boundaries. It apparently did not matter anyway: when they attacked the Piegans in 1870, they were clearly within the reservation established in 1868.

Even with treaties, the problems of whiskey dealing remained and were confirmed by one of the most prophetic local observers of the time. Shirley C. Ashby (or Colonel Ashby as he would be known as a trader) had survived a harrowing trip on the plains to get to Fort Benton in 1867. Traveling in the winter, Ashby felt himself lucky even to reach his new job with Isaac G. Baker, an established trader. He recorded that the "weather was intensely cold, and I suffered very much before I arrived" at a stopping place for the night. "My fingers were frozen, but I had not lost my gloves, as they were tied together with a string, which was thrown over my shoulders." His traveling partner, a man named Anderson, was in worse condition, Ashby said. While they were "in sight of the wagons, I got him behind me, on my pony, rushed to the wagons, got a hatchet cut a hole through the ice, and put our hands in the water. It drew out the frost and formed ice on our hands." When they started the next morning for Fort Benton, Ashby recollected, "it was fearfully cold—forty-degrees below zero. (The reason that I know how cold it was, I had a small thermometer with me.)" Ashby experienced ecstasy when they reached the Marias River, "where there was plenty of dry wood and water. I was never happier in my life, even if I had found a palace, I could not have been happier . . . There has never been a spot, that to me, in all my experience that presented a more comfortable place than on the banks of the river."[50]

Ashby found it strange when he did arrive at his destination that "the Indians coming in to the Ft. Benton bottom would get drunk and sell their robes and furs for whiskey." He found it stranger still that only two firms were licensed by the Indian agent "to go out and trade with the Indians in their own country." "The country north of Ft. Benton was divided," he said. "I. G. Baker and brother received a license to trade in the Indian country north with the Bloods and the North Blackfeet, on the Marias River." Baker had hired a man named "Roche de Rouche, a Frenchman to manage and interpret the Trading Post on the Marias, at a large and handsome salary." This was the same man known as Benjamin Deroche, who received a full square mile section of land under the 1865 Blackfeet Treaty. The other company licensed by the Indian agent was "the Northwest Fur Company, James Hubbell, and John Riplinger, managers," who were "located on the Teton about a mile or two, from the town of Chouteau." Ashby had quickly become acquainted with some of the darker collusions of the fur trade.[51]

Indeed the whiskey trade was so damaging that some of the Indian chiefs tried to stop the traders. One event happened toward the end of 1868, when Jake LaMott, who was employed by I. G. Baker, arrived at "Captain Nels Leavings on the Teton River north of Fort Benton." He was trying to find Charles Conrad, another employee of Baker's company who was trading with the Piegans, but was having a difficult time. The Indians kept pestering him for food and whiskey. He finally broke away and found Conrad, and the two slipped away in the night. The Indians soon overtook them and pleaded to join them again. LaMott and Conrad finally got away at Dead Indian Coulee and went on to the Marias, only to find the camps there "occupied by the traders and agents from Carroll & Steel, Northwestern Fur Co., T. C. Power and Bro., and Captain Nels and Charlie Duvall who there as free traders; all trading whiskey to the Indians." When the Piegan chiefs had seen enough of the drinking, they chased off the traders. Joe Searson, who worked for the Northwestern Fur Company, was almost killed before he was able to get away.

Conrad's wagons were the last to leave and had been sent on their way by an angry group of young warriors in Full Bear's camp and told not to stop until they reached Fort Benton.[52]

It was Mountain Chief of the Piegans who delivered the message that they wanted the whiskey traders out of their camps. "We do not want to see pale faces to come to our villages," he said. "If we desire to trade we will go into their forts, dispose of our robes and leave. There is nothing in common between us." In the midst of reports of whiskey trading and Indian depredations, little attention had been paid to these peaceful intentions of Mountain Chief, then considered to be the main chief of the Piegans, who had been publicly accused of killing John Bozeman in the spring of 1867.[53]

On September 30, 1868, a trader named George Stull wrote from Fort Benton to Colonel G. L. Anderson, the commander of Fort Shaw:

> The Mountain Chief, Chief of the Piegans, is here with a large number of his people. They brought in about thirty head of horses belonging to Whites and now the bearer, All Most a Dog goes to Shaw with said horses, being all he could recover, the Warriors having traded them stolen stock off to the Bloods as fast as they brought them into their camp. He had turned over three head to me, which was stolen from my wagons at Ellis. And he has posted me in regard to who has three more making out the number lost by me. I write you this upon the request of All Most a Dog who I think has done everything in his power for the recovery of horses.[54]

Neither the Seneca Indian Ely S. Parker in Washington nor the sometimes misunderstood Piegan leader Mountain Chief had enough influence to overcome the public opinion created by the passions of the young braves of Mountain Chief's band. In the end it would be Mountain Chief's village that was the target of members of the 2nd Cavalry as they prepared to attack a band that they believed to be his on the morning of January 23, 1870.

SIX

Making a Case against the Piegans

About the 15th of January they will be very helpless and if
where they live is not too far from Shaw or Ellis, we might
be able to give them a good hard blow which will make
peace a desirable object.

GENERAL SHERIDAN TO GENERAL SHERMAN,

OCTOBER 21, 1869

On March 4, 1869, Ulysses S. Grant, forty-seven, stood on the East Portico of the Capitol waiting to be inaugurated as the twenty-first, and youngest ever, president of the United States. He had refused to ride to the event in the carriage of his predecessor, Andrew Johnson, so Johnson did not go at all, preferring to sign last-minute legislation in the White House. In the cold, wet weather Grant read his sparse inaugural address of just more than 1,100 words, handwritten on eleven pages. Words and time were at a premium, but he took a moment to promise a "careful study" of the Indian situation that would "favor any course toward them, which tends to civilization and ultimate citizenship."[1]

Six months later, at his State of the Union speech in December, Grant had a more elaborate plan. Proclaiming the management of the "original inhabitants a subject of embarrassment and expense . . . attended with robberies, murders, and wars," Grant reported that he had "attempted a new policy toward these wards . . . with fair results so far as tried." In an unusual move he had gone outside the bureaucracy to enlist the services of the Society of Friends—the Quakers—to serve as Indian agents. His reason,

Grant said, was they had "succeeded in living in peace with the Indians in the early settlement of Pennsylvania." The Quakers had been given responsibility for a few reservations in the East, and Grant thought that this would work with other tribes and other religious orders. But his plan involved a huge contradiction when he said that for the "superintendents and Indian agents not on the reservations, officers of the army" had been selected. Grant was not ready to give up on using the army as a force to control the Indians, particularly in Montana, where agitation was strong to move against the Piegans. At the time Grant announced his policy, Army Brigadier General Alfred Sully had already been appointed Indian superintendent for the Montana Territory and army Lieutenant William Pease had been named the Blackfeet agent.[2]

Meanwhile, in the Montana Territory, the 13th Infantry was planning to settle into its new forts and transitioning into a more viable force than it had been at its inaccessible Camp Cooke on the Missouri. Personnel changes were also in the offing. On April 18, 1869, Captain R. L. LaMotte, then the commander of the infantry detachment at the new Fort Ellis, wrote to the "District Commander" at Fort Shaw to report on unspecified Indian troubles in the Gallatin Valley, complaining that he had "sent thirty men under Lieut. Codding and have not another man that can ride." Soon Captain. J. T. McGinniss of Fort Shaw advised LaMotte that "four Companies of the Second Cavalry" had been "ordered to Fort Ellis." This would begin the long tenure of the cavalry in Montana. Their new deployment would mean the more mobile army could take aggressive action against the far-flung Indian tribes.[3]

In June 1869 no less a personage than Major General Winfield Scott Hancock, with his full staff entourage, rode over the mountains from the south and started making his way "to Fort Ellis, Montana, and the other posts in that territory." The tall and handsome Hancock was the military commander of the Department of the Dakotas, with headquarters in St. Paul, and had the perfect image to usher in the new aggressive military era in Montana.[4]

General Winfield Scott Hancock

General Winfield Scott Hancock was the commander of the Department of the Dakotas in St. Paul, where his involvement in the planning of the massacre was minimal. His commander, General Philip Sheridan of the Department of the Missouri in Chicago, took over the planning of the attack and handpicked Major Eugene M. Baker to lead it. Courtesy Library of Congress.

As impressive and experienced as Hancock was, he was not yet at the pinnacle of his career that would find him as the Democratic nominee for president of the United States in 1880. After graduating from West Point in 1844 (eighteenth in a class of twenty-five) he served in the Mexican War and was honored for his bravery. As a career military officer, he had served at an ever-increasing rank in a number of posts and in the Civil War, where he commanded a division. Hancock had performed well in the war and was broadly recognized for his accomplishments. At the close of the war he was assigned the grim duty of executing the men and one woman who had conspired to assassinate Lincoln. He supervised their hangings on July 7, 1865. Hancock let it be known that he had objections to hanging some of them whom he thought were less blameworthy, however, particularly when it came to Mary Surratt, the lone woman. "Every soldier was bound to act as I did under similar circumstances," Hancock acknowledged.[5]

At about the same time that Hancock arrived in Montana, Colonel Albert Gallatin Brackett led four companies of the 2nd Cavalry from Wyoming into the territory. On their ride the troops had passed many Indians, mostly Bannocks, who visited the soldiers' camps and sometimes spent the night in camp with them. But Brackett and his men knew that they were being called to a troubled place. The Piegan Indians that they would eventually face in Montana were not of the same disposition as the friendlier Bannocks.

On June 19, after Brackett left Beaver Canyon to a "place on Summit Creek, Idaho Valley, about one mile and a half beyond the station in Pleasant Valley," a messenger approached. He gave Brackett a "dispatch from General Hancock telling us to march across the mountains to Virginia City," where Hancock had ordered supplies for them. The men of the 2nd Cavalry stayed for a few days close to town and then traveled over "a steep hill." On June 28th they were in the mining town of Sterling in the Hot Springs mining district and viewed several quartz-crushing mills. One of them was the Clark and Upson Mining Company, still bearing the name of its co-founder, Gad Upson, the former Blackfeet agent who had died in 1866 in California with the 1865 Blackfeet Treaty still in his possession.[6]

After crossing the Madison River and coming in sight of the Gallatin Valley, Brackett and his troops crossed the west fork of the Gallatin River. They could see a few irrigation ditches for the new agriculture in the valley, which Brackett noted "to be the best farming land in Montana." The group passed through the fledgling community of Bozeman, then "containing perhaps a hundred souls," and moved on to Fort Ellis, two and a half miles east of town. Brackett was pleased to find that it was already a "fort made of logs and surrounded with palisades with two block houses at diagonal corners." Though the fort was small and compactly built, Brackett said that it "seems well adapted for frontier protection." One of its purposes was to allay the fears of the community, and "the Stockade was put up at the request of the citizens of the valley to serve as a place of refuge in case of an Indian invasion."

Fort Ellis was still on the untamed frontier. Even though the cavalry officers could bring their wives and eventually have their own houses there, the only woman who came along on the trek was Amelia Doane, the wife of Second Lieutenant Gustavus Cheney Doane of Company H. The rugged army life in Montana did not favor the marriage, which did not last.[7]

After seeing to it that Brackett's troops were safely at Fort Ellis, Hancock set out to inspect the other military posts. Before his trip was over, he had surveyed a military reservation at the town of Fort Benton, which had a fur-trading fort but not a military fort. While the Fort Shaw post was now up and running, Hancock thought that provisions should also be made for another military fort in Fort Benton, at the head of navigation on the Missouri River.[8]

During the summer of 1869, Brevet Brigadier General Regis de Trobriand, a man who at that time thought highly of General Hancock, arrived in Montana as commander of the military, reporting to Hancock. He was a French immigrant who had fought in the American Civil War. His full name was Philippe Regis Denis de Keredern de Trobriand. Names this complicated were confusing to Americans, so it was generally shortened. His background seemed to be an ill fit for the rugged army life on the plains. He had been born into the aristocracy in France, the son of one of Napoleon Bonaparte's generals who was said to be

Fort Benton street and boat docked scene, 1868

Front street in Fort Benton in 1868, showing a docked steamboat and the trading fort in the distance. The photo was taken in August 1868 by Salt Lake City
photographer Charles R. Savage as he visited Fort Benton at the end of the
steamboating season. Courtesy Overholser Historical Research Center, Fort
Benton, Montana.

a baron of ancient lineage.[9] As a young man de Trobriand studied law, wrote poetry and prose, and published his first novel in
1840. He had a feisty streak and was said to have been an expert
swordsman who fought a number of duels.

Coming to America in 1851, when he was in his mid-twenties,
de Trobriand immediately blended in with the New York social
elite and soon married heiress Mary Mason Jones, lived with
her abroad, and then returned to New York to write and edit for
French-language publications. Ten years after his first arrival in
New York he was in the Civil War as a naturalized citizen, serving as a colonel in the Union Army in command of the 55th New
York Infantry regiment of predominantly French immigrants,
known as the Gardes Lafayette.[10] De Trobriand fought mean-
ingfully at the battle of Gettysburg, where he came out a brevet
brigadier general. When the war ended, he was mustered out
of the army. He then used his writing skills to publish a book in

Colonel and Brevet Brigadier General Philippe Regis
Denis de Keredern de Trobriand

De Trobriand came to the Montana Territory in the summer of
1869 as military commander and clashed with Brigadier General
Alfred Sully, who was serving as Indian superintendent. Courtesy Library of Congress.

France on the Civil War and the Union Army. When it was translated into English and published in the United States in 1889,
its title was *Four Years with the Army of the Potomac.*[11] By 1867 de
Trobriand was back in the regular army as a colonel and was
sent to the plains with the 13th Infantry as commander of Fort

Stevenson, a post close to the Missouri River in the Dakota Territory. He received a brevet promotion to brigadier general on March 2, 1867.[12]

In 1869 de Trobriand was the commander of all the regular army troops stationed in the Montana Territory, which included those at Fort Shaw and Fort Ellis. Even with his new responsibilities, de Trobriand had time to engage in his hobby as an artist. Painting and sketching were among his refinements, and he did scenes of the army posts and forts. A critic noted that as an artist de Trobriand "strove for accuracy in his sketches and oil paintings." Among his works were sketches of Fort Ellis and Fort Shaw done as early as June 1869 and an oil painting of Fort Ellis done in September.[13]

When de Trobriand arrived in the Montana Territory the citizens immediately confronted him with news of attacks, several murders, and thefts of horses by Indians. He soon determined

De Trobriand sketch of Fort Ellis

Sketch of Fort Ellis, done by Colonel Regis de Trobriand in the summer of 1869, probably shortly after he arrived in Montana to become the military commander there. Courtesy C. M. Russell Art Museum.

De Trobriand oil painting of Fort Ellis

Fort Ellis, Montana Territory: oil painting by Philippe Regis de Trobriand, 1869. Original at C. M. Russell Art Museum in Great Falls, Montana. Courtesy C. M. Russell Art Museum.

De Trobriand sketch of Fort Shaw

Sketch of Fort Shaw done by Philippe Regis de Trobriand in the summer of 1869, probably shortly after he arrived in Montana to become the military commander there. Courtesy C. M. Russell Museum.

that two of the tribes of the Blackfeet Nation, the Blackfeet proper and the Bloods, had been on friendly terms with the whites. But this was not true of a third tribe, the Piegans, who had resisted the whites and retaliated whenever they could. The worst of the Piegan bands by reputation was the band of Mountain Chief, who supposedly had killed John Bozeman in 1867.[14]

If de Trobriand thought military dealings with the Indians in the territory were going to be up to him alone, he was mistaken. On July 27, 1869, General Alfred Sully, a tall, gaunt professional military man forty-eight years old, rode into Helena to take up his duties in the Department of the Interior. He was a brigadier general in the regular army. But under the recent policies of the Grant administration, his new assignment was as Indian super-intendent, who reported not to the War Department but to the commissioner of Indian Affairs in the Interior Department. Sully was the first nongovernor to have those duties in Montana and the first Indian superintendent who did not have the powers of a governor to call out a militia.[15]

Sully was an 1841 graduate of West Point, finishing thirty-eighth in his class of fifty-two and had served on the plains both before and after service in the Civil War. A man of contradictions, he was known as an Indian fighter with a hot temper, coupled with vindictiveness toward his fellow officers, a trait that he would display when he and de Trobriand were at odds. Sully had something in common with de Trobriand, however: he too was an artist in his spare time and liked to paint watercolors and oils depicting whatever countryside he was in. He was following in the footsteps of his famous father, Thomas Sully, whose works included portraits of Queen Victoria and presidents George Washington, John Quincy Adams, and Thomas Jefferson, includ-ing the familiar scene of Washington crossing the Delaware. An art critic described Alfred Sully as "a competent artist, less gifted than his father, and inclined toward primitivism, but conveying a sense of realism that adds conviction to western scenes."[16]

Alfred Sully's wife was of French-Indian descent and was a Yankton Sioux tribal member, which only underscored one of his

Brigadier General Alfred Sully
Sully came to the Montana Territory in the summer of
1869 when he was assigned to the Indian Bureau of the
Department of Interior as Indian superintendent. He
clashed with the army and Colonel de Trobriand on how
to deal with the Piegan Indians. Courtesy State Historical
Society of North Dakota, Bismarck.

biggest paradoxes. Sully had earned a reputation on the plains
for severely punishing the Indians. On September 3, 1863, at
Whitestone Hill, Dakota Territory, Sully's troops had destroyed a
village of some five hundred tipis that lodged Yankton, Dakotas,
Hunkpapas, Lakotas, and Blackfeet as a reprisal for the Dakota

Conflict of 1862. Men, women, and children were killed or captured. The troopers' casualties were small. Sully reported: "I
believe I can safely say I gave them one of the most severe pun-
ishments that the Indians have ever received." According to one
of Sully's interpreters, Samuel J. Brown, a mixed-blood Sioux, "it
was a perfect massacre." He found it "lamentable to hear how
those women and children was [sic] massacred."[17]

Sully came under scrutiny for his mistreatment of Indians in
1867, when Congress appointed a commission under James R.
Doolittle to look into "the condition of the Indian tribes and their
treatment by the Civil and Military authorities of the United
States." During the investigation, Sully was targeted and given
a chance to speak out against the charges leveled at him. He advised Congress that since he had "first entered the Army in 1841,"
except for time in the Mexican War and the "first two years of
the Rebellion," he had been "constantly in the Indian Country."
He was able to recount that he had "been with the Seminoles of
Florida, with the various tribes of Indians in Southern California,
Oregon, and the eastern part of California, with all the bands of
the western or Teton Sioux, with the Omahas, Poncas, Pawnees,
Cheyennes, Rees, Mandans, Gros-Ventres and Crows."[18]

Sully recommended to the Doolittle Commission that the "Indian Department unquestionably should be under the War Department." He gave his reasons: "It is to the troops the friendly
Indian looks to for protection against hostile bands, and from the
troops the Agent or Trader looks for protection when his Indians,
exasperated at repeated impositions, threaten to take his life."
Sully believed that the secretary of interior and the War Department might differ on handling certain situations: "frequently, Indians become so troublesome, it is necessary to turn them over to
the hands of the military." After his arrival in Montana as the Indian superintendent under the Interior Department, Sully would
find himself impaled on the horns of the very dilemma that he
had predicted.[19]

Sully had been in Helena only seven days when he wrote to
Ely S. Parker, the commissioner of Indian Affairs, that he feared
"before long we may have serious difficulties between Indians

and whites in this Territory." He immediately tried to get the Interior Department involved in military matters when he added: "I would urge upon you the necessity of applying for an immediate increase of military force in Montana to prevent this." Sully extravagantly overestimated, claiming that he could "safely say that about from fifty thousand to sixty thousand men, women and children is the total of Indians frequently located here." Yet, according to Sully, "there are not over four hundred" troops "in the territory, inclusive of the four companies of the Second cavalry, recently arrived at Fort Ellis." Sully mistakenly believed at that time that the cavalry troops "are to leave and rejoin the Department of the Platte before winter," leaving "about two hundred men." Parker noted: "I heartily indorse General Sully's views and recommendations" and passed the letter on through channels to the War Department.[20]

As the new Indian superintendent, Sully had an unusual interpretation of the cause of the hostilities in Montana. Instead of accusing the Piegans or other local Indian tribes, he placed the blame on Indian tribes who were largely outside the territory: "war parties of Indians from the Powder River country, the British Possessions and from Idaho and Washington Territories." He said that these Indians "frequently visit this Territory and often commit depredations on the whites. The whites retaliate by killing any Indians they may chance to meet, sometimes in the most brutal and cowardly manner."

As a member of the Department of the Interior, Sully was no longer involved in the decisions of the army, something that he struggled against. But he still advocated for military control in the Montana Territory of the "white element in this country which, from its rowdy and lawless character, cannot be excelled in any section, and the traffic in whiskey with Indians in this Territory is carried on to an alarming extent." Sully said that the whiskey trading "frequently causes altercations between whites and Indians, resulting often in bloodshed," but that it could not be stopped because these acts "occur in sections of the Territory where the civil authorities acknowledge themselves to be powerless to act." Sully's proposed solution was to use the army against the whites, because "nothing but military force can at present put a stop to it." He then made a suggestion that hinted strongly of raising a militia—something he did not have the power to do— when he said the "law abiding citizens of Montana . . . would willingly give any assistance in their power to aid the authorities to carry out the laws, if they were backed by force."

At the time Sully wrote his letter to Parker, he thought that he and de Trobriand would get along. In his request for troops he said: "General De Trobriand, commanding this district, has offered me every assistance in his power to enforce the laws; but as you see, his force is very small to do much."[21] As Sully saw it, the two would work together in harmony to end the lawlessness, but this was not about to happen. Soon Sully and de Trobriand would be antagonists over how the Piegans were to be controlled.

Four weeks later, on September 23, Sully sent an incendiary letter to Parker, summarizing the plight of the Blackfeet. According to Sully, "The Blackfeet nation composed of Bloods, Piegans, and Blackfeet proper, number about six thousand men, women and children. They have made treaties by which they have ceded all this land to the government, and confined themselves to a limited reservation. It is to be regretted that their treaty was not ratified, for there is every reason to fear that at least a portion of these Indians intend to make war against the whites." Sully knew full well of General Sherman's policies and the dilemma that the Piegans would face under them: "Indians disposed to be peaceable shall remove to their reservations and remain there or else be treated as hostile." But he had to add that "these Indians have no reservations to go to."[22] This statement was true, because no area had been set aside that was clearly identifiable as the Blackfeet reservation. The 1865 and 1868 treaties, both of which set out the same areas, had never been ratified. Miners and settlers had overrun the area set out in the 1851 Fort Laramie Treaty and the 1855 Lame Bull Treaty.

Regardless of where official boundaries were or were not, the Piegans-Blackfeet traditionally hunted and camped in a certain territory (although with undefined boundaries). A Blackfeet agency was located on the Teton River in that territory. It was Sully's job, immediately after he arrived in Montana, to find an agent for this post. President Grant had officially appointed Lieutenant William B. Pease as Blackfeet agent. But, as Sully told Parker, Pease had "not reached here." It became necessary for Sully, "owing to the threatened hostilities, to place some one in charge of the agency buildings and other valuable government property."[23]

The best man that Sully could find to fill the job of Blackfeet agent temporarily was Fellows David Pease (no relation to William Pease), who had traded on the Upper Missouri for a decade and had been a manager for the Northwest Company until the spring of 1868. He was known to be adept at handling Indian relations. As Sully said, Pease "has been a long time associated with these Indians."[24]

When Fellows Pease reported on August 10, he described the Blackfeet agency as being "located on the Teton river about 75 miles from Fort Benton," noting that the "buildings are very substantial and appropriate." He was greatly concerned about a possible Indian attack and was satisfied that the buildings were "well arranged for defense." Pease was worried because, as he said, "the chiefs and head men complain bitterly against the government for the non-fulfillment of the treaties consummated last fall . . . between themselves and W. J. Cullen, special agent and commissioner in behalf of the government." Pease's anxiety was heightened when he learned the Piegans had killed two white men who were herding cattle: four Piegans were killed in retaliation. Two of the dead Piegans were "notoriously bad Indians," and he said the Indians "do not seem to care so much about the killing of the first two." The other two were "a harmless old man, and the other a boy," however, and "the chiefs are using every exertion to restrain the young men from taking revenge."[25]

The treaty that Cullen had signed with the Blackfeet in 1868, like previous treaties with the tribe, required the government to provide goods, including food, which the Indian Department had always had trouble delivering. This was causing real problems among the Piegans. Fellows Pease said that the Indians needed food, "owing to the scarcity of game," and asked that they be "furnished with beef and flour to subsist them, in order that they may be pacified if possible." He warned: "Unless this is done I fear the malcontents may get control of the tribe and commence hostilities before the department at Washington can be made to realize the critical condition of affairs, and the entire nation be involved in open war." Pease discovered that "British traders and half-breeds have long been trying to excite them to war against the Americans . . . their object being to exchange ammunition and whisky for their horses, robes, furs and in fact everything that is of value to them, at enormous profits."[26]

Fellows Pease may have been reporting more from his general fur-trading experience in the region than from knowledge gained from a current investigation, which he had done in a limited time. He did not live at the agency on the Teton River. Because he was also agent for other tribes he generally stayed at Fort Benton, a more central location.[27]

The ongoing depredations by the Piegans only kept the recent shocking murder of Malcolm Clarke in the public eye. It had occurred only weeks after the arrival of General Sully and General de Trobriand and turned the whole territory against the Piegans. The murder happened when Pete Owl Child of Mountain Chief's band, with a small group of Piegan Indians, visited Clarke's ranch near Helena. The Indians had lured Clarke and Clarke's half-blood son, Horace, outside their house on the night of August 17, murdering Clarke and leaving Horace for dead, but he lived to tell the story.[28]

The murder put Helena in an uproar. Clarke lived in the vicinity and had been attacked at home by Owl Child, who was about two hundred miles away from his tribe. The fear was palpable, and the citizens started calling for retaliation by the military. Unfazed, General de Trobriand reported immediately that he did not think that matters in Montana were serious and described the Clarke affair as "the denouement of a long-standing family quarrel." As to military intervention, de Trobriand's assessment was philosophical: "It is a remarkable fact that when there is no apparent danger, and no cause for apprehension, people will think there is always too much of military, while if a handful of redskins appear upon the bluffs, shaking their buffalo robes, it turns out suddenly that there is never enough of it, according to the same people."[29]

When de Trobriand looked further into Clarke's death, he was given information that led him to believe that Clarke generally had been highly regarded as an early pioneer and a respected citizen of Prickly Pear Valley near Helena. Most of the new citizens around Helena, many of whom had only recently arrived, knew that Clarke had a Piegan wife whose brother was Pete Owl Child. They were the children of Mountain Chief. Clarke also had a young family that included his daughter Helene, a vivacious young child who was popular around Helena. It was a general but mistaken belief that Clarke had lived in peace with the Indians for years. This had apparently ended when Pete Owl Child's burning resentment (growing out of a family matter) compelled him to travel to Clarke's ranch and lure Malcolm and Horace Clarke outside their house that night, murdering Clarke and leaving Horace for dead. According to some, Pete Owl Child had good reason for his savage attack: Clarke had beaten him and seduced his wife.[30]

Clarke's public persona as a solid, law-abiding citizen was only a façade. If the people of Helena had looked into the matter they would have found that he was a known murderer. Only a few years back, in 1863 near Fort Union, Clarke got into an argument over money matters with Kenneth McKenzie's son, Owen McKenzie. Both were drinking, and Clarke shot and killed Owen after the quarrel escalated. His only excuse was that he believed McKenzie was a dangerous man. In an earlier event, Clarke had attempted to murder Alexander Harvey with an ax.[31]

None of these events seemed to have been known to the *Helena Weekly Herald* when it reported the murder, saying only that at "about 12 o'clock last night a party of Indians (supposed to be Piegans) numbering twenty or more" had arrived at Clarke's ranch. One of their number "stepped to the door and asked young Clark [*sic*] . . . to go with him and assist in corralling some mules." As the story was told, when Horace was about "ten rods from the house, the red fiend drew his revolver and shot young Clark, the ball entering near the lower jaw and coming out near the nose." Then it was time for Clarke to meet his end. "Startled at the report of fire-arms, the old man opened the door to see what was the matter, and had no sooner reached the step than another shot was fired, and Malcolm Clark fell to the floor, mortally wounded. Upon examination it was found that the ball had entered the forehead and passed through the brain. He lived but a few moments after the fatal shot."[32]

The *Herald* reported incorrectly that "Mr. Clark was a graduate of West Point, and one of our oldest and most respected mountaineers, having lived in Montana upwards of twenty years." Other than saying that Clarke "leaves a wife and several children," the article did not mention his Piegan wife but praised her daughter, Helene, who was referred to as "Miss Nellie Clarke." The *Herald* said that she had "figured conspicuously in our best society" and that "she is we understand, a niece of Maj. Gen. Van Cleve, of Minnesota." And indeed she was: Clarke's sister, Charlotte Ouisconsin Clark, was married to Van Cleve. The *Herald* also reported that "young Clark, who was shot through the face, and supposed by the Indians to have been killed, is not dangerously wounded, and will probably recover."[33]

Malcolm Clarke's reputation continued to grow in heroic proportions after his death. According to Robert Vaughn, an early territorial pioneer and an Indian agent who knew him well, Clarke "had been a classmate of General Sherman's at West Point." Of course, Clarke and Sherman had attended West Point at distinctly different times and probably had never even met.[34]

Horace Clarke pushed Malcolm Clarke's historical standing even higher, when he wrote some years later that his father had told him that during the "Civil War in 1862, the Government had offered to appoint him a General." But Malcolm Clarke had preferred to be "a special agent, to council and keep the Indians from going to war as the Indians well knew that the great conflict between the north and south would call for all the available men in the Northern states and territories, and that it was an opportune time to attack and rob the settlers."[35]

Charlotte Ouisconsin Clark Van Cleve, who knew Clarke best, told the real history of his early years and his time at West Point. She said that he had challenged a fellow cadet to a duel, which was reported to the commandant: the "next morning at breakfast roll-call my brother stepped out before his company and, seizing his adversary by the collar, administered to him a severe flogging with a cowhide." The result was a court-martial, and Malcolm Clarke headed to Texas on his own to "join the desperate men there in their struggle for independence." More trouble occurred even before he got there. On a ship from New Orleans, Clarke arrested the captain for failing to provide ice and necessaries. He released the prisoner upon landing and went "immediately to General Sam Houston's quarters to give himself up for mutiny on the high seas." No charges were filed.[36]

Shortly after Clarke's death, another man came to Montana who would have influence on the fate of the Piegan Indians. William F. Wheeler was the territory's new U.S. marshal, appointed to his position by President Grant.[37] Wheeler had his own ideas about how to handle the Indian situation and quickly convened a citizens' grand jury in Helena to seek indictments against Pete Owl Child and his companions. The grand jury brought formal charges against Owl Child, Black Weasel, Eagle's Rib, Bear Chief, and Black Bear. Wheeler sent copies of the indictment to the president, the secretary of war, the commander of the U.S. Army, and Alfred Sully as superintendent of Indian Affairs.[38] Sully in turn passed the indictments on to the Indian commissioner in Washington, DC, who soon sent word back to Wheeler ordering him to demand the surrender of the perpetrators from the chiefs of the Piegan tribe. If the chiefs failed to turn the men over, they were to be notified that the government would send soldiers to take them by force.[39]

By October 1869 de Trobriand had been in the territory long enough to become concerned with what was going on. He had abandoned his more placating views and now became a chief agitator for military action against the Piegans. He was supported by the chain of events that included Clarke's murder, Wheeler's indictment of the Indians, and the resulting clamor of the citizens. On October 13 de Trobriand issued orders to Colonel Brackett: "The depredations and murders committed by the Indians during the last two months have excited a great deal of emotion among the residents of the Territory; and it is most desirable that no opportunity be lost to chastise the guilty parties." The 2nd Cavalry was now in place, and de Trobriand ordered Brackett to "send forth a detachment of Cavalry . . . (not however less than twenty-five (25) men) under command of an officer with instructions to spare no effort to capture or kill these bloody marauders." The orders were specific, noting that nearly all of the marauders "belong to the Piegans; and those whom it is especially desirable to bring to justice are: A half-breed by the name of Star, who attacked one of our trains on Eagle Creek and caused one of our teamsters to be butchered by treachery," and "Peter or Pete the assassin of Mr. Clarke, the Mountain Chief's son who attempted to murder the young Horace Clark, and their companions and accomplices: Black Bear; Black Weasel; Bear Chief and others you may hear about."[40]

Lieutenant General Philip Sheridan sought to obtain the backing of General William Tecumseh Sherman to use military force against the Indians. On October 21, 1869, Sheridan laid out a case against the Piegans for Sherman. He first acknowledged "receipt of a letter from the Secretary of the Interior with accompanying reports of General Sully, Mr. Pease and Mr. Culbertson, Indian agents in Montana, on the subject of depredations by the Piegan tribe of Indians." Sheridan had decided that his plan would include no negotiations or arrests. Even though he had not previously had enough troops in Montana "on account of the expiration of enlistments" to "do much against these Indian marauders," he was able to point out to Sherman that "the regiments are now filling up." Given the required troop strength, Sheridan said, "I think it would be the best plan to . . . find out exactly where these Indians are going to spend the winter, and about the time of a good heavy snow I will send out a party and try and strike them." Sheridan knew when to attack the Indians and suggested that "about the 15th of January they will be very helpless and if where they live is not too far from Shaw or Ellis, we might be able to give them a good hard blow which will make peace a desirable object." Sheridan also appealed to Sherman's propensity to take action: "To simply keep the troops on the defensive will not stop the murders; we must occasionally strike here until it hurts; and if the General-in Chief thinks well of this, I will try and steal a small force on this tribe from Fort Shaw, or Ellis, during the winter."[41]

The words of Grant's inaugural speech earlier in the year were to have a "careful study" of the Indian situation that would "favor any course toward them, which tends to civilization and ultimate citizenship." These words now rang hollow and were replaced by words of a winter attack on the Piegans.[42]

SEVEN

Tell Baker to Strike Them Hard

If the lives and property of the citizens of Montana can best be protected by striking Mountain Chief's band, I want them struck. Tell Baker to strike them hard.

GENERAL WILLIAM TECUMSEH SHERMAN TO INSPECTOR GENERAL JAMES A. HARDIE, JANUARY 15, 1870

On November 4, 1869, General William Tecumseh Sherman authorized Lieutenant General Philip Sheridan to proceed against the Piegan Indians. "I have the honor to inform you that your proposed action . . . for the punishment of these marauders, has been approved."[1]

During the Civil War, Sheridan and the other Civil War generals now involved on the plains (Sherman, Hancock, Sully, and de Trobriand) had all been both eyewitnesses and chief executioners under orders resulting in the destruction of men and property. Sheridan had started the scorched earth policy in the Civil War, and Sherman had ended the war with his own scorched earth campaign through the South. As a man who had declared the Indians to be "the enemies of our race and our civilization," Sherman had no apparent compunction about ordering destruction of the Piegan Indian bands. In a report published on December 11, 1869, Sheridan sarcastically decried lenient Indian policy when he avowed that the government "was attempting to govern a wild, brutal and savage people without any laws at all, or the infliction of any punishment for the most heinous crimes." Caustically he added: "This system was not a success. If a white

General Philip Sheridan

Philip Sheridan, who earned the sobriquet "Little Phil" for his short
stature, was the commander in charge of the Department of the Missouri who conducted a western strategy to subdue the Indians. He
personally named Eugene M. Baker to lead the attack on the Piegans.
Courtesy Library of Congress.

man commits murder or robs, we hang him or send him to the
penitentiary. If an Indian does the same, we have been in the
habit of giving him more blankets."[2]

Sherman's analysis, as applied to recent events in the Montana
Territory, failed to consider that while the Piegans charged with
the death of Malcolm Clarke had been indicted, no trial had been

held to find them guilty, as would be expected to follow the same charges against a white person. That matter of due process did not even enter the discussion where the Piegans were concerned.

William Tecumseh Sherman and Philip Henry Sheridan had been associated in the army for many years and had developed an understanding. It is clear that they both distrusted and loathed all Indians. Sheridan had famously been quoted as saying: "The only good Indian is a dead Indian." He is more correctly reported as having said: "The only good Indians I ever saw were dead," which he vehemently denied.[3] Back in 1868, when Sheridan was planning the army attack on Black Kettle's village at the Washita River, Sherman guaranteed him his personal backing, no matter what Sheridan did, promising: "I will say nothing and do nothing to restrain our troops from doing what they deem proper on the spot." He had also given Sheridan permission to use his own judgment in the attack: "You may now go ahead in your own way and I will back you with my whole authority, and stand between you and any efforts that may be attempted in your rear to restrain your purpose or check your troops."[4]

On November 5, 1869, Sheridan notified General Winfield Hancock that he had Sherman's authorization to proceed against the Piegans. He advised Hancock again on November 15, 1869: "General: I enclose you the correspondence which I referred to in my private note of the 5th inst." While Sherman had given Sheridan the authority "to punish the Piegans," Sheridan in turn had directed Hancock "to extend this authority to any of the Blackfeet who may have been engaged in the murders and robberies lately perpetrated in Montana."[5]

It was Sheridan's intention to strike the Indians in total surprise, as he told Hancock: "It will be of no use to make the attempt unless the positions of the villages are well known. Then the greatest care should be taken to keep the Indians from gaining any information on the subject. It will be impossible to strike these marauders unless the greatest possible secrecy is maintained." Sheridan was known for secrecy, as the *Army and Navy Journal* reported later: "In regard to contemplated movements, Sheridan was extremely reticent; with the exception of his chief

of staff, he seldom confided his plans to any one, and, as a consequence, they were seldom betrayed."[6]

Sheridan's letter to Hancock had also alluded to the difficulty
of finding the Indians in their winter camp. The different bands
of the Piegan tribe were known to have wintered on the Marias
River frequently in the recent past, but they did not always winter in the same place. A principal factor that could influence the
location of Piegan camps in any given year was the winter range
of the buffalo and more recently proximity to the fur traders and
their posts. As one early commentator said: the "establishment of
branch posts from Fort Benton on the Marias must have been intended as a move to locate posts where the Indians congregated
for the winter to facilitate trade." However, "once established,
the fact that these posts were on the Marias must have encouraged the Piegans to return to that river repeatedly for their winter camps."[7]

Information on the winter location of Piegan camps came from
the fur traders, who stayed at their posts in the winter months
and kept in contact with the Indians. In 1869–1870 Baker and
Brothers of Fort Benton set up a small branch post on the Marias
River at Willow Round, northwest of Fort Benton. It was also
known that the American Fur Company traders had established
winter trading posts on the Marias that they occupied from October to March.[8]

During the 1860s, the fur trade in Fort Benton was undergo-
ing a haphazard reorganization with the appearance of a number
of small companies and partnerships. A number of independent
traders also populated the area, all being known as free traders.
The larger companies endured in the face of the competition by
dealing with these free traders. During this period, the Chouteaus
turned over the Fort Benton post to a syndicate operating as the
Northwestern Fur Company, not to be confused with the old Canadian North West Company, even though the new organization
was sometimes called the North West Company. Isaac G. Baker
was one of its early managers, as was Francis H. Eastman. John
Riplinger was there in 1868 and was later in charge of Riplinger's
Trading Post on the Marias. He had apparently parted ways with

Baker after first establishing a post on the Teton with him. Once the Teton and Marias posts were known to the Indians, the free traders started to congregate around them, trading whiskey from their wagons for furs. Things became so bad that in January 1869 Riplinger wrote a letter to the commissioner of Indian Affairs: "Last night at 11 o'clock Clarke Tingley passed here with a wagon & a half Bbl. [barrel] of Liquor. He is in Blood camp about two miles above me and has Traded about 100 Robes since he arrived . . . The Indians are Drunk all the time. The camps below all have liquor traders in them. We are doing nothing here; all Indians that don't trade their Robes for liquor here in Camp go to Benton to Bakers & Powers as they report that Baker trades Liquor to them after dark." After he moved his post to the Marias, Riplinger hired Alexander Culbertson, who had fallen on bad times and was out of work and drinking heavily. To make matters worse, his wife Natawista left him for Riplinger.[9]

The Piegans from their winter camps continued the buffalo hunt during the cold months for food and for clothing. The best skins for clothing were taken in the winter when they were thin with long, fine fur.[10] If the buffalo herd moved too far away, the tribe was obliged to follow, while still trying to maintain protection against the winter among the trees on a river bottom. The size and proximity of the winter camps were never known exactly at any time and varied among the bands.

The fur traders knew that one of the best winter camp locations on the Marias River was the broad, partially wooded Marias River valley at what was known as the Big Bend, a place where the river swept north in a broad arc before turning south and then continuing east. The Piegan bands could find protection from wind and snow there amid the aspens and cottonwoods. The usual procedure in establishing camp at such a location would be to pitch the lodges in the open for a few weeks. When the chief sensed that the weather was growing colder, around early December, he would give orders to move the lodges in among the thick timber. After they were assembled, some of the underbrush among the trees would be piled around the base of the lodge to serve as a windbreak. The bands would stay in one place as long as they had grass for horses, wood for fires, and a food supply. But it was also important that the bands winter separately from each other so that the horses could have a large area for forage, with a sizable area of underbrush and trees for the fires of each band. Because of this habit, the fur traders—and the army when the time came—could expect to find the various Piegan bands at separate locations, although in general proximity to each other.[11]

Amid the clamor caused by the Malcolm Clarke murder and more recent events some citizens called for a militia. General Sully as Indian superintendent had no power to raise one but seemingly entertained the idea. General Sherman had been publicly embarrassed by the large expense that the Montana militia had run up in 1867. He now cautioned Sheridan to beware of a similar event in Montana. "I regard the clamor in Montana as identically the same as occurred two years ago, the same Indians the same men and the same stories." He also told Sheridan to keep an eye on Sully, who "was likely to be persuaded by local politicians, and the Interior Department could end up running the campaign."[12] Running the campaign was in fact exactly what Sully proposed. On December 17, after reporting aggressions on that day and earlier on December 13, he recommended to Hancock by telegram that three hundred volunteers be raised in Montana as a militia, to go into the field after the Indians. Not surprisingly, Sully nominated himself to be the commander.[13]

The military activities of Sully and other officers detached from the army and serving in a civilian capacities had already forced Sherman's hand, and he knew that he had to maintain some kind of control. On December 2, 1869, Sherman issued a circular and decreed that "by direction of the President, officers of the Army on duty in the Indian country will give protection to both whites and Indians when outrages are committed on either side, and will make special reports of each case that may occur to the Adjutant-General."[14]

Sully's request for a militia served as a stimulus for the War Department aggressively to take charge and to view the Indian attacks as something that had to be dealt with soon. It was reported that Sully's actions had "assisted to modify the views of General De Trobriand as to the gravity of the situation." The other modifying factor probably came from Sheridan, who had started to make a practice of bypassing General Hancock, de Trobriand's superior.[15]

Even though a large force existed in the Montana Territory, Sheridan had no tested battle officer that he had confidence in to lead an expedition against the Piegans. But he thought that he knew someone he could trust to carry out his orders. He went around both Hancock and de Trobriand in the chain of command to handpick Major Eugene Mortimer Baker. As he told Hancock, "Major Baker, who is now en route to Fort Ellis, is a most excellent man to be entrusted with any party you may see fit to send out." In fact Sheridan had already instructed Baker what he wanted accomplished and told Hancock that he "spoke to him on the subject when he passed through Chicago."[16]

Baker fit the Sheridan and Sherman mold for an Indian fighter ideally. He was described as "a hard-hearted man." A soldier who served under him in Montana said: "He was of middle age [actually thirty-three], was big, powerful, hardy, full-bearded, carried his strong body in erect, soldierly manner. He was a hard drinker, and he was tolerant of alcoholic excesses among his soldiers. In fact, his rough and common ways, his familiar mingling with all subordinates, did much toward bringing them into forgetfulness about some of the reprehensible traits of his character."[17] Baker's superiors knew that they had put a man in charge who would take severe action against the Piegans and ignored Baker's flaws if they knew of them.

Graduating twelfth in his class at West Point in 1859, young Eugene Baker had been commissioned as a second lieutenant in the 1st Dragoons and in 1861 was put on duty on the east side of the Sierras at Fort Churchill, Nevada Territory.[18] His early contact with Indians there had been peaceable; and at one time he had saved white women and children from a wagon train that had been attacked by Indians, without chasing after the attackers.[19] Later he met in peace with a local tribe. When he found that the Indians were starving, he reported with some compassion: "There are no pine nuts this year, and all, or nearly all, of their grass has been cut by the stage company or citizens living on the road." Baker asked for help for the Indians and warned that "if any outbreak occurs it will be because they are driven to it by starvation."[20]

Baker became less compassionate when the Civil War started in 1862. He and the 1st Dragoons (renamed the First Cavalry) were sent east, first in the defenses surrounding Washington until March 1862, when he was promoted to captain. He then joined into the battles of the Peninsula Campaign with the Army of the Potomac in its unsuccessful attempt to take Richmond. In the Battle of Williamsburg on May 4 or 5 Baker was promoted to brevet major, "for gallant and meritorious services." As the Civil War proceeded, Baker's service in action became continuous. He was in the bloody battles at Antietam, Fredericksburg, and Chancellorsville and took part in the pursuit of Lee's army from Gettysburg. He was then put in command of a regiment under Sheridan in the Shenandoah Valley from January to March 1865.[21]

After the war Baker went back west, where he was assigned to Camp Watson, Oregon Territory, for a lengthy period, starting in June 1866. With the bloody experience of the Civil War now ingrained in him, Baker did not have the same benevolence toward Indians that he had displayed at Fort Churchill before the war. While serving as the commander of Camp Watson, on July 8, 1867, he led an attack on a village of Indians, probably Paiutes. Four warriors were killed in the attack (some say that it was only two). Fourteen women and children were captured, along with two horses.[22]

Baker was promoted to major, 2nd Cavalry, on April 8, 1869. A long leave of absence then followed from July to November 1869 before Sheridan sent him to command Fort Ellis, officially commencing on December 1, 1869.[23]

De Trobriand, as a good soldier, had to follow the orders that overrode his earlier personal assessments and started some strategic planning for the attack on the Piegans. He reported on November 26, 1869:

Fort Ellis soldiers

Major Eugene M. Baker and group of army officers in 1871 at Fort Ellis, Montana. Baker is at the center right, with a dark beard and a hand resting on the railing. Photograph by William H. Jackson. Courtesy Montana Historical Society Research Center Photograph Archives, Helena, Catalog #247-248.

The Piegans are divided. The main body [under Mountain Chief] is now on the British Territory, hunting and trading. Although they have plenty of buffaloes, as they have to fight some other tribes, and as the price they get for their robes is much inferior to that paid by Americans, it is thought that they will come back early in the spring to join the other band, if nothing frightens them away. . . . The other band is friendly, under the lead of Heavy Runner, their chief. It is much the smaller of the two. They have their camp on the Marias.

De Trobriand said the knowledge that the cavalry was now stationed at Fort Ellis "kept the Indians on the alert" and predicted: "At the first move they would disappear in the British territory. But let everything remain quiet during three or four months, and in the spring they will come back, supposing that we will let bygones be bygones."[24]

In the meantime General Sully as superintendent of Indian Affairs had made a proposal to proceed to the Indian country himself for a face-to-face meeting with the Piegans. There he would lay down an ultimatum that both the murderers and the stolen horses were to be promptly turned over to him. He did not repeat his earlier nettlesome request that he be allowed to lead a militia against the Piegans. Instead he asked that regular army military support be provided by de Trobriand for his journey. On December 11 Hancock optimistically telegrammed to Sully: "Your dispatch received. I think it would be a good idea if you took charge of it with what troops you wanted. . . . I doubt if we get anything more and think that would have a good result and be sufficient under all the circumstances."[25]

On December 13, 1869, Hancock ordered de Trobriand to furnish the support that Sully had asked for, for the moment subordinating him to Sully. Smarting from the rebuke, de Trobriand said it would result in "putting the military forces of my command virtually at the disposal of the superintendent of Indian affairs in Montana."[26] It became apparent later that de Trobriand and Hancock, the man that he had at one time admired so much, had been at odds over the matter. In a letter to his family long after the fact, de Trobriand said:

> It is not strange, dear Kin, that being so fond of peace, as I am, I find so often in my way some confounded fellow who will bring me out for a fight in some way or other. At any rate it cannot be said that I hunt small game for it happens always that it is with some considerable man that I have to exchange blows. . . . In Montana, it was no less a personage than Major General Hancock with whom I had a fight of two or three months from which I may say that I retired with *"les honneurs de la guerre"* [honors of war].[27]

In fact de Trobriand had not won at all: Hancock had told Sully that he had ordered de Trobriand "to furnish you all the Military assistance you may require to enforce your demands on the Indians of your jurisdiction also to place his troops at such points as you may indicate for the purpose."[28]

As the army's investigations continued, a list of targeted Indians was developed.[29] De Trobriand thought that "no better opportunity can present itself to punish the parties guilty of the murders and depredations committed last summer. The most of them, if not all, are with the band of Mountain chief."[30] One Piegan name placed on the list was White Man's Dog of "one of the lower bands." He was accused of being the chief actor in the theft on December 16 of "thirty valuable mules" belonging to freighter Hugh Kirkendall while he was transporting supplies for the Indian department. Also named were "Star, a half Mexican and half Piegan, a noted murderer; Crow Top, a noted murderer; The Cut Hand, Eagle's Rib (one of the party that murdered Mr. Clarke), Bear Chief (of the party that murdered Clarke), Under Bull, Red Horn, Bull's Head, The White Man's Dog, and the Black Weasel (of the party that murdered Clarke)." The guilty parties also included "Black Bear, and twenty other Indians of Mountain chiefs band were believed to be present on occasion of the murder."[31]

The army's plans for the inevitable attack on the Piegans were supposed to be secretive to avoid arousing the Indians. They could have been predicted by the fur traders, however, who would only have had to watch the increased activity in the forts. Among the fur traders in regular contact with the Piegans were John J. Healy and Alfred B. Hamilton, who operated in Fort Benton and around Fort Shaw at Sun River.[32]

On November 27, 1869, as the army was starting its preparations for an attack, Francis H. Eastman, who was the principal fur trader for the Northwestern Fur Company in Fort Benton, wrote to U.S. marshal William F. Wheeler in Helena, warning him about Healy and Hamilton. He had recently been with Wheeler and had just made some discoveries. "Since I left Helena I have discovered a large sized rat with a very long tail in the woodpile," Eastman wrote. "It is nothing other than a combination of all the old Indian whiskey traders." Eastman had been "put in possession of this item by Mr. Riplinger," the company's trader on the Marias, who had told him that there would be "a party going to leave Benton to go to the [British] Territory mines to prospect

John Healy

John J. Healy (probably in Fort Benton, Montana). Photograph by Root Studio, Chicago (no date). Courtesy Montana Historical Society Research Center Photograph Archives, Helena, Catalog #942–674.

for Gold." Riplinger had identified John Healy and A. B. Hamilton "of Sun River Crossing" as the leaders of the group. Eastman said that "their reputation of course is well known" as having been "engaged in trading liquor to the Indians during the past year." Eastman advised Wheeler that Healy and Hamilton would carefully "not take any liquor out with them, but their intention probably is to reestablish themselves on Elk and Bow River and

Alfred B. Hamilton

Alfred B. Hamilton, fur and whiskey trader (photographer
unidentified). Courtesy Montana Historical Society Research
Center Photograph Archives, Helena, Catalog #957-275.

then the whiskey will be run from Helena, Benton or anywhere
on the road." In Eastman's opinion, "the known reputations of
these men do not leave doubt as to what their intentions are on
the matter. I shall write Genl Sully soon on this matter and you
had better consult him on the subject."[33]

When he wrote to Sully on November 28, Eastman said that he
had "more definite information," received from "Mr Riplinger

who rec'd it from a Half Breed," that "a Co. of all the old Indian Whiskey traders was forming to carry on a regular whiskey
trade this winter." Again he implicated Healy and Hamilton, but
he added that the "rank and file are Half Breeds and white men
who have always been engaged in the trade."[34] What this meant
was that the Piegans would not winter alone; they would have
regular whiskey traders with them at times. On December 14
Eastman had the occasion to telegram Sully from Fort Benton,
reporting that "a party of Indian whiskey traders came in last
night" and that "a large party [of Indians] will come in here in
two days."[35] The trading of whiskey in and around Fort Benton was insidious. As Eastman much later wrote Sully, an Indian
camp near Fort Benton had traded all their horses for whiskey,
and every "loafer and bummer about Benton has from 5 to 10
head of Indian horses."[36]

Amid the planning by the army to send troops after the Piegans, the long-rumored expedition of whiskey traders to Canada headed north out of Sun River on December 28, 1869. John
Healy and Alfred Hamilton had to cross the Piegan lands to get
to Canada. The pretext was that they were going there to mine.
They were actually going there to establish whiskey forts in Canada, about which Eastman had warned Marshal Wheeler. It was
rumored that the two men had obtained a permit to cross the
reservation from Ely S. Parker, commissioner of Indian Affairs,
supposedly upon the recommendation of General Sully. This
also was not true, because the permit, surprisingly, had been issued by Sully himself:

PERMIT TO MESSRS. HAMILTON HEALY TO TRAVEL THROUGH
THE BLACKFOOT COUNTRY

Mssrs A. B. Hamilton and J. J. Healy of Montana Territory having
placed in my honor bonds and security to the amount of $10,000
that they will not trade with any person neither white men negroes
or Indians in this Territory after they leave Sun River Settlement—
and being satisfied that said persons have no intentions to infringe

the laws regulating trade and intercourse with the Indians and by direction of the Commissioner of Indian Affairs at Washington permitted to pass through the Blackfoot Country and cross the Northern boundary line of the United States of America at a point within about 30 miles of St. Mary's Lake. They are also privileged to take with them a party of from 20 to 30 men and six wagons loaded with supplies provided there is no spirituous liquors in the Wagons except a small quantity which may be taken safely for medicinal purposes. Not to exceed.

> Alf. Sully
> U.S.A.
> Supt. Inds.[37]

The ultimate destination of Healy and Hamilton was the confluence of the Belly River and the St. Mary River in southern Alberta, where they established Fort Hamilton, which quickly became known as Fort Whoop-Up.

John Healy and Alfred Hamilton did not navigate the route through the Indian country to Canada alone. They had with them a "short, bowlegged, monosyllabic half-breed." The enigmatic thirty-year-old Jerry Potts had been born in about 1840 to his mother, Namo-pisi (Crooked Back), a member of the Black Elks band of Bloods. His father was Andrew R. Potts, a clerk for the American Fur Company at Fort McKenzie. Andrew Potts had been shot in the face and killed by a disgruntled Piegan, who in turn was killed by his own tribe for the wanton act.[38] Alexander Harvey then adopted the young Jerry Potts. When Jerry was about five, Harvey left the territory out of fear for his life when Malcolm Clarke tried to kill him. Andrew Dawson, a fur trader, then adopted Potts. As he grew older, Jerry Potts moved between the Indian camps and the American Fur Company post in Fort Benton. He became a devoted drinker of ardent spirits, whether it was whiskey or the "firewater" that the fur traders gave to the Indians, which might be made from grain alcohol, burnt sugar, laudanum, and about anything else that was good for flavoring.[39]

Jerry Potts

Jerry Potts, Scottish-Piegan guide and trader
(photographer unidentified). Courtesy Montana
Historical Society Research Center Photograph
Archives, Helena, Catalog #944–419.

As he entered adult life, Jerry Potts did not choose good companions. One of his friends during the 1860s was George Star,
the mixed-blood renegade who had been identified among the
targeted Indians by de Trobriand and the army. The story was
told that Potts and Star were so reckless that when drinking they

were known to stand facing each other at twenty-five paces and try to "trim each other's mustache" with their six shooters.[40] It was inevitable that Jerry Potts would become involved in whiskey trading to the Piegans around Fort Benton.[41]

While Healy and Hamilton were preparing to leave Sun River to establish their whiskey trading fort in Canada, Sully had arrived at Fort Shaw on Christmas Day to make good on his plan to meet with the Indians. Three days after Healy, Hamilton, Potts, and the rest of their party left Sun River, armed with Sully's permit, Sully himself headed out north from Fort Shaw with the protection of twenty-five soldiers that de Trobriand had been forced to give him. He was headed in the same direction and possibly on the same trail as the whiskey traders.

The agency on the Teton was thirty-five miles from Fort Shaw. As Sully reported from Fort Shaw, "I left here on the 1st instant . . . and reached the Teton the same afternoon." When he arrived, his messenger to the Indian camps reported to him that "he found the Indians very much intoxicated, and some of the head-men so overcome with the effects of liquor that it was impossible for them to meet me." His timing was right, and the circumstances were right. Given the speed of a slow-moving wagon train as anywhere from twelve miles a day to twenty-four miles a day if the road was ideal, the Healy and Hamilton wagon train could have arrived on the Teton in time for them to distribute whiskey just before Sully arrived. No one could simply have ordered the Indians to a conference, and the whiskey would have made a good incentive for the Indians to come in to meet with Sully.[42] Even then, "I was able to meet with a very few Blackfeet," Sully said, including "Heavy Runner, Little Wolf, and Big Lake, Piegan chiefs, and Gray Eyes, a Blood chief." He was "disappointed at not meeting more of the principal men of the nation."[43]

Through their interpreters, Sully had a talk with the Indians who were there that night and the next morning at the Blackfeet agency, when they were still intoxicated. He warned them that "the government, tired out with repeated aggressions of their people, were determined to make war against them as the only way to protect the lives and property of the whites." Sully also told them something that was not true. He threatened that "they need not think the northern boundary would stop our troops from pursuing them; that we intended to cross the line and pursue them in the British possessions."[44]

The chiefs, according to Sully, "protested that they were not responsible for the conduct of the . . . Indians; that they were innocent and begged if war must be made, that they might not be involved . . . and finally they agreed to go to their camp, and, with their men, move north and bring back all the stock they could get." But, as Sully reported, "they could not promise me to deliver the principal men connected with late murders . . . However, they agreed to kill them if they could not bring in their bodies." Sully was realistic enough to have "little faith in their carrying out this part of their promise."[45]

It took Healy and Hamilton three weeks to get to the confluence of the Belly and St. Mary's Rivers in Canada, a distance that they could have been expected to travel in less time if they had not stopped along the way.[46] They may have traded with the Piegans on the Marias, because that is where Potts would be expected to spend the winter.[47]

Ely Parker, the Indian commissioner, was not entirely against punishing renegade tribes if it was necessary. When Sully informed Parker of the thefts and murders committed, Parker sent the information on to the War Department with the request that "prompt measures may be taken by the Military to check the lawless acts committed by these Indians."[48] With Sully's interference out of the way, the Interior Department no longer offered any opposition to de Trobriand's designed military campaign against the Piegans. Still, General Philip Sheridan had not felt comfortable in entrusting the planning to de Trobriand alone, so another army officer from outside the Montana Territory had been on the scene at Fort Shaw since January 7. Army inspector general James A. Hardie, forty-six, served in Chicago under Sheridan for the Division of the Missouri. He had been hurriedly sent to investigate the situation in the Montana Territory and make recommendations.

Inspector General James A. Hardie

General James A. Hardie, General Phillip Sheridan's inspector
general, came to Montana just before the massacre at the request of General Sheridan to provide a justification for the attack on the Marias. Courtesy Library of Congress.

Hardie was a West Point graduate whose regular army grade
was colonel, but he had received brevet promotions in the Civil
War to brigadier general and major general. He was now one of
the army's four inspector generals. Hardie had come all the way
from Chicago, leaving there on December 27, the same day he

received his orders from Sheridan, probably traveling by the new railroad as far as Utah and then north by stagecoach. He arrived nine days later in Montana, arriving at Helena on January 5 and at Fort Shaw on January 7.[49]

Sheridan had instructed Hardie: "It will be seen . . . that General De Trobriand and General Sully differ very much in their judgment in reference to the condition of Indian affairs in the district of Montana." As Sheridan explained, "General Sully so represented affairs in Montana as to cause the Secretary of the Interior to apply to the General-in-Chief for additional protection for the people, and on this application as a basis, the General authorized me to punish the Piegan Indians, and orders were sent accordingly to General De Trobriand." Sheridan wanted Hardie to determine the seriousness of the Indian troubles: "On the date of November 22, General De Trobriand makes a report on the condition of Indian affairs, from which it will be seen that the reports of Indian depredations are exaggerated; and also a second report of the date of November 26, from which it appears that the condition of Indian affairs is by no means alarming."[50]

Sheridan was cautious about proceeding with an all-out strike on the Piegans in the face of these conflicting reports. He was also well aware that some of the Piegan bands were friendly and told Hardie that "if there is any danger of Indians being molested who are friendly, you are authorized to suspend all operations under the orders emanating from the General-in-Chief."[51] There was obviously more to Hardie's orders and his visit that did not make the official reports. As de Trobriand later confided to his daughter Lina in a letter, Hardie "came in turn, charged with special instructions for me from the Lt. General."[52]

The scholarly, bespectacled Hardie was analytical in his approach. His final report stated that he found in Montana both people who were interested in "settlement, growth, prosperity, and civilization" and a class of people that "leans toward the Indians, and would be apt to resist belief of evil disposition on their part." Hardie was quick to add that "there are unprincipled and unscrupulous men of all classes who speak and act without reference to the truth and right in pursuit of their private ends or gratifications of their passions." First and foremost, Hardie was a good army man who believed that the army alone should be able to gauge the situation. As he said, the "troops do not court Indian campaigns," so he thought that they were "in a position to estimate more nearly the real danger" and would "turn a deaf ear to clamor." Yet it was in part the clamor over Malcolm Clarke's murder that had brought them to this point and had brought Hardie to Montana.[53]

Having laid the groundwork for his report, Hardie commented on the basis for the troubles in Montana, relying on Sully's belief that much of the "trouble that has disturbed the frontier" was due "to the prevalence of drunkenness among the Indians." He acknowledged that Sully, in his initial letter of August 3, 1869, had "earnestly pressed the use of troops to break up the whisky trade." According to Hardie, there were "plenty of lawless and unprincipled men upon the border who supply Indians with whisky surreptitiously, if not openly, in defiance of the law." He had heard from Sully and passed it on to Sheridan that the "Indian will barter anything for drink, even his horses." It was apparently Sully's belief too "that the need to replace horses sold for liquor frequently incited the Indians to steal." Hardie gave more details, which pointed out the "necessity for military movements, to the disturbance, if not the destruction of the trade."[54] But that was not what brought Hardie to Montana. He was there to assure Sheridan that they had ample reason to attack the Piegans.

Hardie immediately went to work to confirm the information that he had been given on the winter location of the various Piegan bands. He "caused a messenger to be sent to the Marias who knew the Indians well." This man had been previously unknown to Hardie, who did not use his name but described him as a man "whom I heard generally well spoken of, and who had the confidence of General De Trobriand." He was most likely referring to Joe Kipp, a half-blood who had traded with the Piegans and was employed at Fort Shaw as a guide at that time. The guide, whoever he was, "left Fort Shaw January 8, and reached the agency on the Teton, thirty-five miles from Fort Shaw, the same day, and then the Northwest Fur Company trading post, seventy-five miles from Fort Shaw, the next day." He "went among the Piegans on that and the following day, and returned January 12."[55]

On January 13, 1870, Sully wrote to Hardie, attempting to tell him what the army strategy should be. He advocated for orders to the troops to cross into the British possessions to "the camps of the Blackfeet there." His plan was "to give it out when the move is made, that the troops are started to cross the line to recapture stolen stock; that permission has been given our government to do so." Then, "after the troops have passed the Marias, to double on the track at night, so as to reach Mountain chief's camp by daylight." Perhaps the best advice that Sully gave to Hardie was that it would "be a difficult matter to make any movement without the Indians getting information through the half-breeds and whisky-sellers at Sun river and Benton." Sully apparently had come to realize that whiskey traders (likely Healy, Hamilton, and Potts) would surely warn the Piegans and Mountain Chief of the impending strike.[56]

As to his meeting with the Indians, Sully told Hardie: "I hope my mission to the Piegans and Bloods may be a success, yet I am not over-sanguine; two or three weeks will determine." After admitting his lack of confidence in his own efforts, Sully realized that he could no longer be effective and had to leave matters up to the army. He told Hardie: "In the meantime I would recommend the commander of the district not to retard any preparation he may contemplate, so that he may be ready to strike if necessary, should it prove that these chiefs cannot carry out their good intentions with their own people."[57]

The task now was for the military force to find the Indians in a country in which it had no familiarity. The guide, whoever he was, had given Hardie the locations of the hostile Mountain Chief's band. Bear Chief had been one of the Indians indicted for killing Malcolm Clarke. He was no longer known to be a chief, and the guide had given the location of the band that he was in. The guide had also given Hardie the location of the bands that were considered friendly. Even then, there was some concern that the friendly bands might not be distinguishable from the marauding bands. Hardie reported that the guide "thought he could distinguish the marauding bands it was contemplated to strike from those not intended to be punished upon seeing the Indians, and could inform the commanding officer." When Hardie said the guide's details were "sufficiently confirmed by other testimony to entitle them to credit," he seemed less than completely comfortable with the guide's sole judgment on the locations. The guide had also given Hardie his assessment that the Indians did not seem to be making any earnest efforts to fulfill their promises to Sully.[58]

Hardie wanted to make sure of the locations of the bands that were the army's target and wanted to get the Blackfeet Indian agent to sign off on them. On January 10 he sent a telegram to Sully, who was now back in Helena: "I would like to see Lieut. Pease to get detail of information about Indian matters." Hardie politely asked Sully to tell Pease, whom he "believed to be at Benton," to "come and see me here without delay." Pease, who had now been at his post for some weeks, surprisingly informed Hardie that he had no intimate knowledge of Blackfeet affairs.[59]

Hardie had also told Sully that he "would be glad to know what definite period you fix as that beyond which you will wait no further for the compliance of the Indians with their promises to bring in property etc."[60] It was then that Sully's apparent misconception of the goal of the military attack became apparent. Sully's response was unrealistic and seemed out of touch. "I would, if possible, capture Mountain Chief and some of his principal men, and hold them as hostages until the nation fulfills their promises to me," he said. This seemed to reflect an understanding that the military operation planned was only to punish the few perpetrators of crimes and was not the type of campaign that would attack Mountain Chief's entire band. To be sure, only ten days earlier, when Sully had returned from the negotiation with Heavy Runner and the other chiefs, he had made his recommendation that de Trobriand was "not to retard any preparation he may contemplate." Sully wanted the army ready to strike, if it proved the chiefs could not carry through on "their good intention with their own people." Through misconception, resentment at not being included in the planning, or just obstinacy, Sully's most recent recommendation indicated that he may have believed all along that the troops would only be sent into the field to round up Mountain Chief and those who had committed crimes. Sully's statements to the Piegans undeniably seemed to threaten at worst that the troops would follow the bands into Canada if necessary, looking for the perpetrators. They did not threaten annihilation of an entire village, which the army seemed to be planning.[61]

The army's wait for the Indians to comply with the Indian superintendent Sully's demands was at an end. In the meantime Major Baker was already on the trail leading from Fort Ellis to Fort Shaw with his four companies of cavalry ready to proceed against the Indians.

On January 13, the same day that Sully offered his last opinion, Hardie reported by telegram to Sheridan that he had completed his investigation. In telegraphic style he said: "Public excitement not great, but military action a necessity. General De Trobriand thinks impunity encourages Indians, and recommends prompt chastisement." Hardie wrote that Sully's deadline was "really up tomorrow" and that he had "sent messenger to Northwest Fur Company's trading post on Marias River," who "reports feeble efforts only are made for recovery of stock, but there is no great hope of success." Importantly, Hardie said that both the "Bloods and Piegans encamped along Marias River now," although "Mountain Chief's band of Piegans small, but great rascals; encamped separately." "The Bloods do not expect punishment" but did "expect troops to punish bad Piegans."[62]

It was essential that the troops distinguish and strike the right band, and Hardie was aware of Sheridan's authorization for him to call off the campaign if friendly Indians were threatened. He now offered his assurance in a telegram of January 13 to Sheridan that "General De Trobriand thinks he can strike them without molesting friends, either Piegans or Bloods. There is reasonable ground for his opinion; but he wishes to chastise. General Sully is moderate, and now advises that Mountain Chief's band be captured and held as hostages until nation fulfills promise to him." In Hardie's view the "practical result" would be "killing and capturing, both." Hardie also said that he had "not interfered with military arrangements" and raised the question "how far should the opinion of General Sully as to scope of operations govern the military?" In answering his own question, he recommended that Baker should be cut loose to make his own decisions on the march. "I think the military commander (Colonel Baker) should be allowed to proceed generally according to the circumstances under which he finds himself in his operations, having in view securing the fulfillment of promises, etc., and the best interests of the service."[63]

Hardie heard back from Sheridan on January 15. The telegraphed orders were terse and direct. Sheridan had what he wanted to hear from Hardie and gave the blood-chilling order: "If the lives and property of the citizens of Montana can best be protected by striking Mountain Chief's band, I want them struck. Tell Baker to strike them hard."[64]

Hardie telegraphed from Helena to the Headquarters of the Division and informed Sheridan: "The Lieutenant General's telegram received." The die was cast. Hardie added his own recommendation, now unequivocal: "I think chastisement necessary." He also forwarded Baker's agreement: "In this Colonel Baker concurs. He knows the General's wishes." Hardie then announced that he was leaving the next day for Corinne, Utah Territory, to take the train back to Chicago.[65]

The day before Sheridan issued his orders, Major Eugene M. Baker had ridden into Fort Shaw with the four companies of his 2nd Cavalry. Baker had left Fort Ellis on his 200-mile line of march to Fort Shaw "on the 6th of January, with two squadrons of the Second Cavalry." These troops consisted of "H Company, Captain Edward Ball; I Company, Brevet Major Lewis Thompson; G Company, Captain S. H. Norton, and F Company, under the command of Second Lieutenant G. C. Doane."[66]

Henry Kennerly and Joseph Kipp with other Fort Benton free traders
Kennerly and Kipp (both seated, with Kipp to the left) are shown with other
Fort Benton free traders at Sioux City in 1866. Courtesy Overholser Historical
Research Center, Fort Benton, Montana.

The command, in excess of "two hundred strong, rank and
file," did not arrive at Fort Shaw until January 14 "at midday
having made eight camps on the march." Notwithstanding the
bitter cold, the soldiers arrived in good shape and "suffered little," "besides a few frost-bitten fingers and toes."[67] John Ponsford, an enlisted man of twenty-two, said that the temperature

"was 20 below zero on leaving Fort Ellis, and continued until Fort Shaw was reached." They had left even colder days at Fort Ellis and "on the day before Christmas until the day after it was 40 below."[68]

To build up the fighting force that Baker had brought from Fort Ellis de Trobriand assigned him two additional companies of infantry. As Baker said, "On our arrival at Fort Shaw, Brevet Lieutenant Colonel G. H. Higbee was ordered to report to me with 55 mounted infantry, and Captain R. A. Torry, with his company of the Thirteenth Infantry." All the army troops for Baker's expedition had been assembled, and all approvals needed had been issued for him to proceed to the Marias. But the extreme cold weather did not allow them to move.[69] Baker's cavalry had been at Fort Shaw since January 14 and stayed there for five more cold days. Part of the delay was due to the weather. A reporter said that "here we had to remain several days on account of the extreme coldness of weather, the thermometer showing from 15 to 25 degrees below zero during the daytime."[70]

De Trobriand seized the time to write another letter to his daughter Lina: "Here, we have had a terrible cold for five or six days. Last night the thermometer went down to -43 [degrees]. Think of it, forty-three degrees Fahrenheit below zero! Mercury thermometers became useless and have been replaced by alcohol thermometers . . . Meanwhile the terrible cold paralyzes my expedition against the Indians, that is to say, delays it . . . The cavalry is camped near the gate (what weather to be under tents!). As soon as the weather relents I will hurl them at the Indians . . . under the command of Major Baker."[71]

There was also the matter of selecting guides who could lead the army to the Marias. De Trobriand's first selection was Joe Kipp, the scout who was already employed at Fort Shaw and was likely the unnamed messenger sent out earlier by Hardie to find Mountain Chief. Except for his young age of only twenty-one, Kipp appeared to be ideally suited for the task. He was half Mandan, the son of James Kipp, a famous fur trader downriver who had built Fort Berthold in the 1840s.[72] When his father later went to live in Missouri, Joe stayed with his Mandan mother at

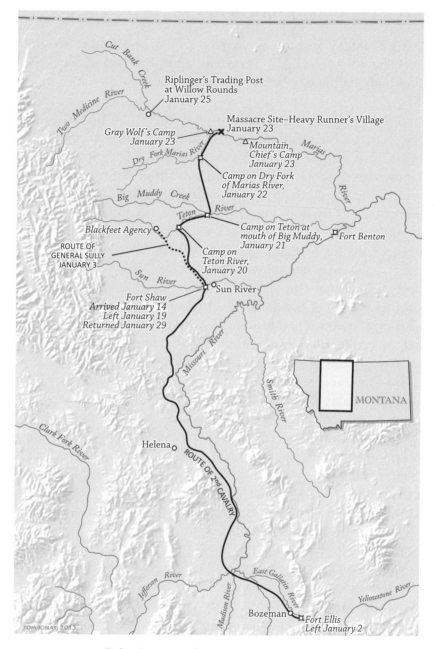

Baker's route of march in January 1870

This map shows the route of march of Major Eugene Baker and the 2nd Cavalry from Fort Ellis to the Marias River in January 1870 and the locations of Fort Shaw, Riplinger's Trading Post, the Blackfeet Agency on the Teton, and General Alfred Sully's route to the agency. Maps by Paul R. Wylie and Tom Jonas, copyright © 2016 by Paul R. Wylie. All rights reserved.

Fort Union, and later they moved to Fort Benton. In 1866, when Kipp was only seventeen, he knew the fur trade well enough to work as a clerk for Carroll and Steele's trading post in Fort Benton. From there he drifted into other fur-trading activities and learned the habits and usual locations of the Indians well enough that in 1869 he was hired regularly as a scout for the 13th Infantry in Fort Shaw.[73] Even though Kipp had worked with the army before, de Trobriand was not totally confident of his ability to handle the duties alone. He looked for an added guide who was older and had more experience in life than the young Kipp but had the same connections to the Piegan tribe and could survive the rigors that lay ahead. He found these qualities in a tall Italian, Joe Cobell.

Cobell had worked at times for the American Fur Company and on one occasion in 1863 had gone with Jerry Potts some four hundred miles downstream on the Missouri to bring back trade goods that had been stranded, returning by wagon to Fort Benton through hostile Sioux Indian country.[74] For some years Cobell had been a "squatter on the fertile tract of land, which lies at the confluence of the two Shonkins, a little less than 20 miles south of Fort Benton." He had moved and was now a neighbor of the deceased Malcolm Clarke on Prickly Pear Creek. Cobell had "a Piegan wife of high degree in her tribe." By 1869 he had a large family of children by three Indian wives. This by no means guaranteed Cobell safety in the Piegan country. As Hardie had noted in his report: "Another settler married to an Indian woman, J. Cable [sic], has been threatened with a fate similar to Clarke's."[75] Cobell also had another score to settle against the Piegans. When Hardie got up a list of livestock stolen by the Indians during the summer of 1869, it showed that six animals, presumably horses, had been stolen from Joe "Cabbell [sic]" of Rock Creek.[76] Mountain Chief and his band were well known to Cobell because his second wife, Mary, was Mountain Chief's sister. According to Blackfeet history, Joe Cobell "was highly skilled with a rifle."[77]

A third guide who had volunteered was along on the trip, whether officially selected by de Trobriand or not: young Horace

Joseph Cobell

Mr. and Mrs. Joseph Cobell. Photograph by Dan Dutro, Fort Benton,
Montana (no date). Joseph Cobell may have fired the shot that killed
Chief Heavy Runner. Courtesy Montana Historical Society Research
Center Photograph Archives, Helena, Catalog #941–763.

Clarke, the son of Malcolm Clarke, whom Pete Owl Child had
tried to kill after he had killed Malcolm. Horace Clarke was in
pursuit of vengeance. He had come to de Trobriand with some
other men who offered to go with the expedition. As it turned out,
Horace's younger brother Nathan was also along on the trip.[78]

Horace Clarke

Horace Clarke and his home, June 1923 (unidentified photographer). Clarke was the son of the murdered Malcolm Clarke and one of the guides for Baker. Courtesy Montana Historical Society Research Center Photograph Archives, Helena, Catalog #941–758.

John Ponsford, an enlisted man, recollected that the guides were "Kipp and Clarke, men who had good reason to see the Indians punished," although it is unclear what Kipp's motive might have been other than a rumor that he had been bested in a fur trade by the Piegans.[79]

James White Calf, a half-blood Piegan, described another group on the expedition: "men who had been supplying whiskey to the Indian camps on Bear River." Perhaps it was no surprise that he identified with this group "Joe Kipp, a half-breed who the Piegans called 'tsoh Keepah' or by his Indian name, Raven Quiver." He also named "three other white men with the group who the Piegans called Brown, Small Neck, and Horn Child."[80]

Private Daniel C. Starr of Company F wrote: "A band of armed civilian volunteer avengers, or adventurers, annexed themselves

Troop F, 2nd Cavalry, at Fort Ellis

Troop F, 2nd Cavalry, Fort Ellis, Montana, 1869 to 1872. Photographer unidentified. Courtesy Montana Historical Society Research Center Photograph Archives, Helena, Catalog #947–242.

to the expedition" and had been with it since Baker "took his
cavalry to Fort Shaw."[81] One of them was Tom LeForge, who
was nineteen in 1870 and was viewed as one of the "armed
volunteers."[82]

Whether it was due to a break in the weather or just because
they had no more time to waste if they wanted an element of
surprise, on Wednesday morning, January 19, Baker and his
command moved out of the gates of Fort Shaw to proceed toward the first low hills and across the frozen plains in quest of
the Indians. By that time "this force numbered about three hundred and eighty men. Company A, Thirteenth Infantry, acted as
guard for the train, while the mounted infantry accompanied the
cavalry."[83]

A man named Peter Gaynor (or maybe the newspapers just
used that name, because his identity is uncertain) said: "We left
Fort Shaw at daybreak on the 19th of January, and marched to

the Teton River, where we lay all day on the 20th. Our command consisted of Companies F, G, H, and L, Second U. S. Cavalry, and a detachment of sixty mounted men from the Thirteenth Infantry, at Fort Shaw. Two companies of the Thirteenth Infantry (dismounted) accompanied us as wagon guard. The whole expedition was under the immediate command of Brevet Colonel E. M. Baker, major Second U. S. Cavalry."[84]

Baker and his command moved slowly through the numbing cold toward the Marias. According to Baker's own version: "I left Fort Shaw on the 19th and marched to the Teton River, where we remained in camp until the evening of the 20th."[85] The *Army and Navy Journal* later printed that at some point on the march "after proceeding about fifty miles" Baker "very wisely left his wagons with their guards, and pushed ahead with all the rapidity possible. From now on, night marches were made, and the command moved along silently, though by no means slowly." The *Journal* story said that "the thermometer still indicated severe weather, but the men, anticipating a brush with the Indians, were so excited that if the mercury had been frozen they would not have heeded the cold." A later story in the *Journal*, authored by Peter Gaynor, said: "Here we left our wagon train and guard, and, taking only a couple of blankets on our saddles and a few pack mules with rations, we commenced a bee-line march across the bluffs for the point where our guide, Joe Kipp, expected to find the Piegans camped."[86]

Martha Plassmann, a journalist, gave her opinion later that there may have been other reasons why the soldiers got through the cold. As she said, "One of the company told me that officers and men 'tried to keep their spirits up by taking spirits down' and, at the end of the journey they scarcely knew what they were doing." The consumption of liquor by the troops would not have been surprising, given the laxity of Major Baker at Fort Ellis. According to William White, who was stationed there as an enlisted man, "drunkenness within the post precincts was not considered a public offense unless the condition prevented performance of routine military duties." He added that "there was no regulation limiting the quantity of liquor that could be bought or sold."[87]

Martha Edgerton Plassmann

Mrs. Martha Edgerton Plassmann (born May 14, 1849,
died September 25, 1936) was a journalist who wrote
about Baker and the Baker Massacre. Photographer
unidentified, no date. Courtesy Montana Historical
Society Research Center Photograph Archives, Helena,
Catalog #944-365.

Baker and his troops remained on the Teton River until the
evening of January 20, when they "left camp and made a night
march to the mouth of Muddy Creek, a branch of the Teton."
There they made camp and stayed "until the evening of the 21st,
and set out for the Marias River, expecting to reach the Big Bend
on the next morning having understood from the guide that was
where the Indians were encamped."[88] Already the troops seemed
to be moving too slowly. The ride the night of January 20 had not

covered a significant distance. From de Trobriand's personal correspondence with his daughter Lina, it is evident that the attack had been planned for Friday, January 21, when in fact on that day the troops still had a long way to go. De Trobriand's plan was for Baker's men "to surprise the hostile Piegans and severely punish them Friday morning at dawn."[89] The delay concerned Baker, because they were losing valuable time and increasing the possibility of Mountain Chief being alerted to the danger.

Much to the dismay of Baker, his column was not able to make it all the way to the Marias even on January 22, as they had hoped. According to Baker: "We were obliged to camp in a ravine on the Dry Fork of the Marias, till the night of the 22nd."[90] A chronicler added more detail: "We marched all night and at early dawn concealed ourselves in a pocket in the bluffs, where we were compelled to pass the whole of a miserably cold day without water or wood sufficient to cook coffee."[91]

Private John Ponsford described how the travel from Fort Shaw after the first day "was done in the night, the soldiers laying off during the day, putting in the time keeping warm or sleeping, in any way they could without fires or tents & only their saddle blankets." He recalled that the "weather was considerable below zero & the snow from 1 to 2 feet on the level."[92] An unnamed correspondent for the *Bozeman Pick and Plow* reported firsthand on the march. This newspaper had just been started three weeks before, on December 31, 1869, by Horatio N. Maguire and John Street.[93] Perhaps the writer was the same Peter Gaynor whose name later appeared on some articles. "At dark on the evening of the 22nd we once more resumed our toilsome march, and at length reached a mighty ravine, which the guide informed us, had never been passed but by two white men. This was readily believed, for the difficulties it presented were truly formidable." The way was treacherous, and it was reported that "here one of our men had the misfortune to break his leg, but rather than be left in such a country with only two companions, he summoned fortitude sufficient to ride his horse twenty miles further, although he was in terrible agony the whole distance."[94]

Sometime during the night of January 22 dissension broke out between Baker and the guides. Baker could not have been happy to spend extra time on the march, and the trouble might have started with Baker "expecting to reach the Big Bend" on the morning of January 22, "having understood from the guide that was where the Indians were encamped." Instead Baker's troops had to spend that day hiding in a ravine. That evening Joe Kipp protested that the trail they were on would not take them to Mountain Chief's camp but rather to the smallpox camp of Heavy Runner. It was apparently Kipp himself who had made a mistake or had wrong information, and he now tried to convince Baker of his error. Despite Kipp's protestations, Baker thought that Kipp was deceiving him and threatened to shoot him if he did not lead as directed.[95] Martha Plassmann wrote: "Horace [Clarke] told me that Joe Kipp tried his best to convince Baker of his [Kipp's] mistake, but that 'officer and gentleman' had been too long in conference with John Barleycorn to heed the warning. . . . On good authority, both officers and men are reported to have been considerably the worse for liquor."[96]

Sometime later that evening, or at least well before dawn the next morning, Baker's command "broke camp and marched to the Marias River, arriving there on the morning of the 23rd." They were two days late in arriving at their target and were ready to attack.[97]

EIGHT

Massacre

*Heavy Runner told everyone to be quiet, that there was
nothing to fear. He said he would show the whites his
"name paper" . . . a shot pierced his heart and he fell,
clutching the paper to his breast.*

SPEAR WOMAN AFFIDAVIT, 1915

The killing of the Piegan Indians began the morning of January 23. Spear Woman, a young girl, saw people in her lodge being "shot mercilessly." Astonishingly, she remained unseen, probably because she was young and little. Finally the firing stopped, and soon after, "the soldiers were gone." At first the only sound she could hear was "the moans of the wounded." Many of them were dying. Soon a new torment was visited on her when she heard "the weeping of the living."

Young Spear Woman found that "her mother and sister survived." They were together again, although she did not know how. Nobody knew in that horrible killing. Her relief was short: their instincts told them to flee. Her mother "grabbed what was needed" for them to leave, and they made it to just outside the camp. Spear Woman and her family were horror-struck when "the soldiers began to return." Her family quickly found cover enough to hide and "dared not move" for fear of even the slightest motion being seen. If the frozen day had gotten warmer, they did not notice.

In the meantime the soldiers had reentered the camp. Spear Woman believed that they "had come back to slaughter again."

She remained hidden and could only watch as the soldiers me-
thodically checked the bodies of the Indians "and anyone yet
alive was shot in the head."

MAJOR EUGENE M. BAKER'S column was in confusion by the time
it reached the bluffs above the Marias River. Dissension had broken out during the night ride to the bluffs. Baker was said to be
drunk and could not comprehend the directions that his guides
were giving him or perhaps just chose to ignore them, with some
justification, because each guide may have had his own agenda.
One of the paid guides, Joe Kipp, was also in the fur trade and
closely aligned with the interests of the whiskey traders. The second guide, the tall, swarthy Italian Joseph Cobell, "a giant of a
man," had his mind on his missing horses stolen by the Piegans
and their serious threat that he would be murdered like Malcolm
Clarke.[1]

The third guide was Horace Clarke, bent on avenging the
death of his father. When word had leaked out in Helena that
General Sully was trying to lead a militia against the Piegans,
young Clarke had seized upon this as a chance for him to avenge
the death of his father. When it became clear that the Indian superintendent, Brigadier General Alfred Sully, would not raise
a militia and that Brevet Brigadier General Regis de Trobriand
would send the regular troops of the U.S. Army against the Piegans, Horace went to de Trobriand to volunteer his services.[2] He
had brought with him a burning hatred for Pete Owl Child and
the other raiders from Mountain Chief's band who had killed his
father and almost killed him too. The night before reaching the
Marias Horace Clarke had watched Baker attempting to lead, but
it was clear to him that it was "an undeniable fact that Col. Baker
was drunk and did not know what he was doing."[3]

After the argument with Baker on the trail all three guides
were sent to the rear, leaving Baker and his troops to find their
own way. The problem that Baker would have in leading, even if
he was sober enough to command, was that the troops could not
simply ride down the river bottom until they reached the camp.

If that tactic had been available to them, they could have inter-
sected the Marias by heading directly north from their day camp
on the Dry Fork and descended down the first ravine that would
take them to the bottom. But Baker was committed to an early
morning surprise attack and wanted his command on top of the
bluffs, where he could fire down on the Indians when they were
found. Without Kipp, Cobell, or Clarke to guide them, all that the
companies of Baker's command could do was proceed on a parallel course with the river, as close to the edge of the ravine-cut
bluffs as possible, while still remaining out of sight. This had not
been easy. Sometimes they were close to the edge of the bluffs,
and at other times they had to point their horses directly away
from the river, to get across the snow-filled shallow ends of the
steep rifts that cut across their path.[4]

Captain Lewis Thompson and L Company were the first actually to reach the Marias. They had arrived there by heading north
with their horses plowing through the trackless snow, "from 1 to
2 feet on the level." It may not have been the best route, because
Baker was "depending upon himself for the direction of the
march." The guides had known which route to take, but when
this information was passed on to Baker, he did not follow it.
Thompson had to find his own way through the snow.[5]

As Thompson and L Company rode down a coulee to the river
bottom, an Indian lodge suddenly appeared before him. Surprised, Thompson thought for a moment that he might have found
the camp of Mountain Chief. Reining in their horses, Thompson
and his company came to a stop. He ordered the troops to dismount. With their arms at the ready, they surrounded the lodge.

Private John Ponsford, twenty-two, was with Doane's F Company as they too approached the Indian lodge and said that he
"thought we had arrived at [Mountain Chief's] camp." When
he heard the order given "to fight on foot," he eagerly jumped
from his horse and rushed with the dismounted troops to the
camp. Then they suddenly stopped, aware that something was
amiss.[6] As they looked around, they expected to see other lodges
of Mountain Chief's band. Instead they felt only an eerie stillness

around them and soon knew the reason. As a few frightened Indians emerged from their tipi, their smallpox was evident.[7]

Instead of Mountain Chief's larger camp, the troops had found the small camp of Gray Wolf. "Two braves and three squaws, were taken prisoner," and the soldiers sought to question them through any means of communication available. They learned that "a large band of their tribe was encamped about ten miles distant on the Big Bend of the Marias." Some of the troops thought that they were clear on exactly what Gray Wolf's small sick band had told them. They had "forced the information that Black Eagle and Big Horn, with the main camp of the Piegans, were at Big Bend, eight miles down the river; and that Mountain Chief, with a few warriors, was camped a few miles further down."[8] Others were not so sure and thought that Major Baker ordered them to start "on a gallop for Black Eagle's camp."[9] The troops now supposed that this was where Mountain Chief's large band was located. Not wasting time, they secured their weapons and mounted their horses, wheeling out of the river bottom, eager to find the Indians and start the attack.[10]

Captain Lewis Thompson seemed sure that he could still find Mountain Chief and gave his L Company troops the command to proceed on their mission. They quickly climbed though a ravine to the top of the bluffs where Thompson thought that they could discover the right route. "Soon a broad trail was found." Thompson's "cavalry started with new vigor, sure that the enemy was close at hand."[11]

Lieutenant Doane and F Company had followed Thompson down to the river bottom and also joined Thompson's L Company on the trail. Doane's Company was under orders from Baker to proceed on down the bluffs, "at a gallop about four miles." Suddenly they came upon "two Indians" who were walking on foot, "with two squaws mounted on ponies." At first the soldiers did not know what Indians they were but soon recognized them as Bloods and not the Piegans they were seeking. The Bloods "were captured without resistance."[12]

Some bands of the Blood tribe were known to be in the vicinity, but their exact location was not known—nor did Baker and his officers care. They were after the Piegans and had specific orders not to attack the Bloods. This had been the understanding from the start. When General Sully, the Indian superintendent, met with the Piegans, he had also met with "Gray Eyes, a Blood chief." Joe Kipp knew that the Bloods had been friendly and had passed this on to Sully and inspector general James Hardie, who in turn had advised Generals Sheridan and Sherman that "the Bloods do not expect punishment" but did "expect troops to punish bad Piegans."[13]

It would not do to let the Bloods they had captured get away to warn the Piegans early in the dark morning, so Sergeant John O'Kelly "disarmed and secured them." The troops swore at the Bloods that "if they didn't just lead the way to their camp that they'd blow their [brains] out."[14] The terrified Indians, thinking that the information was to be in exchange for their lives, told the troops that they were on the right path to Mountain Chief's village and that they would lead them in exchange for their freedom.[15]

Captain Lewis Thompson and L Company kept pushing down the top of the bluffs that morning, but F Company had taken over the lead. Its second lieutenant was in command, ambitious Gustavus Cheney Doane, twenty-nine. He had been third in command of F Company until it left from Fort Ellis. As fate would have it, his superior Captain O. O. G. Robinson was under arrest for being absent without official leave and First Lieutenant William Rowalle was away on allowed leave, leaving Doane in charge, with an opportunity to achieve recognition.[16] As the troops continued, it became apparent that Major Baker was "too drunk" to direct his troops.[17] With whatever clarity he could discern from the orders of his inebriated commander, Doane said that he relied on a direct command by Major Baker to be "sent forward . . . apparently along the trail of the Indians down the river."[18] This Doane did gladly, with visions of a terrible glory in front of him.[19]

Meanwhile, downstream on the bottom of the Marias River, the camp of Heavy Runner had been recently assembled at a place known as the Big Bend, the general location where Baker's command had expected to find Mountain Chief. The camp of Heavy Runner was new. Only the day before a Piegan woman who later became known as Mrs. Frank Monroe came with her father's family and was among the first to pitch a camp on the north side of the river. She remembered that even "before we had camp pitched, most of the party went out after buffalo, and after the camp was pitched another party started out on the hunt." The women and children were left in camp to await the return of the hunters, but instead it was the soldiers who came the next day.[20]

As the troops advanced along the trail and "approached Heavy Runner's camp," the guide Joe Kipp appeared once again.[21] He knew that it was not the camp of Mountain Chief that was at the Big Bend. But when he had advised the major of this during the night Baker thought that Kipp had deceived him and threatened to shoot him if he did not lead as directed. Kipp now protested again that the trail they were on would not take them to Mountain Chief but rather to the camp of Heavy Runner. He was taking a chance by even being with the troops at this point, for fear that Baker might carry out his threat to shoot him.[22]

Kipp's information had come to him just recently. Early that morning he had gone out with Horace Clarke and Joe Cobell to try to find the location of Mountain Chief's camp. During this search Horace Clarke had a surprise encounter on the bluffs with John Middle Calf, nineteen, a member of Heavy Runner's band. It was "scarcely daylight," and "in his excitement at seeing the soldiers" Middle Calf told Clarke that "Mountain Chief had moved about nine miles below on the river." Horace also learned from Middle Calf that Mountain Chief had moved so far down because the whiskey trader Jerry Potts had been there and "warned Mountain Chief's band about the soldiers coming, and Mountain Chief 'moved downstream.'"[23] Armed with this information, the guides tried in vain to communicate it to the soldiers. Their efforts were futile: the column under the orders of Baker bore down on Heavy Runner's doomed camp.[24]

Bear Head, a young boy in Heavy Runner's slumbering village, awoke before light on the morning of January 23, 1870,

Baker battleground

This photo, believed to show the Marias River bottom in the general location of the battle, was part of a set of eight cabinet photos taken from 1886 to 1890. No photographer is identified, but it may have been taken by A. B. Coe. Courtesy Overholser Historical Research Center, Fort Benton.

knowing that "most all of the able bodied men were out on the hunt," so the young boys like himself would have to round up the camp's horses. This was a difficult task, because the horses were left loose during the night up on the bluffs where they were free to forage in the long snow-covered prairie grass. With "about ten boys of various ages," Bear Head "got the horses all rounded up." The bunch was then cut in two, "the better to handle them on account of their being so many." The Piegan boys headed the horses back toward the village. But when they were "on top of a ridge" and "within sight of the camp," Bear Head discerned a movement on "another ridge quite a little distance away." As Bear Head fixed his gaze on the horizon, he was filled with dread as he saw "many riders and wagons" approaching through the icy haze in the early morning light. If he truly saw wagons, these were more likely the wagons of fur traders, because the army's wagons had been left behind to avoid slowing the progress of the cavalry. As he watched the column approach, Bear Head could see that "there was a coulee between them and us." As they came even closer, he made out that they were soldiers. At about that time the soldiers also became aware of Bear Head and his companions and the immense band of horses that they had rounded up. When the soldiers approached him, Bear Head bravely stood his ground, but he was soon left alone to suffer whatever fate he might face at the hands of the soldiers: "all the boys became frightened and all of them . . . made off in the opposite direction."[25]

Then Lieutenant Doane and his company "came in sight" of Bear Head's "large drove of ponies herding on the edge of the bluffs." Doane quickly decided that the horses had to be kept under control so that they would not run to the village, which would be in the vicinity. He ordered Sergeant Henry Williams to take six men "to cut out and drive away the herd." This was risky, as they knew from the presence of the horses that they were now "within range of the village." Williams and his men also faced impending peril because the "ground was full of ravines dangerous to ride over." In fact "the horse of one of the troopers fell into one of these narrow cuts, breaking three of his legs, and was killed in consequence."[26] The horses that had been cut out of Bear Head's herd were soon turned over to "Lieutenant Waterbury, 13th Infantry, who was with Captain Higbee's mounted force."[27]

Fear struck at Bear Head's heart when one of the troopers came up to him and pointed a gun, ready to kill. Seeing that Bear Head was just a young boy, however, the soldier lowered the weapon. Bear Head, who knew no English, could only speak to the man with a word of greeting that they both would understand and in reply heard the same word, "how," from the soldier, who rode on. But the soldiers could not risk setting Bear Head free. The next soldier caught his horse "by the rein and led it along with him," with Bear Head still on its back. "The other soldiers scattered out and surrounded both of the herds of horses and kept them moving in the direction of the camp." At some point Bear Head became aware that the two captive Bloods and their women were being guarded by the soldiers. He heard "one man [say], in Blackfoot, 'Is this Mountain Chief's camp?'" He did not know that it was probably Joe Kipp who had asked him the question. Bear Head replied, "No, his camp is further down. This is Heavy Runner's camp." The man replied: "That is strange— we have two Indians with us who told us that this is Mountain Chief's camp." It was then that Bear Head understood the deception and "knew that these two Blood Indians had misdirected the soldiers to Heavy Runner's camp instead of Mountain Chief's."[28]

While Bear Head was being confronted by Williams and his detachment, the troops of F Company continued on the trail atop the bluffs, which, as Doane observed, "ran parallel with the Marias River." But they could not always see the river, which was "hidden from view in a deep ravine of Bad Lands." This was a problem for Doane, who was afraid that "we should pass some village without seeing it." So he sent out First Sergeant Anderson "alone to the edge of the bluff to look along the river." A short time later Doane looked closely past the edge of the bluffs and saw "smoke from the Indian villages" that "appeared just below." He had reached his goal with his F Company and was the first to arrive.[29]

Peering through the cold winter haze, Doane saw a scattering of Indian tipis settled in among the stark trees along the river bottom. A few tipis were pitched north of the frozen river, but most of them were on the south side. After making a count, Doane noted that the village appeared to have "thirty-two lodges, eleven on the north and twenty-one on the south side of the river." Doane could see that the camp was his for the taking and that he would get the credit for leading the deadly attack if he acted quickly.[30]

Doane determined that in order to keep the Indians from escaping before his troops could kill them he would have to divide his company and send troops across the river to set up part of the perimeter there. Sergeant Charles Moore was close by, but Doane wanted First Sergeant Alexander Anderson to lead the troops across the river. He sent Moore "with several men to report to the First sergeant, with instructions to charge down the bluffs above the villages, cross the stream and deploy on that side."[31] Doane's hastily formed plan was to have the rest of the company "come in below and between the Indians and the herd of ponies." The orders had to be well executed, with both bodies of F Company coming to the edge of the village at the same time and not be exposed to the fire of the Indians, should they choose to fight. His orders given, Doane felt satisfaction as they were "executed to the letter." Just as he and the main part of the company "came down the bluffs on the trail, the First Sergeant was seen crossing the river above the village." Once across the river, Doane could see the first sergeant deploy "his men properly and at a run, and in two minutes the Indians were completely surrounded."[32]

Corporal Daniel C. Starr of F Company was with the troops who surrounded the village. He was a veteran who had had been with the army for some time. This was not his first battle, and he was prepared to fight. As he reached the Indian camp, however, he was surprised that the village did not seem to be on the alert. Quiet prevailed, and he believed that "the Indians were all asleep." Starr did not fully comprehend why, but his experience told him that the stillness might been because "some white men traders had been there a few days preceding" and, he speculated, "there had been much Indian drunkenness, which now was being followed by the usual consequent dullness."[33]

In the stillness of the morning Heavy Runner's sleeping camp was doomed. The soldiers were on its edge, ready for the kill. It would have been a perfect time to take prisoners, but that was not an option for Baker and his command. It certainly was not being considered by Lieutenant Gustavus Cheney Doane, who in his own mind was on the brink of renown as an Indian fighter. He also knew that instructions had come all the way down from General Sheridan through Major Baker to "strike them hard." Word of the instructions had filtered down to Corporal Dan Starr, who knew that "Baker had made known" to his company commanders that "the paramount feature of his military policy when he announced as a motto, 'Nits make lice.'"[34] Starr knew that this "was the customary way of indicating that children were not to be spared." "With this general-extermination idea impressed upon the troops," they were ready for the annihilation of Heavy Runner's camp.[35]

From where he was being held by the soldiers, Bear Head could see the other companies of Baker's command on top of the bluff getting ready for the carnage. He witnessed "the main body of the soldiers approaching the camp and getting off their horses, which some of them held while the rest scattered into line." Bear Head realized that the soldiers would be shooting down into the Indian village from a great advantage.[36]

With Doane's soldiers approaching more closely, some activity at last stirred in Heavy Runner's village.[37] The Indians had been surprised at first. But they were now aware of the soldiers, and their fears had been calmed. They did not believe that they would be harmed. Spear Woman, the little girl in a tipi, had heard Heavy Runner say "there was nothing to fear" and that "he would show the whites his 'name paper.'" After all, they knew that Heavy Runner had met in peace with General Sully on January 2 and been given a paper that he believed would protect him and his band from attack.[38]

Good Bear Woman, twenty-nine, was Mountain Chief's daughter, but she was not in his camp that day. Instead she was in Heavy Runner's camp at the time of the massacre. She saw the soldiers steadily approaching and could see "Chief Heavy Runner . . . come out of his lodge and go to meet the commanding officer." Heavy Runner handed over "some papers, which the commanding officer read, then he tore them up and threw them away." Good Bear Woman then saw Heavy Runner turn "about face" and believed that the "soldiers fired upon him and killed him."[39] Joe Kipp had followed the troops to the village and by this time was within a distance of "probably fifty or sixty yards" from Heavy Runner. He saw Heavy Runner approaching the soldiers:

as the "chief went toward them as if to tell them who he was and explain his mission there . . . they opened fire," killing him.[40]

In the melee that followed the killing of Heavy Runner, the bullets started to come from everywhere: from Doane's troops on the ground around the tipis and from the top of the bluffs above the Marias, where young Bear Head saw the troops dismount. He "could plainly hear the sound of their guns and see the smoke as they began firing into the camp," their empty shell casings falling to the ground.[41]

Joe Kipp was not the only one to see Heavy Runner go down with the first bullet. Spear Woman and Good Bear Woman each saw him fall, but they did not mention where the bullet came from. Many bullets were fired at Heavy Runner, but it probably was not even a soldier who fired the one that killed him. Joe Cobell had come down the bluffs behind the troops and was lurking in back of them when Heavy Runner came out of his lodge. While on the bluffs, Cobell had heard Bear Head say that this was the camp of Heavy Runner and not Mountain Chief.[42] But that would not save Heavy Runner, because Cobell had two reasons to see him punished. First, Mountain Chief was his wife's brother. He wanted Mountain Chief to be spared, which he would be if the troops occupied themselves with Heavy Runner's village. Second, he had a score to settle with Heavy Runner's band, which had stolen his horses. Years later he admitted to family members that he had fired the shot that killed the Piegan chief.[43]

The shot that felled Heavy Runner signaled the start of the killings in earnest. Doane said that a few minutes later "the other companies came up . . . and commenced firing." It seemed to him that this "was continued for an hour." A newspaper report said: "The work of slaughter continued for about three hours." The shots came from everywhere. On the north side of the river "the First Sergeant [Anderson] kept his line effectively, having with him Sergeant Moore and about twelve (12) men." Being on the opposite side of the camp, these men had been put in "great danger, as the dismounted companies were firing in their direction constantly, and they were obliged to maintain an exposed position in order to cut off the Indians who endeavored to break through their line."[44]

Doane's tactic of sending First Sergeant Anderson and his detachment across the river to surround the entire village was a good one: "not an Indian got through," he reported, except that "several were followed high up on the slope of the opposite Bad Lands, and killed with revolvers." Doane gloried in the achievement and heaped praise on "the First Sergeant," who had "especially conducted himself with the utmost bravery and good judgment" and had done "everything that an officer could have done under the circumstances, and in a most creditable manner."[45]

Anderson was not the only one who had crossed the river. "While the firing was going on, Sergeant Amos Wise," who had been in the army since his 1867 enlistment in St. Louis, "with a couple of men, drove off several small herds of ponies which were on the other side of the river." Doane saw him "doing it quickly and with discretion," but Doane's tactic could have led to disaster, because Wise was under fire while he was doing it, with the bullets likely coming from the troops of other companies who may still have been on the bluffs.[46]

Meanwhile several men of Doane's command walked unafraid toward the tipis in Heavy Runner's main village. Corporal Isaac Etheridge went "in front of the Lodges" and fired "into the doors," careless of the danger to his life. Doane watched as he "three times dropped Indians who had bows presented within a few feet of him, with arrows drawn to an aim." But "Etheridge was a splendid shot, and killed several."[47]

Private William Birth, twenty-one, and the rest of K Company of the mounted infantry from Fort Shaw came down the bluffs and dismounted. They had been thrown into the fray. As he and the others approached the village, he was close enough to observe the lodges and said that he was surprised the Indians "did not fight when we came upon their camp." The Indians that Birth saw were all too sick or too frightened to fight and "only sticked their heads out of their tents and went and laid back and covered up again." Without much hesitancy, Birth and the other infantrymen started firing into the tents. They had heard the orders of an officer, which Birth thought was Colonel Baker, who "said to us you know what to do." Even as the shots were being fired into the tipis, the Indians "still . . . would not return the fire." The soldiers around Birth became emboldened: unafraid of any kind of armed resistance by the Indians, they "went up to their tents and took . . . butcher knives and cut open their tents and shot them as they lay under their blankets and buffalo robes." But that was not extreme enough: Birth and his companions "killed some with axes."[48]

More cavalry had come up and dismounted, and on foot they commenced firing at the Indians. In the heat of battle Doane saw a man he thought to be "Private Mullis of the cavalry," who "fought in such a desperate manner as not only to attract the attention of his officers, but also that of nearly the entire command." Doane was proud to report that Mullis "killed alone, and unaided by his comrades, twenty Indians."[49]

Even if the braves in Heavy Runner's camp had not been out hunting, the Piegans would still have been overwhelmingly outnumbered by the five companies of soldiers all shooting into the village: some on the ground, some from across the river, and some from the vantage point of the high bluffs. What resistance the Indians mounted against the torrent of bullets was small. They fired only a few shots themselves, but one of them hit Private Walter McKay of Captain Lewis Thompson's L Company, killing him instantly. Instead of serving as a caution to the soldiers, the loss of one of their number infuriated them. They charged "right in among the tipis . . . shooting down every one they could find." Only a "few squaws and papooses" survived, and "these they made prisoner, together with Wolf Tail, a notorious chief, whom they afterwards killed."[50]

The totality of the ghastly event was beyond description, but a newspaper report attempted to portray the sight:

The scene now presented was one of frightful reality. The hide-covered lodges were ripped with knives by the soldiers, and many a bullet, passing through the opening thus made, laid low the braves within. The uproar was deafening. The sounds of firearms; yells of the infuriated soldiers; yells and death-cries of the redskins; the barking and howling of the Indian dogs, all mingling, made the scene one of terrible interest. Anon, kegs of powder, carefully stowed away in several of the lodges, would explode and kill the inmates. Here, a savage would spring out with rifle in hand, but only fall in his tracks. Their resistance would be made, but the well-directed shots soon caused the effort to cease. Several attempted to pass from one side of the river to the other, but the wide circles of red with Indians in the center, told but too well how vain was the attempt. Though all was in apparent confusion, still the troops kept in such order that not one of their shots hurt a comrade.[51]

The newspaper account told of the grisly fates that befell those who tried to escape:

One Piegan Indian, thinking that his chances for living a long time were few, and eager to have his days prolonged to an indefinite period, in a fit of desperation killed his two squaws, and drew their corpses over his cowardly form. He feigned death, but it availed him nothing, for soon his spirit joined those of his squaws. Six other of the savages ran over a hill on the right bank of the river, and escaped from the main command; but their evil star guided them to a point where a few soldiers were guarding the captured herd, and soon these Indians also lay stiff on the ground.[52]

A young Piegan boy, only about seven years old, escaped this hell with his life. He was "hiding out in the brush when the attack occurred" and "remained hidden while the old men, women and kids were killed." He miraculously got away, but not before his eyes witnessed the horror of young babies being "slung by their heels and heads bashed on rocks." Terrified, he was able some how to run from the camp in the cold winter. He covered about seventy miles to safety near the Rocky Mountains, where he was taken in by a white family and adopted.[53]

From the place where she had sought cover, the young woman in the camp who became Mrs. Frank Monroe could see what the soldiers were doing. "After the firing was over, the soldiers went through the camp and picked out what robes and blankets they wanted for themselves," she said, "and the rest was all got together and burned." She observed the terrifying scene where "all of the lodges and some of the people were burned up." She also saw that her mother was "wounded in the hand by a bullet." Nevertheless, she and her bleeding mother "sneaked away after the firing was over and made . . . way to a camp further up the river."[54]

Buffalo Trail Woman was twenty-two at the time of the attack. Her husband, Good Stab (also known as Yellow Owl), was one of the few able-bodied braves who was not out hunting. When he realized what was taking place, "he prepared for war." He made it to "his mother's lodge, some distance away," where he was shot and killed. Buffalo Trail Woman herself "was wounded on the back and on [her] left ear" and saw "how others in our lodge were shot, including an old man who dug a trench near the fire pit, a kind of fort." Later, when the soldiers fired on the lodge, "the old man got into his trench and covered himself with buffalo skin trimmings."[55]

Spopee, a Blood Indian of about twenty, found himself in Heavy Runner's camp that day and was shot through the hips but lived to tell his story years later, after he had been imprisoned for murder and served thirty years of a sentence before he was pardoned.[56]

The brutal killing of the defenseless Piegans was just too much for Henry Dew, twenty-nine, a private in G Company under Captain S. H. Norton. When he was ordered to use a poleaxe and kill some Indians that were captured during the battle, he could not stomach it; instead he crept out of camp and disappeared into the night. At a later time he rejoined his company.[57]

Young civilian Tom LeForge, nineteen, had followed Baker all the way from Fort Ellis. He someway found himself on the battlefield and in a bad place that day. He was close enough to witness one of the few weak attempts by the Indians to fight back. A Piegan had "slashed his way out from a tipi and let loose an arrow that gashed" LeForge's own hand as it whizzed past. His brush with death continued when he "had the toe-ends of his left foot sheared off by a Piegan bullet." As LeForge was getting away, "he found a young squaw hidden in the brush, nursing her baby." As he approached, "she jumped up, in great fear." She held the infant out toward him, making signs saying "wait until my baby gets its fill from my breast . . . then you may kill me . . . but let the baby live, I give it to you." LeForge was unable to do anything other than turn away and ignore her. When he "again passed that thicket," he "saw the dead bodies of both the mother and child."[58]

Not all of the Indians who were killed that day died in the main attack on the village. Corporal Dan Starr saw that "eight warriors were taken prisoner" and "made attempts at escape." After the "re-capture of two of them who had tried to slip away, the Officer of the Guard lost his temper" and issued a simple order to "kill them—every damned one of them!" As the soldier guards began to get their guns ready, the order came to "get axes and kill them one at a time." Starr himself confessed that he was one of the axe-murderers. When historian Thomas Marquis told Corporal Dan Starr's story some years later he said that "the blame was settled upon his [Baker's] guide . . . a whiskey trader among the Indians." He could have meant Joe Cobell but more likely was referring to Joe Kipp, because Kipp was a known whiskey trader and Cobell did not have that history. Marquis said that this was a "known fact" and that the trader had "used his advantageous position to settle a grudge against this one particular band, some members of which had worsted him in his business dealings with them."[59]

James White Calf, who was then about thirteen years old, had heard of the same thing that Starr was talking about. He had a simple explanation based on what he had been told: "Mountain Chief had been camped with his band on the Bear River (the Marias River), but he had moved his camp further down the river, and Baker could not find him so he attacked the camp of Heavy Runner." But White Calf had come to believe that the men who had been supplying whiskey to the Indian camps on the Marias River guided the troops to the camp. One of these men, he said, was the scout Joe Kipp himself.[60]

Buffalo Trail Woman was wounded in the battle but still conscious and watched as a "scout or interpreter for the soldiers came to where I, and other wounded were." It might have been Joe Kipp. Whoever it was, she heard him tell them "to get our things and they would move us to two lodges that were spared from fire or capture—for hospital purposes, because the rest of the camp furnishings were going to be burned." She "saw the soldiers gather all of the belongings of the camp and set them on fire." She observed from a distance that the soldiers surrounded the lodge where she had been and "fired upon it, killing everyone except those who escaped by chance." This was something that Doane approved of. He had put Sergeant Lewis Howell of F Company in charge of the destruction and was satisfied that Howell had "displayed good judgment in destroying the lodges and in caring for the wounded squaws and children."[61]

Heavy Runner's camp was completely destroyed and became quiet. Most of the soldiers ceased their fire and prepared to go after Mountain Chief, whom they now knew was somewhere down the river. At some point Major Eugene Baker had recovered enough from his inebriation to lead again. He "ordered Lieutenant Doane to remain in this camp and destroy all the property." Together with the other three companies of cavalry and the mounted infantry company, Baker "marched down the river after the camp of Mountain Chief," which he "understood was . . . four miles below." It turned out that Mountain Chief was more like sixteen miles away, and the extra time that it took the troops to get there gave his band members all the time that they needed to disperse.[62]

Arriving at a place on the Marias where Mountain Chief was supposed to be, Baker found nothing but an empty camp. Mountain Chief's small band had been alerted in time, and not an Indian was to be found. All Baker surveyed, to his dismay, was "a camp of seven lodges that had been abandoned in great haste, leaving everything." "The evidence of the hasty departure was simple: the lodges just struck, the pots full of meat still on the fires, and robes and property of every description lying around." Prints in the snow showed the distressed Baker that "the Indians had scattered in every direction, that it was impossible to pursue them."[63]

By this time Baker's troops were suffering from debilitating exhaustion and hunger and could not follow the escaping Piegans anyway. They had "been fasting for thirty-six hours, marching a distance of between seventy and eighty miles and fighting for some hours." All they could do was wait ineffectively for provisions that they hoped would arrive soon at the abandoned camp while Mountain Chief and his band added to the distance between them. It was nearly "three o'clock the next morning" when "pack mules with rations" finally caught up with them. The hungry soldiers "lacked neither inclination nor ability to do ample justice to the frugal fare which awaited them."[64]

As the night of January 23 settled in, Baker was faced with the reality of a double failure. Mountain Chief, their quarry, had escaped. The Indians with him had all survived and by this time were well on their way to Canada. But it was far, far worse that Baker's troops had struck and completely destroyed Heavy Runner's peaceful village. A dejected Baker and his exhausted troops spent the rest of the night at the site of Mountain Chief's last camp. All that Baker could do was destroy what was left in Mountain Chief's village, so that his band could not return for the contents, and the "lodges were burned the next morning."[65]

The real suffering was at Heavy Runner's village, where the survivors were mostly women and the young children they cared for. For them it would still be an ordeal. As the dark descended over what was left of Heavy Runner's village, Doane detailed Sergeant O'Kelly to be on guard. The silence of the cold night was disturbed by the "hideous groans of the wounded," so many that Doane believed that the camp was "full of wounded." Sentinels had been placed around the perimeter of the destroyed village, and the night was punctuated by "firing at intervals all through the night." The scene was made more grotesque by "the howling of dogs, fire breaking out in the woods, and the stampeding of the pony herd in a tremendous wind-storm."[66]

Done with their carnage, Baker and his command "on the evening of January 24" started to find their way back to Fort Shaw, but first they went upstream on the Marias to Willow Rounds. On January 25 they reached John Riplinger's trading post, ostensibly to provide protection against retaliation. Once there, "they learned that a band of Bloods, numbering about five hundred, had left that place the same morning." Baker immediately sent a request to the "leading chiefs to come in."[67] When they did not, Baker went out to find them. In the vicinity of the trading post his party "came upon a large Blood camp, which, however, was rapidly deserted." A "half breed was dispatched after the retreating Bloods, and succeeded in inducing some of them to return; these came laden with buffalo meat as presents to soldiers, and on demand readily gave up what stolen stock they had in their possession." It was the opinion of whoever wrote a report that first appeared in the *New York Sun* before it was picked up in the *Army and Navy Journal* that the Bloods "acted friendly, and will be friendly until an opportunity presents itself for them to scalp and steal, and then seek refuge under the British flag, by simply going no great distance, to where the line of British Columbia keeps back our soldiers from following them further."[68]

While Baker had been in the field, all de Trobriand could do was sit and wait. This gave him time on Sunday, January 23, to pen another letter to his daughter Lina, in which he once again reported that "the thermometer went down at night to 43 degrees Fahrenheit below zero," the same low temperature that he had reported to her the week before. Surprisingly, he told her: "The men barely survived the ordeal . . . [but] . . . they were able to surprise the hostile Piegans and severely punish them Friday morning . . . at dawn." While De Trobriand's information on the thermometer may have been accurate, his day was still wrong, because the ambush had not occurred until two days later on that same Sunday morning. The purpose of his letter was not to give

Lina precise details, however, but rather to keep her involved in the heroic drama that de Trobriand was portraying; yet it never revealed that he had planned the attack for Friday, January 21.[69]

After leaving Riplinger's Trading Post, the soldiers traveled on through the cold: "On the 26th we reached our wagon train, and arrived on the 28th at Fort Shaw where we lay over for a day, and returned to Fort Ellis on the 5th of February, after suffering for thirty-one days more cold and hardships than we had supposed men could possibly endure. Wherever we passed on our return we were greeted with cheers and invited to partake freely of the hospitality of the people."[70]

It could have been a triumphal return for Major Eugene Baker, except that he was not with them. He had been ordered to stay at Fort Shaw.

As THE SOLDIERS HAD headed back to Fort Shaw, they were unaware that a small group was following them. It included Spear Woman, the little girl who stayed hidden as the Piegans were massacred in her lodge. She and her surviving siblings were with their mother, who had decided to follow the soldiers at a distance where they could not be seen. They were starving, and their purpose was to find food left in the soldiers' camps after they had moved on. The little family group camped each night without a fire and each morning would go into the deserted soldiers' camp "looking for any scraps of food," a search that yielded but "bits of hardtack and bacon." On these forays the mother had to leave Spear Woman's infant sister behind. When they returned from one of their scavenging trips they found the baby girl dead in a snowbank. They continued on until they reached the top of a hill from where they could see Fort Benton in the distance. They could also see a camp of friendly Piegans nearby, who took them in.[71]

NINE

The Aftermath

*Lieut Genl. Sheridan requests me to telegraph to Col. Baker
and his command his warmest thanks for the handsome
success obtained in the expedition against the Piegans.*
HANCOCK TO DE TROBRIAND, JANUARY 29, 1870

A t Fort Shaw on January 26, 1870, an anxious Regis de Trobriand finally had a report from the battle. It was not brought in by a soldier or scout but instead "was brought from the trading Post by Mr. Riplinger who had it from run away and wounded Indians." Nor was it the news that de Trobriand wanted to hear. To his dismay he learned from the fur trader whose post the troops had gone to after the battle that Baker had not struck Mountains Chief's camp but another camp, "from which no more than four or five escaped." Nevertheless, de Trobriand rushed to report to General Winfield Hancock that day that "the attack was a complete success." He knew, however, that Mountain Chief's band was the assigned target of the expedition. Riplinger's information was that Baker's "column was going on to strike the camp of Mountain Chief when last heard of." Apparently Riplinger had left his trading post before Baker arrived there with the full news on January 25. De Trobriand reported to Hancock right away that he had not received information from Baker or any of his soldiers but that the village "Baker surprised" was "the camp of Bear Chief a hostile Piegan—thirty lodges on the Marias." Well aware that the Bloods were not to be attacked, de Trobriand cautiously added: "Three Bloods and one whisky trader happening to be in the hostile Camp are reported killed."[1]

At this time the name "Heavy Runner" started to disappear from the army reports, as de Trobriand had failed to mention him in his telegram to Hancock. That same day General Hancock had reinserted himself into the chain of command that had been bypassing him and sent a telegram to Major Baker, in care of de Trobriand at Fort Shaw. It gave direct orders from Hancock for Baker to stay at Fort Shaw. The pretense was that Baker had to be there both for the court-martial of Captain O. O. G. Robinson and to meet with a board to inspect the mounted infantry horses. Baker was then to proceed to Fort Benton for general court-martial duty. Hancock clearly did not want Baker to return to Fort Ellis and Bozeman, with its prying citizens and its newspaper, at least not until a report agreeable to his army command was settled upon. This would end up taking four weeks.[2]

Three days later, on January 29, 1870, when Baker and his weary troops returned to Fort Shaw, de Trobriand learned firsthand the bad news that "Mountain Chief escaped with a few followers leaving everything but the horses they were on." Despite this, on that same day de Trobriand reported to Sheridan "the complete success of an expedition sent against [the Piegans] . . . in which one hundred and seventy-three Indians were killed, forty-four lodges destroyed, and also a large amount of winter provisions, and three hundred horses captured, etc." "Complete success" was of course far from true, because Baker had struck the wrong band, killing their chief Heavy Runner, and was not able to attack Mountain Chief's band. Later on that day Sheridan unhappily had to forward General Sherman the bad news from de Trobriand that "Mountain Chief escaped with a few followers leaving everything but the horses they were on." The only good news for the army was that only "one man [was] killed, and one man accidentally wounded by falling off his horse." But more bad news followed. On January 31 Sheridan telegraphed Sherman a troubling addendum that "Col. Baker had to turn loose over one hundred squaws. He had no transportation to get them in."[3]

Sherman's instructions to Inspector General James Hardie, given just eight days before the massacre, had been to strike

Mountain Chief's band. The instructions from de Trobriand the next day ordered Baker to "chastise the portion of the Indian tribe of Piegans which, under Mountain Chief or his sons, committed the greater part of the murders and depredations of last summer and last month, in this district." At that time de Trobriand explicitly told Baker that the band of Mountain Chief was encamped on the Marias "and can be easily singled out from other bands of Piegans." Even more explicit instructions specified that two of the Piegan bands "should be left unmolested, as they have uniformly remained friendly, viz. the bands of Heavy Runner and Big Lake." As de Trobriand said, "These two chiefs and Little Wolf are the three who met General Sully at the agency, a short time ago."[4]

If de Trobriand did not learn from John Riplinger that Heavy Runner and his band had been killed, he certainly knew it by the time he wrote to General Sheridan on February 2, 1870. He had several days to think about how to paint the massacre in a favorable light and came up with what he must have thought was a creative explanation. He disingenuously decided that he would make the chiefs and the Indians responsible for their own deaths. De Trobriand started his letter to General Sheridan by saying that "Mountain Chief took refuge with his followers in the camp of Big Legs in order to escape more easily." This, according to de Trobriand, put "Big Legs in fear of the consequences": he "wanted to shake them off, and said that if they did not go, he would fight them himself." The fuzzy logic must have been that this explained why Mountain Chief was not where the guide had expected him to be.[5]

"Heavy Runner was also killed, by his own fault," de Trobriand told Sheridan. According to this fiction, Heavy Runner had been "attracted to the hostile camp by the presence there of some whiskey smugglers, . . . he left the trading post where he was perfectly safe, and went to his fate." But de Trobriand knew that Heavy Runner's camp was already on the Marias and that not just the chief but also the members of his band were to remain unharmed. De Trobriand showed some remorse when he said that he "regretted that a friendly chief who had met Genl. Sully in council three weeks before, should have perished by our bullets." He added: "This is well understood by his friends and relatives." De Trobriand's rationalization was that Heavy Runner's death "is not without some salutary teachings by showing the friendly Indians what heavy risks they run in keeping intercourse with the hostile ones." In conclusion, de Trobriand sought to justify other killings of innocents including a number of Blood "young men who were killed like Heavy Runner under the same circumstances. The chiefs had sent for them to leave the hostile camp, but they would not listen to it, and therefore were served right."[6]

On February 13, exactly three weeks after the massacre, the *New York Sun* published an article entitled "The Piegan Fight" from a correspondent in Bozeman. By March 5 it had made its way into the *Army and Navy Journal*. The correspondent seemed either to have been on the march (he used the first person "we" in describing some of the troop movements in detail) or to have been informed by someone on the march. A second article, "Details of the Piegan Fight," appeared in the *Philadelphia Ledger* before it was picked up on March 19 by the *Army and Navy Journal*. It had all the hallmarks of the first article and this time was attributed to Peter Gaynor.[7]

Whoever wrote these two articles included in both of them the list of principal chiefs slain as "Bad Bear, Wolfe's Tail, Heavy Runner, Red Horn, Mountain Chief's son, and others equally prominent, whose names I cannot now recall to mind," as though the writer wanted to leave the list open to add names in the future.[8] Of the slain chiefs named, Wolf's Tail and Red Horn had appeared in Inspector General Hardie's report to General Sheridan before the battle but had not been identified as chiefs.[9]

Another newspaper report by Peter Gaynor on March 19 said that "Big Horn, Red Horn, Heavy Runner, Wolf Tail, and Spotted Wolf, chiefs, were all killed." This list added Big Horn and Spotted Wolf and omitted the name of Bad Bear. A later report by Lieutenant Pease, Blackfeet agent, said that the troops had attacked the camp of Red Horn. After these early articles, the army seemed to prefer saying that it was the camp of Red Horn that had been attacked and avoided mentioning Heavy Runner.[10] Conspicuously absent from these reports was Bear Chief, whose camp had been attacked by Baker, at least according to de Trobriand from what he had heard from John Riplinger.[11] When they were first identified in Hardie's report to Sheridan, before the battle, Bear Chief, Red Horn, and Black Weasel were not identified as chiefs but only as "other Indians" who had been in the party that murdered Clarke.[12]

Some of the newspapers in Montana carried articles soon after the massacre, which only further obfuscated the dates of battle and the identity of the chiefs and camps attacked. The *Helena Daily Herald* reported on January 28 that an Indian had arrived in Fort Benton who gave the news that Baker had "surprised Bear Chief's camp . . . and killed men, women and children." That same edition reported that, based on news coming from the Bloods, who got it "from five Indians who escaped," Baker had attacked "Big Bear's band . . . the morning of the 22d." It reported that on February 2 Baker had "surprised the camp of Bear Chief" and that "Mountain Chief and few other effected their escape." However, as late as April 8 the *Herald* still referred to the massacre as "Col. Baker's fight with Mountain Chief." The *New North-West,* a paper published in Deer Lodge City in the Montana Territory, on February 4 printed that Baker had killed "men, women and children," that "Bear Chief was killed," that "Star, Pete and Mountain Chief escaped," and that "three hundred horses and fourty-four [*sic*] Lodges with all winter supplies [were] captured." On February 25 the same paper published only the official army reports, saying that the "letters explain themselves" and that "they are important to show the authority the Montana officers had for the big 'strike.'"[13]

As the 1870 calendar rolled on into February, something was conspicuously absent from the stories coming from the massacre: Major Eugene Baker's official report. In a day when such reports were usually written out and submitted to commanding officers immediately after a battle, the absence of Baker's official version was troubling. It could be understood that Baker had been in the field and had no time to write his report until his return to Fort Shaw on January 29, but no report came even after he had returned. There seemed to be no excuse, because Baker remained at Fort Shaw under orders even after his cavalry had left for Fort Ellis.[14]

Even without Baker's official report, the army was treating the killings as praiseworthy. On January 29 Hancock sent a telegram to de Trobriand at Fort Shaw, saying that he had been requested by "Lieut Genl. Sheridan . . . to telegraph to Col. Baker and his command his warmest thanks for the handsome success obtained in the expedition against the Piegans." Hancock begged to "add my tribute in the same firm manner." He knew that sooner or later Baker's report was needed, however, and told de Trobriand that "I only await the official details to proclaim in orders my sense of the gallant and arduous service of the troops, and to do full justice to all concerned." In unmistakable terms Major General Hancock, de Trobriand's immediate superior, requested the report immediately: if "a telegraphic dispatch giving a summary of Colonel Baker's report can be made which will do justice to the troops, I beg that you will transmit in advance of the mail."[15] But de Trobriand had bypassed Hancock before and did not feel compelled to rush the report, which still did not come. It was becoming apparent that the report was being withheld until it could be determined exactly what it should say to put the army in a positive light. One issue, of course, was the number of Indians killed.

Even without Baker's report, de Trobriand had determined— or, perhaps more correctly, decided—that the number of Piegans killed would be exactly 173. This number appeared in his first dispatch to Hancock and Sheridan as well as in newspaper accounts that undoubtedly came from army sources.[16] Some were skeptical about whether the bodies could have been counted in such an accurate manner as to set this number so exactly. The various reports indicate that some of the dead were disposed of by burning their tipis, while other Indians who may have been wounded had scattered toward safety and could have died in the ravines and foliage in the vicinity or from exposure on the cold prairie.

The number of 173 dead originated after Doane had arrived on the scene of the battle the next day to assess the grisly aftermath, even as the killing of a few of the wounded Indians reportedly was still going on. His task that morning was to count the bodies of dead Indians and record an exact number. It would not do to give a range or an approximation. Under these conditions and this constraint he arrived at the number of 173 Indians killed. As it turned out, he might better have given just an approximation.

The job of counting the soldiers killed was much easier. All accounts did agree: "Our loss was only one killed—Private McKay, of Company L, Second Cavalry. Wounded—none."[17]

In fact no one could know for sure how many Piegans had died, how many had been in the camp, or how many of the able-bodied men had gone on the hunt. Once the firing started, many in the village were killed immediately by the soldiers' bullets. But Doane also admitted that after the battle the camp was "full of wounded." A few Piegans escaped, with little chance of survival on the plains in the subzero temperatures if they were wounded. Some probably died of their wounds (never having left the camp), and some of the wounded were killed when the soldiers discovered them after the main battle was over. Others might have been burned up in their lodges.[18]

Doane was not the only one counting bodies. Others were doing their own death counts. Their numbers—different from Doane's—appeared in the earliest and most complete reports in the newspapers. One early estimate of the number of Indians killed was attributed to Peter Gaynor. He wrote that "197 Indians had been thoroughly quieted . . . but a few of them had escaped." Another newspaper report said this count "included only those who were found dead in the camp": "it is believed that many more Indians were wounded, who crawled off in the bush to die."[19]

Joe Kipp (who was probably the guide who had helped Buffalo Trail Woman) remained in the camp after the attack. He

personally "counted 217 dead bodies after the firing had ceased."
He believed "all of the able bodied Indians were out hunting"
and was sure that "those who were killed were the Chief and
such Indians as could not hunt." Alfred B. Hamilton, the whiskey trader, said that even more were killed and that "there were
upwards of three Hundred Indians young and old killed by the
soldiers at the time."[20] An obscure man who went by the name
Whiskey Johnston gave an even higher estimate. His story was
told to "Col. Wheeler," who related that Johnston said: "I don't
know how many Injuns thar was, but purty near four hundred, I
reckon; and, as I said afore, only about half a dozen got away."[21]

The Private John Ponsford, who was in the thick of the battle with
Doane's F Company, seemed to think that "about 185 bucks were
killed." If by "bucks" he meant only men, this was a large number, considering that the able-bodied men were thought to be out
hunting. Ponsford also believed that it was not just Indians who
had been killed. He claimed that "the camp had three half-breed
traders in it with supplies of Canadian tobacco and whiskey,"
who "were killed."[22] Not only Ponsford believed that the fur
traders had been in the line of fire. An anonymous newspaper
source reported that "one Spaniard, or perhaps a Mexican, who
was trading with the Indians, was killed with them."[23] This was
most likely a man named Star, who was on the list of Indians
to be punished, identified as "a half Mexican and half Piegan, a
noted murderer."[24]

The report of the Blackfeet agent, Lieutenant William Pease,
said that the troops attacked the camp of Red Horn. Ely S. Parker,
the commissioner of Indian Affairs, said in his annual report that
Baker "attacked a camp of this band—Red Horn being their
chief." Even the Indian Department wanted to avoid the use of
Heavy Runner's name and point to the chastisement of the more
militant Red Horn rather than the peaceful Heavy Runner.[25]

In March Peter Gaynor attempted to have the last word on
the number of Indians killed: "The results of the expedition
have been variously stated by different newspapers, but the correct result is as follows: one hundred and seventy-three Indians
counted dead on the field; thirty-nine lodges destroyed with

all their property; over three hundred horses captured, among them some stolen stock." After stating with great certitude that 173 Indians had been killed, he immediately qualified that number: "It is believed that many more Indians were wounded, who crawled off in the bush to die, the count as above given including only those who were found dead in the camp." This time the number 173 was modified by the phrase "counted dead on the field," serving as a tacit admission that many more had died as a result of the attack. This account said that the chiefs "Big Horn, Red Horn, Heavy Runner, Wolf Tail, and Spotted Wolf" were all killed. Gaynor reported that Black Eagle managed to escape, but "we afterward found out from the Bloods that he was wounded. The squaws and children were given a lodge and a few necessaries, and were left in the camp. The loss of troops was one man killed."[26] Despite what Gaynor or anyone else said, the official number of 173 Indians killed would remain as the permanent official number, repeated in reports and histories to this day.

From the start Regis de Trobriand had treated the surprise attack, bloody massacre, and seizure of Piegan horses as a great military victory. On January 30, after the news of the massacre was already in the newspapers, he wrote to his daughter Lina: "Before this letter reaches you, you will already know through the newspapers that we killed 173 Piegans, destroyed two of their camps and captured more than 300 horses. All those found in the lodges were killed except a hundred squaws and papooses which were set at liberty after the complete destruction of the lodges, provisions, etc." De Trobriand's bragging was unbounded. "Never was anything like it seen in Montana. The settlers haven't raised a statue to me, but I am content that before leaving them soon . . . I shall leave behind me this memory." Ominously footnoted at the bottom of his letter was something that de Trobriand, and probably Lina, would prefer not to know, for it foreshadowed serious charges of cruelty. De Trobriand almost reluctantly told Lina: "There was smallpox among the Indians."[27]

On January 31 Sheridan telegraphed Baker directly at Fort Shaw: "On Saturday last I requested General Hancock to telegraph to you and your command my warmest thanks and now I directly congratulate you and your command on the handsome success of your expedition which will in all probability end all further trouble in Montana."[28] On the same day that Sheridan sent his telegram to Baker, Sully received an ominous letter from Francis Eastman, the chief fur trader in Fort Benton, warning that "Mountain Chief's band is reported on the Milk River and has declared war against the whites!"[29]

While members of the regular army command were busy indulging in self-serving congratulations, they had forgotten one of their own officers, Brigadier General Alfred Sully, the Indian superintendent, who looked askance at their announcements. He would not remain quiet for long. On February 1 Sully reinserted himself into the controversy. His target was de Trobriand, and he chose to challenge him on the accuracy of the number and sex of the Indians killed. Even though Baker's report was not filed until February 18, Sully had heard other reports that women and children were killed. The *New North-West* reported that Baker had killed "men, women and children" and that "no quarter was given."[30] Sully told de Trobriand: "I have seen the reports of Colonel Baker's attack on the Indians where it states that one hundred and seventy-three were killed." He then asked pointedly: "How many of these killed were men?" Sully had his own information on this: "It has been reported to me that there were only twenty or thirty, the rest women and children." Sully gave his source as reports that "come from citizens, half-breeds, and Indians." Then he delivered an ominous warning to de Trobriand, followed up with a gentleman's offer giving him a chance to correct the record. "I have made no report of the affair to the Interior Department," Sully wrote. He was "waiting for some more definite information," which, it was implied, could come from Baker if he so chose.[31] Sully clearly was giving notice that he was going to contest the proposed report if its numbers did not match his.

Two days later de Trobriand threw down the gauntlet and responded angrily to Sully. "I should be sorry to think that you could put any faith in the idle rumors and false reports spread by some whiskey smugglers from Benton, whose poisonous drug was found in plenty in the Indian camps, and by other croakers to whom the peace of the Territory and the security of its residents are of little or no weight, compared with their private interests in trade." Moreover, de Trobriand said that Sully's sources ("citizens, half-breeds, and Indians") could not be trusted. He was not going to let it stop there. De Trobriand, who had already been inventive in his justification for the killing of Heavy Runner, thought he knew another way to prove his case and turned to a mathematical solution. Calculating that there were seven or eight Indians to a lodge, de Trobriand said this proved that "the extreme severity of the weather . . . brought back all the hunters to the camp, and that all the warriors of the band were there." Impressed by his own proof, de Trobriand's sneered: "So much for the report made to you."[32]

Sully was not done. He did not like de Trobriand or his math and sent out the newly arrived Blackfeet agent, W. B. Pease (who told Hardie on January 13 that he had no intimate knowledge of the Blackfeet affairs), to investigate. On February 6 Pease reported back to Sully that he had "visited the camp of Big Jake [Lake], of the Piegan Indians and have seen and talked with several Indians who were in the camp which was attacked by the soldiers." The one number that he knew would not be disputed by de Trobriand was the 173 killed. Pease had somehow determined that of the "one hundred and seventy-three killed, [only] thirty-three were men; of these fifteen only were of the age of fighting men; the remaining eighteen were older; ninety were women, and fifty were children, many of them in their mothers' arms."[33]

It was now apparent that Sully and Pease were not trying to discredit de Trobriand and Baker for attacking the wrong village. They did not choose to question that military mistake. Pease was not even using Heavy Runner's name, instead saying that it had been Red Horn's camp. Sully and Pease, the two officers assigned to the Interior Department, wanted to have the numbers reflect the cruelty to the Piegans. Perhaps this was because Sully himself had been accused of cruelty to the Indians when he was in the Dakota Territory and had been stung by the criticism and the investigation that followed. Now, as Indian superintendent, he did not want de Trobriand and Baker to go without condemnation for their brutal killings of women and children in a camp that had smallpox.

Pease had reported to Sully that "out of two hundred and nineteen belonging to Red Horn's camp, only forty-six survived" and that at "the time of the attack this camp was suffering severely with small pox, having had it among them for two months, the average rate of deaths among them having been six daily."[34]

At about that same time an irrepressible de Trobriand wrote to his daughter Lina again and wanted her to know that the *Rocky Mountain Gazette* had reported a conversation between Lieutenant Gustavus Doane and a settler. "Will the Indians remain quiet now, do you think?" the settler asked when the expedition was returning from the Marias. "Well, I can't say," replied Doane, "but there are one hundred and seventy-three very good arguments in favor of their remaining quiet, lying out on the Marias!" Amid his activities of reading the unsettling reports of the massacre and writing to his daughter, de Trobriand decided that his infantry did not shoot straight enough and appointed an officer "to superintend the target practice."[35]

Plenty of news of the massacre had already reached Washington. Even before Baker submitted his report, the United States Senate had started an investigation. On February 11 it passed a resolution and sent a letter to the War Department "requesting information in relation to Col. Baker's expedition against the Piegans—with copies of all papers which led to the same." The War Department sent the requested papers to the Senate, with a letter dated February 18. The papers were of course incomplete at the time, however, and represented a far less than complete record of the event, which was still being built. The House passed a resolution similar to the Senate's on March 3.[36]

By February 18, the same day the War Department sent its first collection of papers to the Senate, Baker's tardy report was coincidentally completed, but under strange circumstances. De Trobriand sent the report to General Hancock that day, but it apparently was not sent to Sheridan or Sherman at that time. As a result on February 26 Sherman asked Sheridan to forward it. Sheridan replied on February 28 that he would send the report as soon as it was received. Oddly, he said: "Colonel Baker could not make out his report at Fort Shaw, as he was obliged to return immediately to Fort Ellis to get shelter for his horses and men."[37] This would have been contrary to the orders that General Hancock had sent to Baker: that he should not return to Fort Ellis but should remain at Fort Shaw for court-martial duty.[38]

Both Baker and de Trobriand had plenty of time after the Blackfeet agent Lieutenant Pease made his report to reflect on what Sully and Pease had to say. They could not avoid certain facts, and Baker had to admit in the report that the Indians had smallpox. But this was used as a strange justification for his abandonment of the women and children on the plains. Now he was saying that the reason they had been left there was at least partly *because of* the smallpox and no longer solely because of lack of food to supply them. The army's original justification had claimed vaguely that it would have been inconvenient to keep them at Fort Shaw.

Alfred Sully was angered by Baker's report. He had made an offer to de Trobriand to withhold his own report to the Interior Department until Baker was given a chance to file his report reflecting what Sully believed to be the correct number, age, and sex of those killed. He had received only de Trobriand's contentious response to his offer.

At this point Sully had enough and forwarded Pease's report to Ely S. Parker, the commissioner of Indian Affairs in Washington, DC. There it happened to cross the desk of the humanitarian activist Vincent Collyer, who was serving as secretary to the Board of Indian Commissioners. Collyer wrote immediately to Felix Brunot, the president of the board, drawing attention to Pease's "sickening details." His letter immediately made its way to the eastern newspapers.[39]

The publication of Collyer's letter in the press caught Sheridan in an embarrassing moment. On February 28 he telegraphed Sherman: "I see Vincent Collyer is out again in a sensational letter." The infuriated Sheridan continued with a crude and graphic tirade:

> Since 1862, at least eight hundred men, women, and children have been murdered within the limits of my present command, in the most fiendish manner, the men usually scalped and mutilated, their [blank] cut off and placed in their mouths; women ravished sometimes fifty and sixty times in succession, then killed and scalped, sticks stuck up their persons before and after death. I have myself conversed with one woman who, while some months gone in pregnancy, was ravished over thirty times successively by different Indians becoming insensible two or three times during the fearful ordeal; and each time on recovering consciousness mutely appealing for mercy if not for herself, for her unborn child. Also another woman ravished with more fearful brutality, over forty times, and the last Indian sticking the point of his saber up the person of the woman. I could give the names of these women were it not for delicacy.[40]

With the congressional investigation ongoing and the matter now fully in the public's eye, Sherman took a few days to respond to Sheridan. The reason for the delay was that he wanted time to publicize Sheridan's letter. When he did respond, he told Sheridan: "The substance of your letter about the Piegans has been read by the Secretary of War to the Cabinet and will be given to the press." Sheridan of all people would not seem to be someone who needed any bolstering, and Sherman would not seem to be a person to offer it, but he did. "Meantime, don't be unhappy about Indian affairs," he told Sheridan. "There are two classes of people, one demanding the utter extinction of the Indians, and the other full of love for their conversion to civilization and Christianity. Unfortunately the army stands between and get the cuffs from both sides." Surprisingly, Sherman did all of this before he had even read Baker's full official report. He asked Sheridan: "Let us have Baker's full report as soon as possible."[41]

On March 7 Sherman more actively entered the fray and started to lay out a case that would shift the blame for the massacre to the Interior Department. He wrote again to Sheridan, enclosing "a couple of slips from the *Morning Chronicle* of yesterday and today." They were sent "to show you that your communications have been given to the public, and what the first impressions are." Sherman left no doubt what he wanted the army's official position to be when he told Sheridan flatly to say that the "Piegans were attacked on the application of Gen. Sully, and the Interior Department." Sherman was sure that Sully and the Interior Department should not be "shocked at the result of their own requisitions, and [their] endeavor to cast blame on you and Col. Baker is unfair." Sherman then took full aim at Sully and leveled ethical charges: "Gen. Sully by communicating by telegraph for the use of Mr. Collyer did an un-officer like and wrong act, and this will in the end stand to his discredit."[42] These words were a stinging rebuke for General Sully, who still had his commission in the regular army and would likely return to duty under Sherman's command sometime in the future.

In the meantime the loud uproar from the East was already being heard in the Montana Territory. De Trobriand traveled to Helena on March 9. As he wrote to Lina on that day, the residents of Helena had a large meeting "to express in vigorous terms the opinion of the residents of Montana of our expedition against the Indians, and by a solemn approbation respond to the criticisms of so-called Eastern philanthropists who, in the press and in Congress debate foolishness, about which the west is indignant." But the eastern criticisms had not slowed de Trobriand's string of self-compliments, and he was still basking in his glory. After he had addressed the group in Helena, he told Lina: "I astonished the natives by an improvised talk which was interrupted twenty times by applause."[43]

Applause was something that General Sherman and the army were not getting in the East. Congress was now raising questions about the cruelty to women and children. Sherman knew that the investigation was not going away and had to take a deeper look at the accusations against Baker.

On March 14, 1870, Sheridan had a telegram sent to Baker at Fort Ellis: "In accordance with instructions from Genl Sherman, the Lieut Genl directs that you report specific as possible to the number sex and kind of Indians killed in your affair with the Piegans. Report immediately by telegraph."[44]

By March 18, 1870, de Trobriand, now back at Fort Shaw from Helena, had been sobered somewhat by knowledge of Sherman's inquiry and by the criticism from the East. His letter to Lina on that day was far from the mood of elation that had characterized his earlier writings. He told her that "the only point on which one could base all this fuss is the death of a certain number of squaws killed during the attack."[45]

Many eastern newspapers had become fully invested in the controversy, including the *National Anti-Slavery Standard* of New York, which under the title "Sheridan and the Indians" republished an article from the *New York Evening Post*: "We must express our absolute horror at the cold blooded massacre of women and children—ninety women and fifty young children—perpetrated by the United States soldiers in Montana recently." The *Standard* also published another letter from Vincent Collyer to Brunot: "Sir: Gen. Sheridan strikes out at me almost as wildly as he did at the poor Piegans, and with about as much justice."[46]

On the other side of the controversy, an article of February 10, 1870, from the *Bozeman Pick and Plow* was republished in the *Army and Navy Journal*. It reported the resolutions of a mass meeting in Bozeman: "[We] Resolve, 1. That the Indian of poetry and romance is not the Indian of fact: the former is said to be noble, magnanimous, faithful, and brave; the latter we know to be possessed of every attribute of beastly depravity and ferocity . . . and Resolve, 5. That our thanks are due, and are hereby gratefully tendered, to Col. Baker and his men, for their toilsome march in an inclement season to chastise our savage robber foes, and for the deserved though terrible punishment inflicted upon them."[47]

On March 18 Sheridan again wrote to Sherman, saying that he had not yet received Baker's further report. He took the opportunity to vent some of his frustration. "In taking the offensive, I have to select that season when I can catch the fiends; and if a village is attacked and women and children killed the responsibility is not with the soldier, but with the people whose crimes necessitate the attack." Sheridan of course had served under Sherman in the Civil War and knew exactly what further points to make:

> During the war, did anyone hesitate to attack a village or town occupied by the enemy because women or children were within its limits? Did we cease to throw shell into Vicksburg or Atlanta because women and children were there? If the women and children were saved in these places, it was because they had cellars to go into; and should any of the women and children of the Piegans have lost their lives, I sincerely regret that they had not similar places of refuge, though I doubt if they would have availed themselves of them, for they fight with more fury than the men.[48]

Finally Baker sent his supplemental report from Fort Ellis. It was now March 23, fully two months after the massacre. At this remote date he had *quadrupled* Pease's number of men killed and added a new exact number of 140 captive women and children who were released. The full report stated:

> In answer to your telegram received on the 22d instant, I report that after having made every effort to get the judgment of the offices of the command, I am satisfied that the following numbers approximate as nearly to the exact truth as any estimate can possibly be made; that the number killed was one hundred and seventy-three. Of those there were one hundred and twenty able men, fifty-three women and children; that of captives (afterwards released), there were of women and children one hundred and forty.
>
> I believe that every effort was made by officers and men to save the non-combatants, and that such women and children as were killed were killed accidentally. The reports published in the Eastern papers, purporting to come from General Alfred Sully, are wholly and maliciously false, and if he has authorized them he knew them to be false; if he has given authority to these slanders, I can only suppose it is that attention may be drawn away from the manifest irregularities and inefficiency that mark the conduct of Indian affairs

under his direction in this Territory. It seems incredible that the false assertions of two officers, General Sully and Lieutenant Pease, neither of whom have made any effort to inform themselves in the matter, should outweigh the reports of those who were engaged in the fight, and who feel they have nothing to palliate or concede in their conduct. All the officers of this command ask at the hands of the authorities is a full and complete investigation of the campaign, and less than this cannot, in justice, be conceded to them.

For the first time Baker and the Army backed off from any claim to the exact accuracy of the number of 173 Indians killed. The numbers he gave were now conceded to be both "approximate" and an "estimate."[49]

The *New York Times* had previously remarked that "the slaughter of the Piegans in Montana is a more serious and a more shocking affair than the sacking of Black Kettle's camp on the Washita." The editors were not about to let this second vague report go unchallenged. In its March 30 edition the *Times* noted that even Baker's "rude estimate admits of the killing of no less than fifty-three women and children." What incensed the *Times* most was Baker's report of "140 women and children captured and released." "Released to what?" the Times asked, and then answered: "To starvation and freezing to death."[50]

TEN

A General Dictates the History and a False Priest Brokers the Peace

I prefer to believe that the majority of the killed at Mountain Chief's camp were warriors.

WILLIAM TECUMSEH SHERMAN TO PHILLIP HENRY

SHERIDAN, MARCH 24, 1870

It appears that he has deceived the Jesuit fathers even better than he has me.

FATHER ALBERT LACOMBE OF THE OBLATES

The backbiting between Colonel de Trobriand of the army and Brigadier General Sully and Lieutenant Pease of the Indian Department could have gone on longer had it not been for the intervention of General William Tecumseh Sherman. The army's top commander had had enough of the wrangling when, on March 24, he wrote to Lieutenant General Sheridan that he was adopting Major Baker's second late report. There was to be no further reporting from Baker or anyone else.

Something had set Sherman off. The House of Representatives had been considering a bill that would "transfer the control of Indian affairs to the War Department," which Sherman wanted. When John A. Logan, a congressman from Illinois and chair of the Committee on Military Affairs, "read the account of the Piegan massacre his blood ran cold in his veins, and he went and asked the committee to strike out that section and let the Indian

Bureau remain where it is, and the committee had agreed to that."[1] This had obviously upset Sherman enough to send out a warning that there would be trouble for anyone in the army who contested the number, age, and sex of the Piegans killed on the Marias. As part of his public relations fight, Sherman had told Sheridan on March 28 to "assure Colonel Baker that no amount of clamor has shaken our confidence in him." Sherman wanted to validate Baker's reports and did not want any other reports written on the subject. As a final threat Sherman warned that "if any responsible party will father the Reports that have been so extensively published we will give him the benefit of an Official Investigation." In other words, anyone coming forth with reliable numbers different from Baker's would certainly face an inquiry, which probably would not be pleasant.[2]

Sherman wanted to communicate even more to Sheridan. He forcefully dictated the way in which the history of the event should be written: "I prefer to believe that the majority of the killed at Mountain Chief's camp were warriors; that the firing ceased the moment resistance was at an end; that quarter was given to all that asked for it; and that a hundred women and children were allowed to go free to join the other bands of the same tribe known to be camped near by, rather than the absurd report that there were only thirteen warriors killed, and that all the balance were women and children, more or less afflicted with smallpox." Sherman wanted the "history" written this way because the army must both "protect the settlers, and, on proper demand . . . protect Indian lands against the intrusion of the settlers. Thus we are placed between two fires, a most unpleasant dilemma, from which we cannot escape and we must sustain the officers on the spot who fulfill their orders."[3]

Until March 26 the editors of the *Army and Navy Journal* had printed accounts of the massacre that came to them from other newspapers. They now stood up and took an editorial stance on the massacre: strongly in favor of the army. In an editorial titled "The Piegan Fight" the *Journal* lauded the performance of Baker, saying: "Colonel Baker's report of his scout against the hostile

Piegan and Blood Indians shows incontestably that the march itself was a heroic one . . . and we agree with Colonel Baker that 'too much credit cannot be given to the officers and men of the command for their conduct during the whole expedition.'"[4]

The *Journal*, like the army, no longer mentioned Heavy Runner as a casualty as it once had; nor did it mention Bear Chief or Red Horn. The *Army and Navy Journal* reasoned in its March 26 editorial that it "was not known how strong the Indians might be, and huddled as they were indiscriminately in camp, the first fury of the attack fell alike on all ages and sexes." Maintaining that the warriors were not out hunting but in the camp, the journal nevertheless said that many of the warriors, "it seems, fled; at all events, the great majority of those left were women and children, some of whom perished at first, though over one hundred were captured." In the view of the editors: "The two Piegan camps were divided, and our troops had fallen on the weaker, with an easy victory; but the alarm was of course taken by Mountain Chief's camp of seven lodges encamped at some distance." Just how a camp with forty-four lodges was weaker than a camp with seven lodges is unclear, but this obvious point apparently did not faze the *Journal* in its quest for justification. The editorial finished with another statement, which blamed the Interior Department: "One other fact is noteworthy. This blow fell on a guilty tribe, and was delivered in consequence of the representations of their own agents."[5] The *Journal* was clearly referring General Sully and Lieutenant Pease as the agents. Sherman's campaign to shift the blame from the War Department to the Department of the Interior was catching on.

De Trobriand now loathed Lieutenant William Pease even more than ever before. On April 7, 1870, Pease sent a letter to Sully, his superior in the Indian Department, complaining about de Trobriand's personal treatment of him. When Pease had arrived at Fort Shaw on March 27, on the way to his post at Fort Benton, he "called on Brevet Brigadier General de Trobriand . . . for the purpose of evincing, as an officer, my respect for the commanding general of the district and post" in what he believed was the "fulfillment of the obligations of ordinary courtesy."

Expecting an officer-like response, Pease "was received by him in his apartment in a manner anything but courteous, or as an officer of the Army."[6]

De Trobriand "opened the conversation by interrogating" Pease as to his "business at the post," to which Pease replied that he was "visiting an acquaintance, an officer of the garrison" and that he "had called on him as commanding officer of the post." After asking Pease again why he was there and again receiving the same answer, de Trobriand accused Pease of "making false statements, and of slandering the Army." Pease "disputed the truth of his assertion, using words to the effect that [he] . . . was not given to slander." The matter soon escalated to a yelling match. An indignant Pease was too furious to "recollect what reply I made" and he "did not fully hear" de Trobriand's remarks. Feeling that he had been "subjected to gross indignity and outrage," Pease "withdrew and closed the door, not hearing what he [De Trobriand] was saying." Probably the door was slammed.

After the shouting match with Pease, de Trobriand told a soldier that if Pease ever came to the post again he would be ejected, and this of course was passed on to Pease. It was then that Pease decided that he had to tell Sully that his feud with De Trobriand had actually started even before the massacre. "You are aware, general," he wrote, "that this is not the first time that General De Trobriand, in his official capacity, has cast damaging and infamous aspersions against my character in my official capacity, charging me with complicity with traders and of bringing Indians to Benton, 'apparently for traders' interests.'" Because he believed that many "will prejudge me and harshly . . . until the matter . . . has been fully investigated," Pease requested "that such investigation be speedily made, that I may be relieved from grave imputations against my integrity and honor." Pease claimed innocence of any charge that he had criticized "Colonel Baker's *discharge of his military duties*, or to cast odium upon the Army" because it "was as foreign to the purport of my correspondence as it was contrary to my inclination." Nevertheless, Pease's report had become the source of the outrage against Baker and the army for the massacre.

The taciturn Baker had been stung by the criticism of him. When de Trobriand wrote one of his regular letters, this time to Lina's husband, Albert Kintzing Post, on April 13, 1870, he was feeling sorry for Baker: "Poor Baker has been roughly handled by the organs of the Indian ring or the so-called philanthropists who know nothing of the Indians and the condition of affairs in the Great West. The worst is that he feels it so sorely." To de Trobriand it was just something that should be shrugged off: "if I was in his place, I would not care a bit."[7]

The matter was starting to die down. On April 8, 1870, the *Helena Herald* not surprisingly gave a simple opinion supporting Baker: "General Sheridan ordered men to hunt them down, just as we hunt down wolves. When caught in camp they were slaughtered, very much as we slaughter other wild beasts, when we get a chance. And if the government means to protect its frontiers, we do know that it is possible to avoid just such adversity, whenever a tribe proves that it cannot be reached by kindness and good faith."[8]

Several weeks later de Trobriand and his entourage left Montana forever and rode to his new assignment as commander of Fort Douglas in Utah Territory. His departure gave occasion for him to receive some of the public praise that he had wanted. A Helena paper wrote: "Gen. De Trobriand leaves the Territory with the kindest regards and best wishes of all good citizens. He has been an active and efficient commander of this district, has put forth zealous endeavors to preserve us from Indian depredations, and through his endeavors, Baker's successful and efficacious expedition was organized and sent out against the murdering Piegans."[9]

While all this was going on Francis Eastman, the chief fur trader in Fort Benton, wrote Sully on April 21, 1870, that "Mr. Riplinger . . . writes there will be no trouble with these Indians this season, and they are all anxious to make peace." This was good news coming from Eastman, who had told Sully three months before that "Mountain Chief's band is reported on the Milk River and has declared war against the whites!" Now, according to Eastman, things among the Indians were much calmer but still in a chaotic state. "Big Lake's camp has been close to Benton . . . and they have traded all their horses for whiskey." The result was that "every loafer and bummer about Benton has from 5 to 10 head of Indian Horses." The chief whiskey trader was none other than Jerry Potts, who may have narrowly escaped with his life from the Baker Massacre. He was still trading whiskey to the Indians, on the outskirts of Fort Benton. According to Eastman, the "night before last, Jerry Potts with several other half-breeds and two white men went to their camp with 10 gals. Whiskey and the result was a general row that resulted in the killing of Bear Shirt and wounding of another Indian."[10]

A rather bizarre illustration appeared in the April 30, 1870, edition of *Harper's Weekly Magazine*. It was an engraving showing a Piegan brave bringing the head of "Pete" Owl Child to General de Trobriand on a platter. This was likely in reference to the deal that General Sully hoped he had struck with Heavy Runner and the other chiefs who met with him on January 2. The caption to the engraving noted that there had been no Piegan Indians within 100 miles of the military post since the massacre and that "Pete escaped at the time, and afterwards died of small-pox. Father D. baptized and buried him."[11]

The Catholic clergy in Montana and in Canada also became involved in the aftermath of the massacre and helped to calm things down. Father Camillus Imoda, a Jesuit from the St. Peter's Mission in Montana, on March 17 had visited "the Indian camps on Belly River in the British possessions" and "met a large camp of Piegans, most of whom were those that fled from the Marias after their misfortune of January last." Father Imoda was "called by Mountain Chief into his lodge" and reported that the chief "spoke at length of their late misfortune and of the desire he and his people have of making a lasting peace with the whites." Mountain Chief complained to Imoda of the "false report of his having declared war against the whites." The chief "said he had been stripped of his lodge and made poor, but he is satisfied that his young men have been beaten and thinks that now they will mind their chiefs and not go any more to trouble the whites."[12]

AN INDIAN PEACE-OFFERING.

Harper's Weekly magazine, 1870

An April 1870 edition of *Harper's Weekly* showed this print of "Pete" Owl Child's head being delivered to General de Trobriand.

On May 13, 1870, however, the *New York Tribune* published an article with a dateline from Fort Shaw that introduced the involvement of a new priest. On June 11 the *Army and Navy Journal* republished the article, in which an unidentified source quoted facts provided by "Father Devereaux," a Jesuit priest in Canada, including excerpts from a letter that the priest was said to have sent to President Grant. Devereaux, the newspapers said, "comes from the Blackfeet Indians, among whom he has been living for nine years." The priest was quoted as saying that "all who escaped at that time went directly to the principal Blackfeet camp on Belly River, North of our line." The author of the article, whoever it was, provided an extract of the casualties from Devereaux's report: "In the Piegan camp, Jan. 23, 1870, there were 44 lodges, 37 at one camp and 7 near by, containing 484 souls;

132 were warriors, of whom 36 escaped; 190 persons were killed, as follows: 96 warriors, 33 women and 61 children; 294 escaped. The small pox appeared four days after they arrived at Belly River." The unnamed author continued: "I myself add to this that 17 women and children died of wounds after the engagement, but the warriors were all killed on the spot. There were, therefore, killed outright, 96 warriors and 77 women and children. Father Devereaux confirms the report that some Indians killed their own squaws."[13]

The newspapers got some of the account of the Devereaux involvement with the Blackfeet correct but missed widely on two major points. First, "Devereaux" was not the priest's name. Second, he was not even a priest. His name was Jean L'Heureux. While he passed himself off as a Jesuit in Montana and an Oblate in western Canada, he had not been ordained by either order. Correspondence in 1861 indicated that L'Heureux wanted to work for the Oblate order. During that summer, however, he stayed at St. Albert Mission, just north of Fort Edmonton, where he was caught in an illegal act and had to leave. The priests arranged for L'Heureux to join a band of Blackfeet who were traveling back to Montana after trading. When he donned the cassock of the Oblates he was able to pass himself off to the Jesuits as a secular priest. By the spring of 1862 he had helped save some Stoney Indians from being killed by the Bloods and was praised as "the priest at the Chief Mountain." Later that summer L'Heureux returned to St. Albert, apparently posing as a Jesuit who had built a church at Chief Mountain. Discovering the dual existences, Father Albert Lacombe of the Oblates wrote: "It appears that he has deceived the Jesuit fathers even better than he has me."[14]

Over the next several years L'Heureux lived with the Blackfeet tribes in Canada, often wearing a cassock and performing baptisms and marriages. Somehow he stayed on as a false priest among the Indians. They accepted him and gave him the Blackfeet name Nio'kskatapi (Three Persons), after the Holy Trinity. The Catholic clergy and the fur traders scorned him, but he was valuable to both groups because he was able to bring the Indians in to trade and achieved a significant number of religious

Jean L'Heureux

Jean L'Heureux, the false priest, is shown in 1880 with three Blackfoot chiefs. At one time he had fooled both the Jesuits and the Oblates into believing he was a priest in the other order, when neither had ordained him. Courtesy Glenbow Archives, Calgary, Alberta, Na-2968–4.

conversions and baptisms. As an embarrassment to the Oblates in Canada and the Jesuits in Montana, he is seldom mentioned in their histories. After the Baker Massacre it was not only Mountain Chief's band that fled across the border but also many if not most of the Piegan bands, which were afraid to return to the

Marias. They placed their confidence in L'Heureux to act as a peace emissary and draft a letter to the Montana Indian superintendent, General Alfred Sully. The letter set down what the Piegan chiefs wanted. It stated that "Three-Persons [L'Heureux] will go to your lodge. He will give news to you that our will is all good . . . We pray for peace with your white children." After L'Heureux delivered the letter Sully forwarded it to the Department of Interior.[15]

In the fall of 1870 a summary of the Baker Massacre was included in a 400-page report by the commissioner of Indian Affairs, Ely S. Parker. The report covered all of the Indian tribes in the United States. Parker noted in the beginning that "no serious outbreaks or demonstration of hostility, threatening to involve any tribe in a war with the Government, have occurred." The exception was the Baker Massacre. In only the third sentence of the report he had to mention that "those with whom we have had, perhaps, the greatest trouble are the Piegan Indians." Parker wrote that "this resulted in the killing of 173 of their number, among whom were, it is reported, many women and children." According to Parker, Baker had "attacked a camp of this band—Red Horn being their chief." Apparently he had taken Red Horn's name from the previous reports of Sully, Pease, and the army. The bands of Bear Chief and Big Horn were not mentioned. Red Horn, a presumed chief who had somehow been identified as more militant than the peaceful Heavy Runner, was still being blamed.[16]

Twelve years after the massacre, in 1882, Lieutenant General Philip Sheridan had a book published recording the engagements within the Military Division of the Missouri from 1868 to 1882, while he was commander. In describing Baker's attack and battle, Sheridan had gone back to calling the villages struck the camps of "Bear Chief" and "Big Horn." He had forgotten about Red Horn and of course made no mention of Heavy Runner. The attack, he claimed, resulted in "killing one hundred and seventy-three Indians," the usual number stated, and "wounding twenty."[17]

ELEVEN

The Spoils of War

*This was a very rich camp. A large number of skins, furs,
and robes were stored in the different lodges; but smallpox
having been known to prevail in the village at this time,
it was therefore deemed advisable to give everything up to
the torch.*

ARMY AND NAVY JOURNAL, MARCH 5, 1870

*Those who were not killed were left homeless and penniless.
Thirteen hundred head of horses and several thousand
buffalo robes were taken from the people.*

HORACE CLARKE AFFIDAVIT, NOVEMBER 9, 1920

On April 13, 1870, Brevet Brigadier General Regis de Trobriand was in his last few days at Fort Shaw in the Montana Territory and continuing his regular correspondence with
his daughter Lina. He told her that he would soon be on his way
to Utah, where he was to be the commander of Fort Douglas. He
also wrote her that when he left Montana, he would take with
him "one of the Piegan horses captured in our famous expedition, which I bought for my servant to ride along."[1]

Through the fog of events of that terrible day on January 23 Joe
Kipp had seen the soldiers round up many Piegan horses, starting before the battle and continuing afterward. It was not just the
horses belonging to Heavy Runner that Kipp saw but also those
of other chiefs. He estimated, and probably drastically overestimated, that "the soldiers . . . rounded up something like five
thousand head of horses belonging to the Indians." As to those

horses belonging to the village that had been destroyed, he believed there were "some four or five hundred head of horses belonging to Chief Heavy Runner."[2] Other accounts also reported large numbers of horses being taken by the soldiers. "The whole herd, amounting to over three hundred horses, was driven in, and a guard put over it," according to newspaper accounts, and "over three hundred horses captured, among them some stolen stock."[3] Major Baker himself reported that they had "captured over three hundred horses," and of course his account became the official estimate.[4] Alfred B. Hamilton, the whiskey trader, confirmed a similar number. He "knew that Heavy Runner had several Hundred Head of Horses" because in "those days an Indian would not be considered a chief unless he had several hundred head of horses."[5] In sad fact it might have been Heavy Runner's desire to accumulate horses that brought the bullet that killed him, if the story that Joseph Cobell fired the shot because Heavy Runner's band had stolen horses from him is true.

In the meantime, even with issues of abandonment of women and children and smallpox taking front stage, de Trobriand could not seem to stop his extravagant claims of victory, which now turned triumphantly to the number of horses captured. In a letter to General Hancock on May 2 de Trobriand claimed that "two hundred and eighty-five horses" which were "nearly all Indian ponies" had arrived at Fort Shaw.[6] Of those, "only thirty-four horses were claimed and returned to known resident citizens who 'proved property.'" This would leave some 250 unclaimed Indian horses. As much as de Trobriand might have wanted to keep them all, army regulations said that they were to dispose of the horses. He made arrangements himself for an auction. Even then de Trobriand did not follow the regulations exactly, for to do so would have required him to consult on the issue of ownership with Lieutenant Pease, the Blackfeet Indian agent whom he so despised.[7]

Before the auction de Trobriand gave special orders that the horse known as "Blackfoot" be assigned to "Lieutenant Waterbury for his exclusive use while he is on duty with the Mounted detachment." Other horses may have been put into use by the army. The horses that de Trobriand described as "poorly looking animals" were auctioned off.[8] It did not occur to the victorious de Trobriand that the Indian horses could have been returned to the Piegans, once the stolen livestock was separated.

De Trobriand happily reported to Hancock that "the sale of the Indian horses captured during the last expedition against the Piegans, took place as announced on Saturday April 30th and was terminated on the following day (yesterday) with a remarkable success." "Everybody was very much surprised at the price brought . . . which was about double of what was generally expected." It was de Trobriand's estimate that "the proceeds of the sale amounting to nearly three thousand dollars more than covers for the government the expense of the expedition."[9]

With the captured horses disposed of, a new problem arose when buffalo robes suspected of being infected with smallpox appeared in the fur trade. There was no direct suggestion that the robes had come from Heavy Runner's or Mountain Chief's villages, but circumstantial evidence was strong.

After the killing stopped at Heavy Runner's camp, Baker had ordered Lieutenant Doane to destroy the village. A horrifying description appeared in the newspapers over a month later: "This Piegan village has vanished with its inmates. Nothing now remains to show its existence save blackened spots where the lodges and stores were destroyed by fire, ghastly corpses strewn around, ravens flitting to and fro, and cowardly wolves snarling and snapping over their feast."[10] Despite this report of a total destruction in flames, controversy still arose over what happened to the valuable buffalo robes in the camp. Private William Birth of the mounted infantry K Company thought that they had "burnt all the blankets and buffalo robes." He remembered that "the Colonel wouldn't let us take anything" and did not "want anything that belonged to them, for they had the smallpox among them." But Birth could not have seen everything that was going on in the chaotic aftermath.[11]

Horace Clarke said later that "several thousand buffalo robes were taken from the people."[12] Clarke did not make nearly as direct a statement when historian David Hilger interviewed him much later about the massacre. At that time Clarke said that "civilian camp followers tried to steal robes and furs from the Heavy Runner camp after the massacre, but soldiers recovered and burned the loot, including about a thousand robes."[13] Still later in a 1920 affidavit Horace Clarke had a different number: "Thirteen hundred head of horses and several thousand buffalo robes were taken from the people." He added: "Those who were not killed were left homeless and penniless."[14] This left an unclear record, so it will never be known if all the robes in the camp were burned or some were taken. But in any case infected buffalo robes entered the market not long after the massacre. Their origins were with the whiskey traders John Healy and Alfred Hamilton, who, along with Jerry Potts, may have been in the vicinity of the Marias River at the time of the massacre.

As early as June 26, 1870, the army had been informed that infected buffalo robes were suspected of having entered the fur trade. This information was passed on to General Hancock, who reported it to Washington, DC. The secretary of war became involved and sent back instructions to Hancock that "all practicable precaution be taken by post commanders in this Department to prevent any attempts to evade by land route shipments existing orders and instructions relative to shipment of infected robes and furs."[15]

The matter lay quietly for several months until the robes were actually found. On November 7, 1870, J. A. Viall, who signed as "Supt. Indians," reported that there were "detained at Sun River Crossing a large lot of Buffalo Robes the property of Henry Thompson" of Helena. He said that they were the "same robes formerly owned by Msrs. Healy and Hamilton." Instead of asking that the robes be embargoed or destroyed, Viall added: "I would respectfully request you to release" them. According to Viall, "Mr Thompson has filed in this office satisfactory proofs going to show that these robes were not purchased from among tribes of Indians where the small pox prevailed and that these robes are in no wise infected with that disease." Yet the robes must have had suspicious origin, and Viall went on to state a case that "proofs have been filed showing that a large number of robes belonging to this same lot have been sold and disposed of in this City and that they have not spread or caused any contagion or disease among persons handling or using them."[16]

This information was forwarded to the War Department, together with "reports of Assistant Inspector General A. Baird and Surgeon J. F. Head, in relation to disinfecting Buffalo robes." The matter was complicated by bureaucracy in Washington, DC, and the War Department gave orders to Hancock, who was advised that "after consultation with Surgeon General Barnes he has concluded to order the release of all robes whose owners will, by affidavits properly sworn to, state that they have used all means to disinfect them, which they can use without destroying the robes."[17] Even after being given that permission, however, Colonel John Gibbon had to write back to Hancock that "there is no action on the subject called for at this Post, no robes being held at this place under the instruction of the War Dept."[18]

Apparently the robes were at Fort Benton, where "over 200 tons of buffalo robes . . . were embargoed by the federal government because of smallpox the previous winter among Indians." The embargo was not lifted for months. In September I. G. Baker shipped 3,000 robes to Helena for government inspection and got them cleared. This portion had been traded for with the Assiniboines, who did not suffer from the disease.[19]

A year and a half later, on November 11, 1871, the *Cincinnati Enquirer* noted: "Prominent gentlemen here attribute the spread of the small-pox in Philadelphia and other cities to the sale of buffalo robes there, taken from the Blackfeet and Piegan camps, where the disease prevailed two years ago."[20]

After the massacre Joe Kipp became even more closely involved with the Piegans as a whiskey trader. In opposition to the Fort Whoop-Up trading post started in Canada by Healy and Hamilton on the Belly River, Kipp had his own whiskey trading operation at Fort Standoff, built at the confluence of the Belly and Waterton Rivers. The name "standoff" came from a confrontation when Kipp was a short distance south of the unmarked Canadian boundary and stood up to a U.S. marshal by telling him that he was actually north of the line.

Kipp had his reputation tarnished when Calf Shirt, a Blood chief, showed up at his trading post and was killed by the traders in an epic assassination that involved poisoning, shooting, and finally drowning before the nearly invincible Indian lost his life.[21] Kipp later married Double Strike Woman, one of Heavy Runner's daughters, whose white name was Martha. Kipp adopted several of Heavy Runner's children and raised them. The story of his suspected duplicity in the massacre did not fade, and it is said that many on the Blackfeet Reservation who have his name hold him in contempt. Neither his Mandan heritage nor his whiskey trading helped his reputation.[22]

Horace Clarke fared better. He himself was half Piegan, and he married a Piegan woman. They moved first near the Highwood Mountains in the Piegan country and then up next to the Rockies at what is now East Glacier. When Clarke made a sworn statement in 1920, he acknowledged that he had been in the battle. He also said: "The hostile camp was Mountain Chief's, and it was the camp we intended to strike, but owing to too much excitement and confusion and misinformation the Heavy Runner camp was the sufferer and the victim of circumstances."[23]

Joe Cobell lived out the rest of his life in the Piegan territory. There would always be a question about whether he had fired the first shot that killed Heavy Runner, but this seemingly did not serve to darken the Cobell name.[24]

TWELVE

Drunk Again

CHARGE—Drunkenness on duty.
SENTENCE—To be dismissed from the service.

COURT-MARTIAL OF EUGENE M. BAKER,
AT FORT CUSTER, MONTANA TERRITORY, 1881

Baker continued to command Fort Ellis after the massacre. No formal inquiry into his inability to direct the troops against the Piegans on the Marias in 1870 was ever made, despite the many observations that he had been drunk.

The Indian threat in Montana had somewhat abated, but there was still concern that the Indians would attack wagon trains and settlers moving along the roads. After the killing of Malcolm Clarke, the miners at Diamond City in Confederate Gulch asked for protective measures, as did the citizens who had moved into the upper Smith River valley to start farms and ranches. Baker was ordered to scout out a location for a new camp, to be named Camp Baker after him. The plan was that some of his cavalry could be garrisoned there, but he was against the idea. "In my opinion," Baker said, "there is no more necessity for a company at Camp Baker, than there is in front of Headquarters of the Commanding General." By summer the camp had been established anyway at a point some eighty miles above the Missouri River along the quiet flowing waters of the Smith River. There the post remained with little or no activity until it was renamed Fort Logan in 1877 and moved farther up the Smith River to the mouth of Camus Creek.[1] The name Camp Baker was a tribute to

236

Eugene Baker and the massacre that dominated his reputation. He had become known in the territory as "Piegan Baker," but this was not necessarily laudatory. Opinions about him would always be mixed.

On August 20, 1870, Elizabeth Chester Fisk, twenty-four, the wife of Helena newspaperman Robert Fisk, and her young cousin Mae Fisk arrived in Bozeman. "In the evening," said Elizabeth in a letter to her mother, "we had a grand reception of the entire party and a number of officers from Fort Ellis." The two young women had "made the acquaintance of Col. Baker of the 'Piegan Massacre' notoriety." In her first assessment, Elizabeth found the man who had led the slaughter to be "one of the quietest most gentlemanly of men, generous and sensitive." Sensing the pain that Baker was seemingly trying to drink away, she noted: "He feels most keenly the many unjust things said of him and his punishment of the Indian depredations." Despite Baker's melancholy, he and young Mae Fisk were attracted to each other. Soon she declared that she had fallen in love with him. They became engaged, with a ring, but they did not set a wedding date. Almost a year later Baker and Mae Fisk were not yet married. In July 1871 Elizabeth and Mae (still with her engagement ring) were traveling back to Montana after a visit to the East. At Omaha they "met Col. Baker and two of his staff . . . and with them . . . journeyed through to Helena," Elizabeth said; but still the marriage date was not set.[2]

Two years after the engagement the romance was going nowhere. Elizabeth Fisk's opinion of Baker had become anything but complimentary. At the time when Baker was "out hunting Indians with the North Pacific R. R. Surveying party" Elizabeth wrote to her mother: "There is no possibility that he and Mae will ever be married." It was an understatement, because the marriage had been doomed for some time by Baker's drinking. Baker had been in Helena visiting Mae the previous Christmas but "was more than half drunk all the time he was here." A wedding had been planned for January. But Elizabeth said that "Col. Baker changed his plans" and "delayed his visit to Helena for

Cousin Mae Fisk at 18.

Cousin Mae at 30.

Mae Fisk

Two portraits of Mae Fisk at eighteen and at thirty.
She was engaged to Eugene Baker (unidentified
photographer: copy of picture in Fisk Scrapbook
loaned for copying by Bruce Fisk, Seattle). Courtesy Montana Historical Society Research Center
Photograph Archives, Helena, Catalog #942–315.

two or three weeks." Soon Mae stopped hearing from him altogether. When Elizabeth's husband, Robert Fisk, visited Baker at Fort Ellis a few months later, he reported back to her that Baker had "told him he hoped to be married some time but was in debt and saw no way of getting out." To the Fisk family this was "equivalent to a dismissal of all hope, since he was drinking and gambling worse than ever." Finally Elizabeth wrote her mother the sad news: "Mae waited about six weeks, and, hearing nothing from him and receiving no reply to the letters she sent, she returned his ring bidding him farewell."[3]

When Robert Fisk had told Elizabeth and Mae that Baker was out hunting Indians with the surveying party, he was referring to Baker's duty as the commander of a survey escort near Pryor's Fork of the Yellowstone River. Baker was surprised by a Sioux war party, and his troops exchanged shots with the Indians, but he was reported to be too drunk even to acknowledge that a battle was going on. Paul McCormick, the civilian freighter who had been with Baker on the Marias expedition, was with him again on the Yellowstone. As he said, "I had charge of the transportation at Baker's battle field on the Yellowstone which is on the same side of the river that Billings is and 11 miles East." McCormick recalled later: "At this fight he had 800 men but if it had not been for the 'hangers on,' for whom he did not have much respect, he would have been whipped."[4]

Baker was put under arrest for drunkenness on August 14, but nothing came of it. Even though Baker was often referred to as "colonel" he remained a major in rank the rest of his career, which could only be described as a series of disasters. His inebriation on the Yellowstone was but one such event. Just a short time later he was placed "in arrest" from October 15, 1872, until January 11, 1873, on charges proffered against him by Capt. S. H. Norton, who had commanded G Company of the 2nd Cavalry at Fort Ellis. In a strange turn of events Norton claimed that Baker, who was drunk at the time, had wrongfully put him under arrest. The matter was dropped.[5]

Baker then began a long series of stopovers of short duration, sometimes serving as commander of various forts and posts in Wyoming and Nebraska. His health began to fail during this time, and he was granted sick leave from May until November 1875 on his own certificate of disability. At some point he was again granted sick leave until March 1876, with "disorder of spleen and liver, splenic pain and jaundice." He did not return to duty until November 1, 1876, for short assignments at posts in Wyoming. After an absence of five years he was returned to Montana at Fort Keogh on the Yellowstone River and remained there intermittently until September 1879.[6]

Then came a long period of ordinary leave for a year starting in October 1879. In November journalist Martha Plassmann encountered Baker at the Overland Hotel in Fort Benton and noted that he had been drinking to excess. By November 1880, after Baker's leave was up, he was nowhere to be found. He did show up three days later at Fort Keogh, saying that he had been unavoidably detained.[7]

Eleven years passed from the time of the Marias River massacre before any formal action was taken on an episode of Baker's drinking. On February 22, 1881, while he was commanding the 11th Infantry at Fort Custer on the Yellowstone River, Baker was intoxicated on duty, and some of the junior officers decided that they finally had enough. In the face of the invulnerability that Baker seemed to carry with him after the Piegan massacre, the subordinate officers fearlessly put their commander under arrest. Formal charges were filed. A court-martial was convened at Fort Custer on May 12, 1881, with the tribunal composed of army officers from posts and regiments throughout the West.[8]

The testimony opened with questions by the prosecutor, Captain Erasmus Corwin Gilbreath of Baker's own command. Gilbreath had an identity problem right away, because he had happened to be the officer of the day when Baker was found inebriated and uncomfortably had to call himself as his first witness. When he awkwardly asked himself if he had found Baker intoxicated, he gave the answer that his commander was so much "intoxicated to be without the full control of his mental and physical faculties."[9]

Finished with his own testimony and relieved to have someone other than himself to question, Gilbreath called Captain Samuel Todd Hamilton as the next witness. When Gilbreath asked Hamilton if he had seen Baker drunk on duty on February 22, Hamilton responded that Baker "had been drinking and . . . he ought not to be in the Office and I advised him to go home and lie down." Pressed further for details, Hamilton said that Baker "made some reply which I failed to understand," because "it was spoken in a low tone so that I did not know what he did say." At that time Hamilton, who was called Sam, said that he heard a more audible response: "All right Mr. *Sampleton*" (emphasis added). Hamilton reluctantly gave the crucial testimony required to convict Baker: "I do not think he was in condition to perform his duties as Commanding Officer at the time I saw him." Gilbreath's next witness was Lieutenant Charles T. Roe, who had seen Baker on the day he was drunk and testified that he saw him "under the influence of intoxicating liquor so much as to be in a maudlin state."

The time had come for Baker to present a defense, and he decided to do it himself. He knew Roe well and could expect that the junior officer would not try to incriminate him if he could avoid it. When Baker began to cross-examine Roe, his questions were precise and to the point. Roe's answers seemed to favor Baker.

Question: "Were you a witness to any improper acts on my part?"

Answer: "I didn't witness any improper acts on the part of the Major."

Question: "Did you observe anything at variance with gentlemanly courtesy in my treatment of yourself or of any who came to my office that morning?"

Answer: "I did not."

With these answers from Roe, Baker was satisfied that he was making some headway in his defense and did not call any further witnesses himself. Baker's hopes faded as Gilbreath put on more witnesses against him, however, reaching a total of five in all, who testified they had seen Baker both drunk and unfit for duty.

When the testimony came to an end, Baker asked the panel to consider his record of accomplishments in the military. As a first matter, he asked the court to consider General Philip Sheridan's commendation to him for the Piegan massacre. Baker had also obtained other written statements from army generals that praised him. These were given to the court to be read and then included in the record of the proceeding. They were impressive. Gilbreath himself admitted that the documents, "from the rank and character of the writers, are entitled to the most careful consideration." Typical was the statement that Baker had obtained from General George Crook: "I take pleasure in stating that I consider you [Major Baker] a gallant, skillful, and efficient officer, a cultivated and estimable gentleman, and a thoroughly honorable man."[10]

While they might have preferred to rule otherwise, the members of the court were faced with the overwhelming evidence against Baker and found him guilty of the charges. They sentenced him "to be dismissed from the service." Having done their duty, they quickly added that the "members of the Court, without exception . . . recommend Major Baker to the clemency of the reviewing authorities." This plea was based upon their "knowledge of Major Baker's character and services, and in view of the documents as to his previous record from distinguished officers, which are appended to the proceedings."

During Baker's appeal, which went up through the army command, the War Department filed a "Court Martial Brief." It pointed out that "the Judge Advocate General, in his report on the case, gives his entire concurrence in the recommendation of the Court, and thinks that Major Baker's services justify the most lenient consideration at the hands of the Executive in deciding upon punishment." The War Department' brief noted: "The well being of the Army and the demands of discipline may perhaps forbid the entire remission of the sentence; but it is recommended that the Executive, in taking final action on the case, give to Major Baker's past career and services and present character, the amplest weight to which they are justly entitled."

With a letter of June 13, 1881, D. E. Gromin, the judge advocate general of the army, submitted the record of the trial to Robert T. Lincoln, secretary of war, for his review.[11] The matter was then referred to William Tecumseh Sherman, general of the army.[12] Eleven years earlier Sherman had ordered Baker to attack the Piegans and then protected him against public outcry afterward. Not surprisingly, he protected Baker again and recommended leniency. The matter was sent to President James A. Garfield, who on June 30, 1881, modified the sentence "to suspension from rank and forfeiture of one-half pay for the period of six months."[13]

Three years later, while on his way to Fort Walla Walla, Washington, Baker was taken ill. He had previously been diagnosed with "aortic insufficiency complicated by chronic gastritis." He died on December 18, 1884, after six weeks in quarters at the fort at the age of forty-seven. The stated cause of death was "disorder of spleen and liver, splenic pain and jaundice." The army paid $150 for Baker's casket but not for the transportation of the body to his hometown of Fort Ann, New York, for burial.[14]

Baker's mother, Salome Baker, filed a claim for Baker's pension two years later, claiming that she was in poor health and nearly blind. She said that she depended entirely on Baker's pay for support except for a "small amount received from the sale of an old piano." In her affidavit she stated that her son left neither widow nor child to claim the pension and that she wished to be saved "from want and embarrassment."[15]

AFTER THE BATTLE Doane and his troops had "returned to Fort Ellis in February." His military record showed that Doane was the "first and last man in Piegan Coup Jan'y 23, 1870, . . . troops having surrounded village and captured Indian stock before the command came up. Greatest slaughter of Indians ever made by U.S. Troops."[16] This was at least some of the recognition that

Doane wanted as an Indian fighter, even though the attack was against the wrong village, which did not seem to matter to him.

At the end of the day on January 23, 1870, when the firing had stopped, Doane had looked over Heavy Runner's devastated village, full of the dead bodies of innocent Indians. With some satisfaction he later recalled: "I remember the day when we slaughtered the Piegans, and how it occurred to me, as I sat down on the bank of the Marias & watched the stream of their blood, which ran down on the surface of the frozen river over half a mile, that the work we were then doing would be rewarded, as it has been."[17]

Notes

ABBREVIATIONS

LC   Library of Congress, Washington, DC
MHS   Montana Historical Society, Helena
MSU   Montana State University, Bozeman
NARA   National Archives and Records Administration, Washington, DC

PREFACE

1. James Welch with Paul Stekler, *Killing Custer: The Battle of the Little Bighorn and the Fate of the Plains Indians* (New York: W. W. Norton, 1994).

2. "The Slaughter of the Piegans," *New York Times*, February 24, 1870; "The Piegan Village Slaughter," *New York Times*, March 30, 1870.

3. Francis B. Heitman, *Historical Register and Dictionary of the United States Army, from Its Organization, September 29, 1789, to March 2, 1903*, 2 vols. (Urbana: University of Illinois Press, 1965), 1:184 (Baker), 1:370 (de Trobriand)..

CHAPTER 1

1. Reuben Gold Thwaites, ed., *Original Journals of the Lewis and Clark Expedition, 1804–1806* vol. 5 (New York: Antiquarian Press, 1959), 183–227 (quotation on 220: all subsequent Lewis quotations are from this source unless otherwise noted); Thomas Jefferson, "Jefferson's Confidential Message, Recommending a Western Exploring Expedition," January 18, 1803, in *President's Messages: Inaugural, Annual and Special, from 1789 to 1846*, comp. Edwin Williams, vol. 2 (New York: Edward Walker, 1846), xxvi, as cited in Eric Jay Dolin, *Fur, Fortune and Empire: The Epic History of the Fur Trade in America* (New York: W. W. Norton, 2010), 170–173.

2. "Camp Disappointment" is marked by a monument and sign at milepost 233 on U.S. Highway 2 between Browning and Cut Bank, which is four miles

directly south of the actual campsite reached on July 23, 1806. Lewis's idiosyncratic spellings and punctuation are preserved throughout, without the use of "[*sic*]." See http://www.browningmontana.com/campdis.html.

3. Lewis selected "Werner, Frazier and Sergt Gass" to meet him on the Missouri. Thwaites, *Original Journals*, 185, entry for July 1, 1806.

4. Ibid., 185, entry for July 3, 1806.

5. Ibid., 218, 219, entry for July 26, 1806.

6. Milo M. Quaife, ed., *The Journals of Captain Meriwether Lewis and Sergeant John Ordway: Kept on the Expedition of Western Exploration, 1803–1806* (Madison: State Historical Society of Wisconsin, 1965), 382–383.

7. Thwaites, *Original Journals*, 219–221, entry for July 26, 1806.

8. John C. Ewers, *The Blackfeet: Raiders on the Northwestern Plains* (Norman: University of Oklahoma Press, 1958), 126–136.

9. Thwaites, *Original Journals*, 221, entry for July 26, 1806.

10. Ibid., 223.

11. Lewis wrote on August 14, 1805: "The means I had of communicating with these people was by way of Drewyer [Drouillard] who understood perfectly the common language of jesticulation or signs which seems to be universally understood by all the Nations we have yet seen." Frank Bergon, ed., *The Journals of Lewis and Clark* (New York: Viking Penguin, 1989), 232.

12. Thwaites, *Original Journals*, 221–223, entry for July 26, 1806.

13. Quaife, *The Journals of Captain Meriwether Lewis and Sergeant John Ordway*, 382–383 (quotations); Thwaites, *Original Journals*, 23, entry for July 27, 1806.

14. Thwaites, *Original Journals*, 224–228, entry for July 27, 1806. The location of the fight has been settled as being on the Marias River, just south of where Cut Bank, Montana, is today and nineteen miles southeast of Camp Disappointment. It is known as the Two Medicine Fight. See http://www.browning montana.com/campdis.html.

15. Thwaites, *Original Journals*, 224–228, entry for July 27, 1806.

16. Ibid., 224–228, entry for July 28, 1806.

17. Ibid., 227, 228.

18. "Blackfeet recollections differ from those recorded in Lewis' journal," *Great Falls Tribune*, April 23, 2003, http://archive.greatfallstribune.com /communities/lewisandclark/stories/183232.html.

19. A Blackfeet recounting of the encounter was published in a newspaper story in 1919, which was more consistent with Lewis's journal. George Bird Grinnell, known as one of the fathers of Glacier National Park, recounted an interview he had conducted in 1895 with a Blackfeet chief called Wolf Calf, who was then 102 years old. When Wolf Calf was 13 years old, he was present at the fight scene. The chief directed the young men to try to steal some of the Lewis party's things, according to Wolf Calf. The old chief located the fight scene as on the hill immediately south of Birch Creek, where the town of Robare then

stood in 1919 in Teton County. "In reply to an inquiry as to any attempt to pursue Lewis' party, Wolf Calf declared that the Indians were badly frightened, that they were bitterly hostile to the whites after the incident and ashamed because they had not killed all the white men." Fred Tasker, "Commemoration a Chance to Tell Different Stories," *Salt Lake Tribune*, January 26, 2003. See also Eric Newhouse, "Blackfeet Recollections," *Great Falls Tribune*, April 23, 2003. According to Darrell Kipp, "They would have thrown the medal away or destroyed it." The result of that encounter, he said, "was that the Blackfeet closed their territory to all whites for the next eighty years, attacking and killing any intruders they could find within their borders."

20. Newhouse, "Blackfeet Recollections."

21. Alexander Henry, *The Journal of Alexander Henry the Younger, 1799–1814*, ed. Barry M. Gough (Toronto: Champlain Society, 1992), 2:376–377 (all subsequent Henry quotations are from this source unless otherwise noted, preserving his idiosyncratic spellings and punctuation without the use of "[sic]").

22. K. G. Davies, "Kelsey, Henry," in *Dictionary of Canadian Biography* (Toronto: University of Toronto Press, 1969; revised 2013), http://www.biographi.ca/en/bio/kelsey_henry_2E.html; Henry Epp, ed., *Three Hundred Prairie Years: Henry Kelsey's "Inland Country of Good Report"* (Regina: Canadian Plains Research Center, 1993); John Warkentin, *The Kelsey Papers* (Regina: Canadian Plains Research Center, 1994), http://jetson.unl.edu/cocoon/encyclopedia/doc/egp.ea.023. Henry Kelsey (ca. 1667–1724) seems to be credited as being the first European to see the northern plains Indians and to witness a buffalo hunt conducted on foot before horses were acquired.

23. James G. MacGregor, *A History of Alberta* (Edmonton: Hurtig Publishers, 1972), 15–21; J. B. Tyrrell, ed., *David Thompson's Narrative of His Explorations in Western America, 1784–1812* (Toronto: Champlain Society, 1916), https://archive.org/details/davidthompsonsna00thom. David Thompson, an early explorer and trader for the Hudson's Bay Company, left a journal that included accounts of his time wintering with the Piegans on the Saskatchewan River in 1787–1788, in what is now southern Alberta.

24. George Bird, *Story of the Indian* (New York: Appleton Publishing, 1895), cited in Peter Nabokov, ed., *Native American Testimony* (1978), revised ed. (New York: Penguin Books, 1999), 42–44 (quotations) ; MacGregor, *A History of Alberta*, 15–21; Tyrrell, *David Thompson's Narrative*.

25. Grinnell, *Story of the Indian*, cited in Nabokov, *Native American Testimony*, 482n5 (attributed to "Wolf Calf, *Piegan*").

26. Tyrrell, *David Thompson's Narrative*, 328–332. In 1797 Thompson left Hudson's Bay Company to join the North West Company.

27. Arthur S. Morton, *A History of the Canadian West to 1870–71* (Toronto: Thomas Nelson & Sons, 1939), 19–21.

28. MacGregor, *A History of Alberta*, 15–18.

29. John G. Jackson, *The Piikani Blackfeet: A Culture under Siege* (Missoula: Mountain Press Publishing, 2000), 14–17.

30. Morton, *A History of the Canadian West to 1870–71*, 480–481.

31. Henday was described as a laborer who had worked on the shore of Hudson's Bay at York Factory. Morton, *A History of the Canadian West to 1870–71*, 244; Barbara Belyea, ed., *A Year Inland: The Journal of a Hudson's Bay Company Winterer* (Waterloo, Ontario: Wilfred Laurier University Press, 2000); Jas. G. MacGregor, *Behold the Shining Mountains* (Edmonton: Applied Art Products, 1954). Those who have examined the Henday journals have noted that only four hand-transcribed copies exist, with inconsistencies between them. MacGregor, *A History of Alberta*, 74–75, 109–110.

32. MacGregor, *A History of Alberta*, 26–27.

33. Cocking's journals are quoted in Morton, *A History of the Canadian West to 1870–71*, 286.

34. Jackson, *The Piikani Blackfeet*, 9; Morton, *A History of the Canadian West to 1870–71*, 9–21.

35. W. L. Morton, "The North West Company: Pedlars Extraordinary," *Minnesota History* 40, no. 4 (Winter 1966); Paul Chrisler Phillips, *The Fur Trade* (Norman: University of Oklahoma Press, 1961).

36. Morton, *A History of the Canadian West to 1870–71*, 480–481; Tyrrell, *David Thompson's Narrative*, 375 (quotation); Rowland Bond, *The Original Northwester: David Thompson and the Native Tribes of North America* (Nine Mile Falls, WA: Spokane House Enterprises, 1970), 61. At that time Thompson was headed west to go over the mountains and follow the Columbia River to the sea and likely would have preferred to go through the Piegan territory.

37. Alexander DeConde, *This Affair of Louisiana* (New York: Charles Scribner and Sons, 1976), 29ff.

38. Richard Edward Oglesby, *Manuel Lisa and the Opening of the Missouri Fur Trade* (Norman: University of Oklahoma Press, 1963).

39. Quaife, *The Journals of Captain Meriwether Lewis and Seargeant John Ordway*, 13–23.

40. DeConde, *This Affair of Louisiana*, 27–39. See Blake A. Watson, *Buying America from the Indians: Johnson v. McIntosh and the History of Native Land Rights* (Norman: University of Oklahoma Press, 2012), 170–171.

41. Oglesby, *Manuel Lisa*, 54–58.

42. Ibid., 3–6, for Drouillard's killing of a deserter who refused to return to the party. He was eventually tried for murder and acquitted.

43. See http://lewisandclarktrail.com/drouillard.htm; Paul O'Neil, *The Rivermen* (New York: Time-Life Books, 1975), 64 (quotation)–67 (handwritten list of Drouillard's belongings on 66). See Stephen T. Gough, *Colter's Run* (Stevensville, MT: Stoneydale Press Publishing, 2008), for a fictional account of another member of Lisa's party who would have fared no better than Drouillard if he had not had the ability to run away from the Indians.

CHAPTER 2

Epigraph: Ewers, *The Blackfeet*, 33.

1. Thomas Forsyth to Lewis Cass, Secretary of War, "State of the Fur Trade in 1831," August 1, 1831, Manuscript Department, State Historical Society of Wisconsin, reproduced in Hiram Chittenden, *Fur Trade of the Far West* (1935), 2 vols. (Lincoln: University of Nebraska Press, 1986), 2:909–914 (all subsequent Forsyth quotations are from this source unless otherwise noted).

2. Lewis Cass to A. J. Dallas, Acting Secretary of War, July 20, 1815, in Clarence E. Carter, ed., *The Territorial Papers of the United States* (Washington, DC: U.S. Government Printing Office, 1934), 10:574–575, cited in Francis Paul Prucha, *Documents of United States Indian Policy* (Lincoln: University of Nebraska Press, 2000), 25–26.

3. Dolin, *Fur, Fortune and Empire*, 194–198; Hiram Chittenden, *The American Fur Trade of the Far West* (1935), 2 vols. (Lincoln: University of Nebraska Press, 1986), 1:167–169.

4. W. L. Morton, "The North West Company: Pedlars Extraordinary," *Minnesota History* 40, no. 4 (Winter 1966): 157–165. See generally Phillips, *The Fur Trade*, 306–347.

5. Morton, *A History of the Canadian West to 1870–71*, 738–743.

6. Lesley Wischmann, *Frontier Diplomats: The Life and Times of Alexander Culbertson and Natoyist-Sissina'* (Spokane, WA: Arthur H. Clark Company, 2000), 35.

7. Charles Larpenteur, *Forty Years a Fur Trader on the Upper Missouri: The Personal Narrative of Charles Larpenteur, 1833–1872* (Chicago: Lakeside Press, 1933), 106–108 (quotation); Chittenden, *The American Fur Trade of the Far West*, 1:355–363; George Catlin, *Letters and Notes on the Manners, Customs and Conditions of N. American Indians* (1844), 2 vols. (New York: Dover Publications, 1973), 1:21.

8. See generally LeRoy R. Hafen, ed., *The Mountain Men and the Fur Trade of the Far West*, vol. 2 (1965) (Lincoln: University of Nebraska Press, 1995); and John C. Jackson, *Shadow on the Tetons: David E. Jackson and the Claiming of the American West* (Missoula: Mountain Press Publishing, 1993). Other mountain men who worked for the company were Joseph Meek, Robert Newell, George W. Ebbert, and Kit Carson.

9. *U.S. Statutes at Large*, 4:564, as reproduced in Prucha, *Documents of United States Indian Policy*, 62.

10. Ewers, *The Blackfeet*, 55; Anne F. Hyde, *Empires, Nations, and Families: A New History of the American West, 1800–1860* (New York: Harper Collins, 2011), 61–62.

11. Ashley eventually was elected to the U.S. House of Representatives from Missouri.

12. See generally Watson, *Buying America from the Indians*. When Lewis and Clark set out on their expedition in 1803–1804, it was under the name of the "Corps of Discovery." This was a fitting designation, because the rights to

the Louisiana Purchase territory that they had explored had been claimed by France under the discovery doctrine and sold to the Americans.

13. Ibid. The more conventional spelling "McIntosh" has been used instead of "M'Intosh."

14. Prucha, *Documents of United States Indian Policy*, 35–37.

15. Albert D. Richardson, *Beyond the Mississippi: From the Great River to the Great Ocean: Life and Adventure on the Prairies, Mountains, and Pacific Coast, 1857–1867* (Hartford, CT: American Publishing, 1867), 19.

16. See generally Dolin, *Fur, Fortune and Empire;* and Chittenden, *The American Fur Trade of the Far West,* vol. 1.

17. Thomas Forsyth to Lewis Cass, Secretary of War, "State of the Fur Trade in 1831," August 1, 1831, Manuscript Department, State Historical Society of Wisconsin, reproduced in Chittenden, *The American Fur Trade of the Far West,* 2:909–914. See Prucha, *Documents of United States Indian Policy,* 52, 53.

18. George Washington to James Duane, September 7, 1783, in Prucha, *Documents of United States Indian Policy,* 1–2.

19. Prucha, *Documents of United States Indian Policy,* 52–53. The Indian Removal Act was signed into law by President Andrew Jackson on May 28, 1830. The act authorized him to negotiate with the Indians in the southern United States for their removal to federal territory west of the Mississippi River in exchange for their homelands. The affected Indians were the Cherokee, Chickasaw, Choctaw, Creek, and Seminole tribes. The Removal Act paved the way for the reluctant—and often forcible—emigration of tens of thousands of American Indians to the West.

20. This quotation is attributed to Thomas Harkins (or Nitikechi), a Choctaw chief, who also wrote "A Farewell Letter to the American People," which was widely published in newspapers following the removal. George W. Harkins to the American People, February 25, 1832, http://www.ushistory.org/documents/harkins.htm. Subsequent removals occurred in later years. See Theda Perdue and Michael D. Green, eds., *The Cherokee Removal: A Brief History with Documents* (Boston: Bedford/St. Martin's, 1955).

21. Ewers, *The Blackfeet,* 33 (quotation), 57; Chardon, *Chardon's Journal,* as cited in Kennedy and Reeves, *An Inventory and Historical Description of Whiskey Posts.*

22. W. Raymond Wood, "James Kipp: Upper Missouri Fur Trader and Missouri River Farmer," *North Dakota History* 77, nos. 1 and 2 (2011): 2–35. On March 21, 1821, the North West Company merged with the Hudson's Bay Company.

23. Ibid. Somewhere along the way, Kipp married a Mandan woman and became proficient in her language.

24. Chittenden, *The American Fur Trade of the Far West,* 1:333–336, 2:328–329; John G. Lepley, *Blackfoot Fur Trade on the Upper Missouri* (Missoula: Pictorial Histories Publishing Company, 2004), 85–86.

25. Wood, "James Kipp"; Hugh A. Dempsey, *A Blackfoot Winter Count*, Occasional Paper No. 1 (Calgary: Glenbow Foundation, 1965), 9. Kipp's presence was noted on the Blackfeet Winter Count for 1831. See Rudolph Friederich Kurz, *The Journal of Rudolph Friederich Kurz*, trans. Myrtis Jarrell (Lincoln: University of Nebraska Press, 1970). For more information on Kurz, see Hyde, *Empires, Nations, and Families*, 411–416.

26. Lepley, *Blackfoot Fur Trade on the Upper Missouri*, 88–90.

27. Dempsey, *A Blackfoot Winter Count*, 9; Chittenden, *The American Fur Trade of the Far West*, 1:336; Hafen, *The Mountain Men and the Fur Trade of the Far West*, 2:35–39, 41–46; Ewers, *The Blackfeet*, 58.

28. Ewers, *The Blackfeet*, 73.

29. Paul F. Sharp, *Whoop-Up Country: The Canadian–American West, 1865–1885* (1955) (Helena: Historical Society of Montana, 1960), 58.

30. Reuben Gold Thwaites, ed., *Early Western Travels, 1748–1846* (1906), vol. 23 (New York: AMS Press, 1966), 90–123. See Jackson, *The Piikani Blackfeet*, for details of the Catlin and Bodmer visits.

31. John Rowand to James Hargrave, January 1, 1840, in George Parkin de Twenebroker, ed., *The Hargrave Correspondence, 1821–1843* (1938) (New York: Greenwood Press, 1968), quoted in Kennedy and Reeves, *An Inventory and Historical Description of Whiskey Posts*.

32. Morton, *A History of the Canadian West to 1870–71*, 741; Kennedy and Reeves, *An Inventory and Historical Description of Whiskey Posts*.

33. John Rowand, to James Hargrave, January 11, 1834, in Twenebroker, *The Hargrave Correspondence*, 133.

34. John C. Jackson, *Jemmy Jock Bird: Marginal Man on the Blackfoot Frontier* (Calgary: University of Calgary Press, 2003), 65.

35. Trade and Intercourse Act, Sec. 21; *U.S. Statutes at Large*, 4:729–735; in Prucha, *Documents of United States Indian Policy*, 63–68. A final Trade and Intercourse Law was passed on June 30, 1834.

36. Chittenden, *The American Fur Trade of the Far West*, 1:355–363; Lepley, *Blackfoot Fur Trade on the Upper Missouri*, 100, 101.

37. On June 30, 1834, Congress prohibited distilleries in the Indian territory.

38. Larpenteur, *Forty Years a Fur Trader on the Upper Missouri*, 106–107.

39. Dolin, *Fur, Fortune and Empire*, 194–198; Chittenden, *The American Fur Trade of the Far West*, 1:167–169, 1:355–363; Larpenteur, *Forty Years a Fur Trader on the Upper Missouri*, 106–108; Chittenden, *The American Fur Trade of the Far West*; Catlin, *Letters and Notes on the Manners, Customs and Conditions of N. American Indians*, 1:21, as quoted in Wischmann, *Frontier Diplomats*, 36.

40. Kennedy and Reeves, *An Inventory and Historical Description of Whiskey Posts*.

41. Some buffalo meat was used for subsistence in the form of pemmican at the trading posts and forts.

42. Henry A. Boller, *Twilight of the Upper Missouri River Fur Trade: The Journals of Henry A. Boller*, ed. W. Raymond Wood (Bismarck: State Historical Society of North Dakota, 2008), 21–22, 226; Ray Mattison, "James Kipp," in *Fur Traders, Trappers, and Mountain Men of the Upper Missouri*, ed. Leroy R. Hafen (Lincoln: University of Nebraska Press, 1995), 35–39; Kurz, *The Journal of Rudolph Friederich Kurz*; W. Raymond Wood, William Hunt, and Randy Williams, *Fort Clark and Its Indian Neighbors: A Trading Post on the Upper Missouri* (Norman: University of Oklahoma Press, 2011). Steamboats began arriving at Fort Clark in 1832, delivering trade goods to the fort and returning to St. Louis with beaver pelts and bison robes.

43. David J. Wishart, *The Fur Trade of the American West, 1807–1840* (Lincoln: University of Nebraska Press, 1979), 66–69, 109; Chardon, *Chardon's Journal*, 253.

44. Dempsey, *A Blackfoot Winter Count*, 9.

45. Wischmann, *Frontier Diplomats*, 109–116.

46. Lepley, *Blackfoot Fur Trade on the Upper Missouri*, 145–147; Chittenden, *The American Fur Trade of the Far West*, 2:961–963.

47. Joel Overholser, *Fort Benton: World's Innermost Port* (Helena: Falcon Press, 1987), 1–4.

48. Dempsey, *A Blackfoot Winter Count*, 11–13. As early as 1848 a winter count showed that Bad Head took a large band of Bloods to stay near Fort Benton.

49. On Missouri River travel, see generally Richardson, *Beyond the Mississippi*.

50. Paul R. Wylie, *The Irish General: Thomas Francis Meagher* (Norman: University of Oklahoma Press, 2007), 302–303.

51. Overholser *Fort Benton*, 14, 15.

52. Nicolas Point, *Wilderness Kingdom: Indian Life in the Rocky Mountains, 1840–1847: The Journals and Paintings of Nicolas Point, S.J.*, trans. and introduced by Joseph P. Donnelly (Chicago: Loyola University Press 1967), 13.

53. Lawrence B. Palladino, *Indian and White in the Northwest: A History of Catholicity in Montana, 1831 to 1891* (Lancaster, PA: Wickersham Publishing Company, 1922), 185–192; Point, *Wilderness Kingdom* 13 (quotations).

54. Dempsey, *A Blackfoot Winter Count*, 10–12.

55. Office of the Adjutant General, "U.S. Military Applications Egbert M. Clark," *Records of the War Department* (Washington, DC: National Archives and Records Service, 1957), 17–32.

56. Dempsey, *A Blackfoot Winter Count*, 11. Harvey was known by the Blackfeet as Running Wolf. Six Indians were killed and several wounded, as recorded in the winter counts of both the Northern Blackfeet and Southern Piegans. A simple notation in the 1844 winter count translates to "Blackfeet kill a trader. Traders retaliate."

57. Wischmann, *Frontier Diplomats*, 81–84; *Bradley Manuscript*, Contributions to the Historical Society of Montana 10 (Helena: Montana Publishing, 1940), MHS, 3:231.

58. John E. Sunder, *The Fur Trade on the Upper Missouri, 1840–1865* (Norman: University of Oklahoma Press, 1965), 89; T. H. Harvey to Andrew Drips, March 13, 1846, in Chittenden, *The American Fur Trade of the Far West*, 2:687–688n2; Wischmann, *Frontier Diplomats*, 141ff. Harvey later started a rival company, Harvey, Primeau and Company, which competed with the American Fur Company at Fort Lewis, Fort Union, and Fort Pierre: Sunder, *The Fur Trade on the Upper Missouri*, 94.

59. Larpenteur, *Forty Years a Fur Trader on the Upper Missouri*, 68–74, 224–226 (quotations). *Bradley Manuscript*, MHS, 3:241, mentions Culbertson's intervention, which is not noted in Larpenteur. See Wischmann, *Frontier Diplomats*, 121.

60. Larpenteur, *Forty Years a Fur Trader on the Upper Missouri*, 224–226; Thaddeus A. Culbertson, *Journal of an Expedition to the Mauvaises Terres and the Upper Missouri in 1850*, ed. John Francis McDermott, Bureau of American Ethnology, Bulletin 147, Smithsonian Institution (Washington, DC: Government Printing Office, 1952).

61. Culbertson, *Journal of an Expedition*.

CHAPTER 3

Epigraph: D. D. Mitchell to H. R. Schoolcraft, St. Louis, January 26, 1854, in Schoolcraft, *Information respecting the History, Condition, and Prospects of the Indian Tribes*, 685–687. "Mitchell explained further: 'It is true, they killed and scalped a great many of the mountain trappers; but it must be considered, that they were under no treaty obligations, so far as the United States were concerned. They found strangers trespassing on their hunting grounds, and killing off the game upon which they relied for subsistence; any other tribe, or even civilized nation, would have done the same with less provocation.'"

1. LeRoy R. Hafen, *Broken Hand: The Life of Thomas Fizpatrick, Mountain Man, Guide and Indian Agent* (Lincoln: University of Nebraska Press, 1973), 168.

2. Hafen, *The Mountain Men and the Fur Trade of the Far West*, 2:35–39, 2:41–46.

3. Douglas C. McChristian, *Fort Laramie: Military Bastion of the High Plains* (Norman: University of Oklahoma Press, 2008), 51–61; Jackson, *The Piikani Blackfeet*, 168–170.

4. It is estimated that approximately 90,000 people arrived in California in 1849—about half by land and half by sea. Perhaps 50,000 to 60,000 of these were Americans, and the rest were from other countries. See Kevin Starr and Richard J. Orsi, eds., *Rooted in Barbarous Soil: People, Culture, and Community in Gold Rush California* (Berkeley: University of California Press, 2000), 50–61; and Susan Johnson, *Roaring Camp: The Social World of the California Gold Rush* (New York: Norton, 2000).

5. William Medill to Thomas Ewing, June 15, 1849, in the Records of the Office of Indian Affairs, NARA Group 75, as quoted in Francis Paul Prucha, *American Indian Treaties: The History of a Political Anomaly*, 237.

6. Prucha, *Documents of United States Indian Policy*, 84 (quotation); McChristian, *Fort Laramie*, 51–61; Jackson, *The Piikani Blackfeet*, 168–70.

7. Jackson, *The Pikani Blackfeet*, 168–170.

8. Charles J. Kappler, ed. *Indian Affairs: Laws and Treaties*. 2 vols. (Washington, DC: Government Printing Office, 1904), Treaty with the Flatheads (1855), 2:722–725.

9. Stan Hoig, *The Chouteaus: First Family of the Fur Trade* (Santa Fe: University of New Mexico Press, 2008), 191 (quotation); Merrill Mattes, *Great Platte River Road: The Covered Wagon Mainline via Fort Kearny to Fort Laramie* (Lincoln: Nebraska State Historical Society, 1969), 466.

10. *Missouri Republican*, November 9, 1851, as quoted in Prucha, *American Indian Treaties*, 216–217. See Prucha for signatures on the treaty.

11. Overholser, *Fort Benton*, 14, 15. Prince Maximilian of Wied had noted in his diary about his travels in the "Interior of North America, 1832–1834" that the Blackfeet "dwell between the three forks of the Missouri of which the Jefferson River is the most northerly; the Madison River, the western or central; and the Gallatin the most southerly or easterly. They live, however, especially the Piekanns, as far down as Maria River, in the prairies of which they move about, and where all the three tribes sometimes meet to trade with the American Fur Company." Quoted in Thwaites, *Early Western Travels, 1748–1846*, 23:96. See Jackson, *The Piikani Blackfeet*, 169–170.

12. Jackson, *The Piikani Blackfeet*, 169–170; Ewers, *The Blackfeet*, 215–221; also see Institute for the Development of Indian Law, *Treaties and Agreements of the Indian Tribes of the Pacific Northwest* (Washington, DC: Institute for the Development of Indian Law, 1974).

13. Institute for the Development of Indian Law, *Treaties and Agreements of the Indian Tribes of the Pacific Northwest*. The wording of the treaty was "commencing at the mouth of Muscle-shell River; thence up the Missouri River to its source; thence along the main range of the Rocky Mountains, in a southerly direction, to the head-waters of the northern source of the Yellowstone River; thence down the Yellowstone River to the mouth of Twenty-five Yard Creek; thence across to the head-waters of the Muscle-shell River, and thence down the Muscle-shell River to the place of beginning."

14. "Treaty of Fort Laramie, U.S.-Sioux-Cheyenne-Crow-Assinaboines-Arrapahoe-Mandan [*sic*]," September 17, 1851, reproduced in Prucha, *Documents of United States Indian Policy*, 84–85; and Pierre-Jean de Smet, 1851 Map, MHS.

15. Prucha, *American Indian Treaties*, 440–441.

16. Hazard Stevens, *The Life of General Isaac I. Stevens*, 2 vols. (Boston: Houghton Mifflin, 1901), 1:348. More specifically, Steven's journals say that he advised the Indians to give up hostile exchanges with the Crows, Assiniboines, Crees, and Snakes and to stop hostilities with the "Blackfoot, Sans Arc, and Auncepaps bands of Sioux."

17. Stevens, *The Life of General Isaac I. Stevens*, 1:348–363; Jackson, *The Piikani Blackfeet*, 170–171; James Doty to Isaac Stevens, Fort Benton, December 28, 1853, Indian Office Records, quoted in Ewers, *The Blackfeet*, 213 (all subsequent Doty quotations are from this source unless otherwise noted); "The *Fort Benton Journal*, 1854–1856, and the *Fort Sarpy Journal*, 1855–1856," *Contributions to the Historical Society of Montana* 10 (1940), MHS. Stevens and Doty had learned of the continuing warfare between the Blackfeet and Gros Ventres tribes who roamed east of the Rocky Mountains. Stevens, *The Life of General Isaac I. Stevens*, 1:348 (quotation).

18. D. D. Mitchell to H. R. Schoolcraft, St. Louis, January 26, 1854, in Schoolcraft, *Information respecting the History, Condition, and Prospects of the Indian Tribes of the United States*, 685–687.

19. Doty's comments are quoted in Jacob Piatt Dunn, *Massacres of the Mountains: A History of the Indian Wars of the Far West, 1815–1875* (1886) (Mechanicsburg, PA: Stackpole Books, 2002), 514–515. See Stevens, *The Life of General Isaac I. Stevens*. For the Piegan trade with Hudson's Bay Company, see Thwaites, *Original Journals*, 5:183–227.

20. Dunn, *Massacres of the Mountains*, 428–429.

21. "Treaty of Hellgate, U.S.-Flathead-Kootenay-Upper Pend d'Oreilles," July 16, 1855, http://www.cskt.org/documents/gov/helgatetreaty.pdf. The treaty was not ratified by Congress until March 8, 1859.

22. Ibid., for the boundaries; Stevens, *The Life of General Isaac I. Stevens*, 2:86–90.

23. "Treaty with the Blackfeet, U.S.-Blackfeet," October 17, 1855, in Kappler, *Indian Affairs*, 2:736–740. See the treaty for more details on the boundary-defining provisions.

24. Ibid.

25. David A. Walter, ed., "Montana Episodes: The 1855 Blackfeet Treaty Council, a Memoir by Henry A. Kennerly," *Montana The Magazine of Western History* 32, no. 1 (Winter 1982), http://www.jstor.org/stable/4518633. See also Alex Johnston and Andy A. den Otter, *Lethbridge: A Centennial History*, ed. Hugh A. Dempsey (Lethbridge: City of Lethbridge and Whoop-Up Country Chapter, Historical Society of Alberta, 1985), 27. Kennerly found Lame Bull's tribe "at the junction of the Modern Belly and Oldman Rivers." Walter, "Montana Episodes." Names such as "Champagne"/"Champaign" and "Schucette"/"Shucette" were frequently spelled in different ways, and it is not clear in many cases which are the correct spellings.

26. Walter, "Montana Episodes" (quotations); Overholser, *Fort Benton*, 15, 21–22, 288. Little is known of Champagne; but as Kennerly remembered, "later on Baptiste lost his eyesight and died in poverty and misery."

27. President Franklin Pierce nominated Edwin A. C. Hatch of Minnesota Territory to be Indian agent for the Blackfeet and other neighboring tribes on March 1, 1855. Later agents (and their appointment dates except when given in

the main text) were Alfred J. Vaughn, Luther Pease, Henry W. Reed, Gad Ely Upson, George B. Wright (April 10, 1866), Nathaniel Pope (acting, August 25, 1868), Lieutenant William B. Pease (June 11, 1869), M. M. McCauley (September 9, 1870), Jesse Armitage (February 25, 1871), William F. Ensign (July 23, 1872), Richard F. May (November 6, 1873), John S. Wood (October 24, 1874), and John Young (October 20, 1876). See Blackfeet Indian Agency (Montana), "Agents and Appointment Dates," www.familysearch.org/learn/wiki/en/Blackfeet _Indian_Agency_(Montana).

28. Genevieve McBride, *The Bird Tail* (New York: Vantage Press, 1974), 1–21.

29. Palladino, *Indian and White in the Northwest*, 198, 205.

30. Ibid., 200–209. See also McBride, *The Bird Tail*, 9–21.

31. Sharp, *Whoop-Up Country*, 32, citing Captain John Pallisar's journals.

32. Merrill Burlingame and K. Ross Toole, *A History of Montana*, 2 vols. (New York: Lewis Historical Publishing Company, 1957), 124–127. The gold mining camp at Bannack was originally part of the Idaho Territory, after Congress established it on March 4, 1863, with its territorial capital at Lewiston.

33. Merrill G. Burlingame, *The Montana Frontier* (Bozeman, MT: Big Sky Books, Montana State University, 1980), 132–133.

34. Helen McCann White, ed., *Ho! For the Gold Fields: Northern Overland Wagon Trains of the 1860s* (St. Paul: Minnesota Historical Society, 1966).

35. *Bradley Manuscript*, 3:252. See generally White, *Ho! For the Gold Fields*.

36. Jeffrey Safford, *The Mechanics of Optimism: Mining Companies, Technology, and the Hot Spring Gold Rush, Montana Territory, 1864–1868* (Boulder: University Press of Colorado, 2004), 36–37; "The County Election," *Montana Post*, September 16, 1865.

37. Gad Upson to D. N. Cooley, October 2, 1865, in *Report of the Commissioner of Indian Affairs for the Year 1865* (Washington, DC: Government Printing Office, 1865), 510–515 (quotations on 511, 515).

38. Statutes at Large, 38th Cong., 2nd Sess., March 3, 1865, 559.

39. Ibid.

40. *Report of the Commissioner of Indian Affairs for the Year 1865*, 250–252.

41. Gad Upson to William P. Dole, July 12, 1865, in ibid., 250.

42. Lepley, *Blackfoot Fur Trade*, 227, 241.

43. *Montana Post*, May 28, 1865.

44. Heitman, *Historical Register and Dictionary of the United States Army*, 1:856. In some publications, including Heitman's, Sackett's surname is listed as "Sacket," but that is not the preferred spelling. For a history of the Sackett family, see Charles H. Weygant, *The Sacketts of America: Their Ancestors and Descendants, 1630–1907* (Newburgh, NY: published by the Author, 1907).

45. Burlingame, *The Montana Frontier*, 117–122; Rodger Huckabee, "Camp Cooke: Montana Territory's Forgotten First U.S. Army Post," *Montana The Magazine of Western History* 62, no. 4 (Winter 2012), 60–67.

CHAPTER 4

Epigraph 1: Sherman to Meagher, February 16, 1866, Terr. 2, Montana Territorial Papers, MHS.

Epigraph 2: Sherman to Meagher, May 9, 1866, Terr. 2, Montana Territorial Papers, MHS.

1. Wylie, *The Irish General*, 221–247.

2. *Montana Post,* January 17, 1866; Meagher to Wheaton, October 20, 1865, State Department Territorial Papers, Montana, NARA—M 356, Roll 1. On Meagher's aspirations at the time, see Meagher to Seward, December 14, 1865, State Department Territorial Papers, Montana, NARA, M 356, Roll 1.

3. Gad Upson to William Dole, Fort Benton, July 12, 1865; William Dole to Gad Upson, Washington, DC, March 24, 1865, in *Report of the Commissioner of Indian Affairs for the Year 1865*, 250–252.

4. Wylie, *The Irish General,* 221–247; Thomas Meagher to Father de Smet, Virginia City, December 15, 1865, in Thomas Francis Meagher, "A Journey to Benton," *Montana The Magazine of History* 1, no. 4 (October 1951): 46–49, 48–49nn3–6, http://www.jstor.org/stable/4515758. Also with the group were George J. Wood, sheriff of Edgerton County, where Last Chance Gulch and Helena were located; and Cornelius Hedges, a young lawyer from Helena.

5. Palladino, *Indian and White in the Northwest*, 200–209.

6. James Hamilton, *From Wilderness to Statehood: A History of Montana, 1805–1900* (1907), 2nd ed., ed. Merrill Burlingame, (Portland: Binfords & Mort, 1957), 181; "The Wagon Road to Benton," *Montana Radiator,* January 27, 1866 (quotations); Thomas Meagher to Father de Smet, December 15, 1865, in Meagher, "A Journey to Benton," 46–48, 48–49nn3–6.

7. The Indians were to receive $5,000 annually for twenty years with the money to be expended by the United States for livestock and farm implements and other goods and services for the Indians' benefit. Hamilton, *From Wilderness to Statehood*, 183.

8. The western boundary was the Continental Divide and the eastern boundary was the mouth of the Milk River. "Treaty between the United States and the Blackfoot Nation of Indians, etc., November 16, 1865," in Kappler, *Indian Affairs*, 4:1133–1137; Hamilton, *From Wilderness to Statehood*, 182–183. The *Montana Post* reported on December 9, 1865: "The interpreters, and other whites having influence among the natives" were seated at the negotiation.

9. "Treaty between the United States and Blackfoot Nation of Indians, November 16th 1865," handwritten copy from the files of the Overholser Archives in Fort Benton. The treaty was never ratified. *Montana Post*, December 9, 1865; Hamilton, *From Wilderness to Statehood*, 181. French names were frequently spelled in different ways.

10. While the Blackfeet "Nation" was fully represented, the "tribes" of the Bloods and Blackfeet proper were not. Only a single chief representing the

Blackfeet tribe attended the negotiations, and the Bloods had no representatives at all. The reason was that the unrepresented tribes had already retreated across the border to the British territory. Meagher to Cooley, Virginia City, December 14, 1865, in *Report of the Commissioner of Indian Affairs for the Year 1866*, 196. The Bloods, who were accused of murdering eleven whites in April, had departed immediately for the border and had not been in the territory since. When Upson had dispatched messengers to try to bring in the Blackfeet from Canada, a tribe of Kootenai Indians turned them back. Hamilton, *From Wilderness to Statehood*, 183.

11. *Report of the Commissioner of Indian Affairs for the Year 1865*, 30–31. The eastern Blackfeet agent oversaw the Gros Ventres and various tribes of Blackfeet, including Piegans, Bloods, and Blackfeet proper; the western Flathead agent supervised the Flatheads, Pend d'Oreilles, and Kootenais. The agents were required to report to the governor regularly, a duty that they sometimes chose to ignore. The estimated numbers of Indians of various tribes were as follow: Gros Ventres of the Mountains, about 1,800; various tribes of Blackfeet Indians: about 1,870 Piegans, 2,150 Bloods, and 2,450 Blackfeet proper; and a western group with about 550 Flatheads, 900 Pend d'Oreilles, and 270 Kootenais. *Report of the Commissioner of Indian Affairs for the Year 1866*, 197.

12. Hamilton, *From Wilderness to Statehood*, 183; Gad Upson to Cooley, April 6, 1866, in *Report of the Commissioner of Indian Affairs for the Year 1866*, 197; Safford, *The Mechanics of Optimism*, 44.

13. Hiram Upham to Gad Upson, January 9 and February 2, 1865, in *Report of the Commissioner of Indian Affairs for the Year 1866*, 197–199.

14. "Letter from Fort Benton: Indians on the War Path—Shocking Murders—Heavy Robberies of Stock—Determination on the Part of the Settlers to Kill the Last Indian," *Montana Post*, February 3, 1866. H. A. Kennedy, Joseph Hill, George Steele, J. J. Healy, William T. Hamilton, and A. B. Hamilton signed the letter. Hamilton was then the agent of the *Montana Post* in Fort Benton. For the vigilante activities around Bannack and Virginia City, see Mark C. Dillon, *The Vigilantes of Montana, 1863–1870: Gold, Guns and Gallows* (Logan: Utah State University Press, 2013).

15. *Report of the Commissioner of Indian Affairs for the Year 1866*, 197.

16. Wylie, *The Irish General*, 126–134 (quotations).

17. Sherman to Meagher, February 16, 1866, Terr. 2, Montana Territorial Papers, MHS. The letter was addressed to Meagher as "Secretary of Montana," even though he was acting governor at the time.

18. Ibid. See also Sherman to Grant, June 10, 1867, in John Simon, ed., *The Papers of Ulysses S. Grant*, 32 vols. (Carbondale: Southern Illinois University Press, 1967–2012), 17:174.

19. Burlingame, *The Montana Frontier*, 117–122; Huckabee, "Camp Cooke," 60–67.

20. There was a small trading post settlement at the mouth of the Musselshell River, eighty miles downstream. Kim Allen Scott, ed., *Splendid on a Large Scale:*

The Writings of Hans Peter Gyllembourg Koch, Montana Territory, 1869–1874 (Helena: Bedrock Editions & Drumlummon, 2010), 60–67, 325n6.

21. Reports and Circulars, 7/11/1866–3/31/1870, Camp Cooke, Montana Territory, Record Group 393, National Archives, Washington; Huckabee, "Camp Cooke."

22. Huckabee, "Camp Cooke."

23. "L. M. Brown's Account," in White, *Ho! For the Gold Fields*, 189–190. According to Brown's assessment, "The Milk River is the largest and most important northerly branch of the Missouri, and for long distance lies almost parallel with the Missouri about one hundred miles north of the latter." See also accounts of the Fisk, Holmes, and Davy wagon trains.

24. Martin F. Hogan to Andrew O'Connell, July 21, 1866, Martin Hogan Papers; D. C. Donoghue-Montgomery Collection, SC 864, MHS.

25. Special Orders 46 and Special Orders 40, December 1, 1866, in Special Orders 7/11/1866–3/11/1870, Camp Cooke, Montana Territory, Group 393, NARA.

26. *Montana Post*, December 1, 1866.

27. *Montana Post*, December 29, 1866. Sheriff William Hamilton wrote: "The soldiers are gentlemen of the first order and no lovers of Indians and would sooner fight than eat. However, they might as well be in New York as where they were . . . they are no account to the citizens where they are." Mortuary Record of Internments in National Cemetery at Camp Cooke, MT T., January 1, 1868, Camp Cooke files, NARA. Three other bodies of soldiers who died in 1866 are recorded, two with death dates of December 17 and one with a death date of December 27.

28. *Montana Post*, August 18, 1866.

29. Upham to Cooley, July 25, 1866, in *Report of the Commissioner of Indian Affairs for the Year 1866*, 202–203.

30. G. B. Wright to G. C. Smith, July 5, 1867, in *Report of the Commissioner of Indian Affairs for the Year 1867*, 253–259.

31. Smith was ordained in 1869 and was the pastor of the Baptist Church in Frankfort, Kentucky. He also became a temperance advocate and was the candidate of the National Prohibition Party in 1876, getting 9,522 votes in the presidential election of that year.

32. "Miscellaneous Items," *Montana Post*, October 6, 1866; Meagher to Barlow, October 26, 1866, in Samuel Latham Mitchell Barlow Collection, Huntington Library and Archives, San Marino, California.

33. "The Telegraph between Great Salt Lake and Virginia City Is Finished! Montana Forms a Part of the Civilized World! Citizens! Hang Your Banners on the Outer Walls!" *Montana Post*, November 3, 1866 (quotation); "Miscellaneous Items," *Montana Post*, October 6, 1866; Robert G. Athearn, *Thomas Francis Meagher: An Irish Revolutionary in America* (Boulder: University Press of Colorado, 1949), 155; petition to President Andrew Johnson from Anson L. Potter et al., August 1866, SC 309, MHS; "Miscellaneous Items," *Montana Post*, October

13, 1866; *House Journal*, 38th Cong., 1st Sess., December 10, 1863, and April 8, May 6, and May 10, 1864, http://memory.loc.gov/ammem/amlaw/lwhj.html; *House Journal*, 38th Cong., 1st Sess., May 11, and May 13, 1864. While Bruce did obtain the presidential nomination as secretary, the Senate Committee on Territories "reported adversely thereon." *Senate Executive Journal*, 39th Cong., 2nd Sess., February 23, 1867, http://memory.loc.gov/ammem/amlaw/lwej.html; *Senate Executive Journal*, 40th Cong., 1st Sess., March 21, 1867, http://memory .loc.gov/ammem/amlaw/lwej.html. On March 1 the Senate refused to "advise and consent" to Bruce's nomination and on March 21 President Andrew Johnson nominated James Tufts to replace Meagher "in the place of John P. Bruce, rejected." But Tufts was on the East Coast, and it would take him a long time to get to Montana.

34. *Montana Post*, November 3, 1866. To the military stationed in Montana, the telegraph meant that the higher commands to the east and the top generals, Sheridan and Sherman, could be involved in the management of military maneuvers and that the citizens also had access to timely communication with the government in the East.

35. Susan Doyle, ed., *Journeys to the Land of Gold: Emigrant Diaries from the Bozeman Trail, 1863–1886* (Helena: Montana Historical Society Press, 2000), 1:7–8.

36. "Indian Affairs," *Helena Herald*, January 17, 1867.

37. *Montana Post*, November 3, 1866.

38. Nathaniel Coates Kinney to His Excellency the Governor of Montana, February 8, 1867 (marked as "recd Jan. 7, 1867"), MHS. Kinney warned that the Crows would attack if the obligations of the Fort Union treaty were not met.

39. Simon, *The Papers of Ulysses S. Grant*, 17:54.

40. Sherman to Smith, April 2, 1867, Territorial Governor File, MHS; Sherman to Smith, April 4, 1867, Territorial Governor File, MHS. Sherman had some reason to be generally skeptical of the overall severity of the Indian threat, because many of the reports of Indian depredations in the West had proved to be highly exaggerated. Among the newspaper articles to reach Sherman's desk, for example, was one that ran in the *Yankton Union and Dakotaian* on March 20, 1867, reporting the "massacre" of the entire garrison at Fort Buford at the confluence of the Missouri and Yellowstone Rivers. Soon that report was completely discredited. A few weeks later the *Union and Dakotaian* corrected another false report: the story circulated by the *Council Bluffs Nonpareil* that Indians had scalped and killed the entire crew and all passengers on the steamboat *Miner* was also untrue. "Reported Massacre of the Garrison at Fort Buford," *Union and Dakotaian*, March 20, 1867; "Fort Buford No. 2—Council Bluffs in the 'Massacre' Business," *Union and Dakotaian*, May 13, 1867.

41. "Shall We Aid or Abandon," *Montana Post*, April 6, 1867 (Bozeman quotation); *Montana Post*, April 13, 1867 (Blake quotation). Blake then assailed members of the Montana Democratic Party and John Bruce, editor of the rival *Montana Democrat*, for quibbling about political matters in the presence of the

Indian threat: "There is a most surprising lethargy exhibited in this matter, be-side which our local political issues are minor considerations." See the articles "Turn Out! Turn Out!" and "The War Meeting."

42. Grace Raymond Hebard and E. A. Brininstool, *The Bozeman Trail: Historical Accounts of the Blazing of the Overland Routes into the Northwest and the Fights with Red Cloud's Warriors*, vol. 1 (Lincoln: University of Nebraska Press, 1922), statement on April 1, 1896, by George Reed "Crow" Davis, 223, 224.

43. "Benton Items," *Montana Post*, May 16, 1868.

44. "News About Towne—Murder of Little Dog and His Son," *Montana Post*, June 9, 1866.

45. "Indian Affairs," *Montana Post*, July 20, 1867.

46. Ibid.

47. Sherman to Meagher, May 3, 1867, Territorial Governor File, MHS; Townsend to Hosmer, in the *Montana Post*, May 4, 1867;

Sherman to Castner, May 6, 1867, Territorial Governor File, MHS; Sherman to Hosmer, May 7, 1867, Territorial Governor File, MHS; Sherman to Meagher, May 7, 1867, Territorial Governor File, MHS; Sherman to Meagher, May 9, 1867, Territorial Governor File, MHS.

48. Sherman to Meagher, May 9, 1867, Territorial Governor File, MHS. The arms finally did arrive, but not until July. They were offloaded at Camp Cooke, two hundred hard-travel land miles away from the conflict.

49. Sherman to Lewis, May 29, 1867, Territorial Governor File, MH; "Gone to the Front," *Montana Post*, May 18, 1867; *Report to Accompany Bill S. 519*, 41st Cong, 2nd Sess., Report No. 31, 2.

50. *Report to Accompany Bill S. 519*, 41st Cong, 2nd Sess., Report No. 31, 1 (quotations: also cited in *Report to Accompany H. Res. 23* below); Davis Willson to "Folks at Home," May 29, 1867, 1407, Willson Collection, Montana State University Special Collections; *Report to Accompany H. Res. 23*, 42nd Cong., 2nd Sess., Report No. 82, 13, 25–27.

51. *Report to Accompany Bill S. 519*, 41st Cong., 2nd Sess., Report No. 31, 2–3. Lewis also testified before Congress that he had received the May 24 dispatch from Sherman but had replied that he could not raise troops. Lewis did not receive Major William Clinton's response to his request for troops until after he had returned to Salt Lake City. Simon, *The Papers of Ulysses S. Grant*, 17:104–107. Grant forwarded Stanton several reports by military officers in the West, most importantly, the repeated dispatches from the governor of Texas and its citizens; Major William Clinton to Acting Governor Thomas Francis Meagher, Letter, April 17, 1867, Letters Sent 8/1866–12/1869, Camp Cooke Files, Montana Territory, Group 393, National Archives, Washington, DC; "Action of the Executive," *Montana Post*, April 13, 1867. Grant also said: "In substance this same reply was made to Gn. Meaghr's first dispatch."

52. *Virginia City Tri-Weekly Post* of May 30, 1867, cited in Leland J. Hanchett Jr., *Montana's Benton Road* (Wolf Creek, MT: Pine Rim Publishing, 2008), 78.

53. Wylie, *The Irish General*, 294.

54. Simon, *The Papers of Ulysses S. Grant*, 17:159–160. Note that Sherman's earlier authorization to Major Lewis was for three months, while his report to Grant said that it was two months.

55. *Report upon the Montana Indian War Claims of 1867*, 41st Cong., 3rd Sess., H. Ex. Doc. No. 98, 8. This view was shared by Inspector General James A. Hardie, who investigated the matter four years later and said: "During the month of May, and especially toward its close, the correspondence between the governor, the Lieutenant General, and the War Department . . . was assumed to exhibit the facts of the recognition on the part of the United States of the call for militia and of an engagement to pay the necessary expenses incurred therefor."

56. Robert G. Athearn, *William Tecumseh Sherman and the Settlement of the West* (Norman: University of Oklahoma Press, 1956), 163–164; circular issued by Sherman, Headquarters Military Division of the Missouri, St. Louis, June 21, 1867, Territorial Governor File, MHS.

57. Simon, *The Papers of Ulysses S. Grant*, 17:173–174, 179; *Report to Accompany Bill S. 519*, 41st Cong., 2nd Sess., Report No. 31, 2. A few years later, when bills for services and supplies were submitted by Montana citizens, Sherman categorically denied that he had ever authorized troops and blamed the entire fiasco on Meagher, clearly stating that when Meagher assembled the Montana troops: "He had no authority from me, but such authority was emphatically withheld." Wylie, *The Irish General*, 293–297 (Sherman and Grant quotations).

58. Davis Willson to "Folks at Home," May 29, 1867, 1407, Willson Collection, MSU Special Collections.

59. Simon, *The Papers of Ulysses S. Grant*, 17:173–174, 179.

60. Ibid., 176–177.

61. Wylie, *The Irish General*, 293–297, 11; Meagher to Barlow, June 15, 1867, Huntington Library, San Marino, California.

62. Phillips, *Forty Years on the Frontier*, 2:64; Thomas Leforge and Thomas Marquis, *Memoirs of a White Crow Indian* (1928) (Lincoln: University of Nebraska Press, 1974), 17; Francis Xavier Kuppens, "Thomas Francis Meagher, Montana Pioneer," *Mid-America: An Historical Review* 14, no. 3 (1931–1932): 138–139.

63. Thomas Meagher to Thomas Meagher, Sr., June 15, 1867, National Library of Ireland.

64. Wylie, *The Irish General*, 304–331.

CHAPTER 5

Epigraph: Simon, *The Papers of Ulysses S. Grant*, 17:22.

1. William H. Armstrong, *Warrior in Two Camps: Ely S. Parker, Union General and Seneca Chief* (Syracuse, NY: Syracuse University Press, 1978), 110.

2. Ibid., ix–x, 108–111.

3. Ibid., 109–121 (quotation on 113).

4. Ibid., 114. The tribes were the Creeks, Choctaws, Chickasaws, Cherokees, Seminoles, Osages, Senecas, Shawnees, Quapaws, Wyandottes, Wichitas, and Comanches.

5. Ely Parker to Charles E. Mix, June 20, 1866, RG 107, NARA; Ely Parker to Louis Bogy, December 13 and 22, 1866, Office of Indian Affairs Letters Received, RC75, NARA; Parker to N. H. Parker, June 6, 1866, typed copy in Ely S. Parker Papers, Buffalo and Erie County Historical Society, Buffalo, New York, quoted in Armstrong, *Warrior in Two Camps*, 209n16.

6. Armstrong, *Warrior in Two Camps*, 109–121.

7. Parker had appended detailed recommendations later printed in House Miscellaneous Documents, 39th Cong., 2nd Sess., H. Ex. Doc. 37, 1–8. On the Fetterman massacre, see Nathaniel Coates Kinney to His Excellency the Governor of Montana, February 8, 1867 (marked as "recd Jan. 7, 1867"), Territorial Governor Papers, MHS.

8. Simon, *The Papers of Ulysses S. Grant*, 17:173–181 (quotations); letter from Sherman to the Secretary of the Interior, communicating in compliance with a resolution of the Senate of the 8th Instant, information touching the origin and progress of Indian hostilities on the frontier, 40th Cong., 1st Sess., S. Ex. Doc. 13, 1867, serial 1279, 3 (Taylor's recommendations on 1–6; Sherman's statement on 121); Robert M. Utley, *Frontier Regulars: The United States Army and the Indian, 1866–1891*, Bison Books edition (Lincoln: University of Nebraska Press, 1984), 130–132, 139; Annual Report of the Secretary of War, 40th Cong., 1st Sess., 1868, H. Ex. Doc. 1, serial 1367, 271–272; and Athearn, *William Tecumseh Sherman*, 226–230.

9. Simon, *The Papers of Ulysses S. Grant*, 17:22, 23.

10. Ibid., 18:257–258. Sherman had his own beliefs on how to integrate with the Indians. One of the things he wanted to try was using Indians as soldiers. Report of Lieutenant General Sherman, Headquarters Military Division of the Missouri, St. Louis, Mo., October 1, 1867, addressed to Major George K. Leet, Assistant Adjutant General, Headquarters of the Army, Washington, DC, *Annual Report of the Secretary of War to Congress, 1867*, Report of General Sherman, Division of the Missouri (Ft. Leavenworth: Combined Arms Research Library, KSD00998 roll no. 3, 1867), 33.

11. Other members of the Peace Commission, besides Sherman, were Major General William S. Harney (retired), who had taken part in earlier conflicts with the Cheyenne and Sioux along the Platte River; Brigadier General Alfred H. Terry, commander of the Military Department of Dakota; Senator John B. Henderson of Missouri, chair of the Senate Indian Appropriations Committee, who had introduced the bill that created the Peace Commission; Colonel Samuel F. Tappan, formerly of the First Colorado Volunteer Cavalry and a peace advocate who had led the U.S. Army's investigation of the Sand Creek massacre; and Major General John B. Sanborn, formerly commander of the Upper Arkansas

District, who had previously helped to negotiate the Little Arkansas Treaty of 1865. Major General Christopher C. Augur, commander of the Military Department of the Platte, replaced Sherman after he was recalled, as a temporary appointment. Stan Hoig, *The Battle of the Washita: The Sheridan-Custer Indian Campaign of 1867–69* (Lincoln: University of Nebraska Press, 1980); Jerome A. Greene, *Washita: The U.S. Army and the Southern Cheyennes*, Campaigns and Commanders Series, vol. 3 (Norman: University of Oklahoma Press, 2004); Simon, *The Papers of Ulysses S. Grant*, 17:257.

12. Simon, *The Papers of Ulysses S. Grant*, 17:241.

13. Letter of the Secretary of War, 41st Cong., 3rd Sess., S. Ex. Doc. No. 8, December 21, 1870, report of Holabird from Department of Dakota, Office Chief Quartermaster, Saint Paul, Minn., October 15, 1869 (quotation). Holabird also said: "Had the troops at Camp Cooke been placed at Benton, they also would have been of service." The worst stretch of that portion of the Missouri was known as Dauphin rapids.

14. Alfred Terry, Brevet Major General Commanding, to W. A. Nichols, Assistant Adjutant General, St. Paul, September 27, 1867, in *Annual Report of the Secretary of War to Congress, 1867* (all subsequent Terry quotations are from this source unless otherwise noted).

15. Once in the Gallatin Valley, Terry could see that its broad expanse encompassed the water courses of the Madison, Jefferson, and Gallatin Rivers, all of which came together in one spot to form the headwaters of the Missouri. Terry had been impressed that "great alarm was honestly felt by the people of this valley" and was "satisfied many of them left their farms untilled, and repaired to the towns or places of safety," while "many others made preparations for leaving their homes, but, as I have said before, nothing which happened within the Territory justified this alarm, and but for occurrences elsewhere it would not have been felt."

16. "Headquarters Military Division of the Missouri," St. Louis, Mo., October 1, 1867, in *Annual Report of the Secretary of War to Congress, 1867.*

17. Terry reported: "On several occasions boats have been fired into by hostile Indians, one man having been killed and a few wounded; but navigation has not been materially interfered with." Alfred Terry, Brevet Major General Commanding, to W. A. Nichols, Assistant Adjutant General, St. Paul, September 27, 1867, in *Annual Report of the Secretary of War to Congress, 1867.*

18. Huckabee, "Camp Cooke"; Alfred Terry, Brevet Major General Commanding, to W. A. Nichols, Assistant Adjutant General, St. Paul, September 27, 1867, in *Annual Report of the Secretary of War to Congress, 1867.* Terry told Sherman that a site was under investigation for "a new post not yet named, on the Yellowstone river, near the mouth of Twenty-five-mile creek, Montana Territory, about thirty miles east of Gallatin City, commanded by Captain R. S. LaMotte, thirteenth infantry, and garrisoned by companies D, F, and G, of the same regiment." Alfred Terry, Brevet Major General Commanding, to W. A.

Nichols, Assistant Adjutant General, St. Paul, September 27, 1867. Twenty-Five-Mile Creek was actually called Twenty-Five-Yard Creek, which today is the Shields River.

19. Simon, *The Papers of Ulysses S. Grant*, 17:150–151; Wylie, *The Irish General*, 299–301; Henry Blake to Henry Wilson, October 15, 1867, in Simon, *The Papers of Ulysses S. Grant*, 18:150–151 (quotations). Congress took until March 1873 to approve payment of $513,343 with a joint resolution of the House and Senate. See *Report to Accompany Bill S. 519*, 41st Cong, 2nd Sess., Report No. 31, 4.

20. "Report of Lieutenant General Sherman, Headquarters Military Division of the Missouri," St. Louis, October 1, 1867, addressed to Major George K. Leet, Assistant Adjutant General, Headquarters of the Army, Washington, DC, in *Annual Report of the Secretary of War to Congress, 1867* (KSD00998 roll no. 3: 1867, 33).

21. Ibid.

22. As reported: "The troops did not get into barracks until late in the fall and after the weather became quite cold. The officers were somewhat late in getting into their quarters. None of the buildings occupied were completed further than to afford habitable shelter. Early in the spring of 1868 the building of the post was resumed, and during the season the walls of the remaining buildings at the post were put up and roofed."

23. "Surgeons Report 1870," *Reports and Circulars*, 7/11/1866–3/31/1870, Camp Cooke, Montana Territory, Record Group 393, 92–95, National Archives, Washington, DC.

24. "Information Furnished by Surgeon P. C. Davis and Assistant Surgeon Clarence Ewen, United States Army," *Circular No. 4* (Washington, DC: War Department, Surgeon General's Office, December 5, 1870); "A Report on Barracks and Hospitals, with Descriptions of Military Posts" (Washington, DC: Government Printing Office, 1870).

25. Letter of the Secretary of War, 41st Cong., 3rd Sess., S. Ex. Doc. No. 8, December 21, 1870, Report of S. B. Holabird from Department of Dakota, Office Chief Quartermaster, Saint Paul, Minn., October 15, 1869.

26. "Indian Massacre," *Montana Post*, February 15, 1868, in Hanchett, *Montana's Benton Road*, 79–80.

27. "The Indians—Protection for the Road," *Montana Post*, February 15, 1868, in ibid., 80.

28. "Appeal for Arms," *Montana Post*, February 22, 1868, in ibid., 80–81. Over a hundred "citizens of Trinity Gulch and Little Prickly Pear Valley" petitioned the governor of Montana for "arms and ammunition."

29. "Another Indian Murder—The Blackfoot Hostile," *Montana Post*, May 2, 1868, in ibid., 80–81.

30. "Indians Captured," *Weekly Montana Democrat*, May 29, 1868, in ibid., 82–83. The article was apparently copied from an article appearing in the *Montana Post*.

31. G. B. Wright to G. C. Smith, July 1, 1868, in *Annual Report of the Commissioner of Indian Affairs for the Year 1868.*

32. Ibid. (quotations); Robert Vaughn, *Then and Now; or, Thirty-Six Years in the Rockies, 1864–1900* (1900) (Helena: Farcountry Press, 2001), 80–81; Hanchett, *Montana's Benton Road*, 82–83.

33. G. B. Wright to N. G. Taylor, Fort Benton, June 11, 1868; G. B. Wright to N. G. Taylor, Fort Benton, June 15, 1868; N. G. Taylor to Orville Browning, Washington, DC, June 30, 1868; Orville Browning to William Seward, Washington, DC, July 2, 1868; State Department Territorial Papers, Montana, 1864–1872, microfilm roll M356–1, NARA. On June 30 Taylor wrote Browning, advising that "I have to say that, on the 3rd. inst., I addressed a communication to the Governor, directing him to at once pay over to Agent Wright the residue remaining in his hands of the funds remitted to him, per requisition issued on the 23rd of January last." Taylor reported that "no reply has been received" and forwarded Wright's letter of June 11.

34. Rodger D. Touchie, *Bear Child: The Life and Times of Jerry Potts* (Victoria and Vancouver: Heritage House Publishing Company, 2005), 98; Hugh A. Dempsey, *Firewater: The Impact of the Whisky Trade on the Blackfoot Nations* (Calgary: Fifth House, (2002), 27–28.

35. On August 7, 1868, Taylor sent Wright's written retraction to Browning. On July 2 Browning had forwarded Wright's original complaint to Seward for action. On August 10 Browning sent Seward a letter forwarding Wright's retraction of June 15, 1868. State Department Territorial Papers, Montana, 1864–1872, microfilm roll M356–1, NARA.

36. Ibid. (quotation); Browning to Seward, July 2, 1868; N. G. Taylor to Orville Browning, Washington, DC, April 18, 1868, in *Report of the Commissioner of Indian Affairs for the Year 1868* (Washington, DC: Government Printing Office, 1868), 223–224. It seems that the letter to Smith from the State Department had been sent to Montana, but Smith was not there. Instead the letter reached him when he was in Washington, DC.

37. George B. Wright, "Annual Report," Fort Benton, July 1, 1868, in *Report of the Commissioner of Indian Affairs for the Year 1868*, 203–208.

38. Green Clay Smith, "Proclamation," March 25, 1868, State Department Territorial Papers, Montana, 1864–1872, microfilm roll M356, NARA.

39. Ulysses Grant to Edwin Stanton, Washington, DC, March 10, 1868, in Simon, *The Papers of Ulysses S. Grant*, 18:187–188.

40. Officially this was the "Treaty with the Sioux—Brulé, Oglala, Miniconjou, Yanktonai, Hunkpapa, Blackfeet, Cuthead, Two Kettle, Sans Arcs, and Santee—and Arapaho" (1868): Kappler, *Indian Affairs*, 2:998–1007.

41. W. J. Cullen to N. G. Taylor, Fort Benton, September 2, 1868, in *Report of the Commissioner of Indian Affairs for the Year 1868*, 221–222.

42. Ibid.

43. Kennerly is quoted in Lepley, *Blackfoot Fur Trade*, 250. The newspapers had accounts of the treaty actually happening. Cullen had signed it as commissioner on the part of the United States, in the presence of George B. Wright, Blackfeet Indian agent, former Indian agent Alfred J. Vaughn, the enigmatic Malcolm Clarke, Father Camillus Imoda, S.J., and 2nd Lieutenant Thomas Newman of the 13th Infantry. Others on hand were the ever-present Alexander Culbertson (apparently as a U.S. interpreter this time) and the ever-opportunistic Baptiste Schampin (Champagne/Champaign), who like Clarke had been given a full square mile (640 acres) of land under the terms of the unratified 1865 treaty. The treaty document showed that over twenty "chiefs, headmen and delegates of the . . . nation and tribes of Indians parties to this treaty" made their marks.

44. Pratt to McGinnis, June 7, 1869, Fort Shaw Files, NARA. Cullen was concerned about this attack on Mountain Chief because it was something, he said, "I know to be true." W. J. Cullen to N. G. Taylor, Fort Benton, September 2, 1868, in *Report of the Commissioner of Indian Affairs for the Year 1868*, 221–222; Nathaniel Pope to N. G. Taylor, October 9, 1868, in *Report of the Commissioner of Indian Affairs for the Year 1868*.

45. W. J. Cullen to N. G. Taylor, Fort Benton, September 2, 1868, in *Report of the Commissioner of Indian Affairs for the Year 1868*, 222.

46. W. J. Cullen to N. G. Taylor, Helena, August 22, 1868; W. J. Cullen to N. G. Taylor, Fort Benton, September 2, 1868; N. G. Taylor to Orville Browning, Washington, DC, April 18, 1868, in *Report of the Commissioner of Indian Affairs for the Year 1868*, 216–224.

47. *Report of the Commissioner of Indian Affairs for the Year 1868*, 216–224.

48. W. J. Cullen to N. G. Taylor, Washington, DC, December 4, 1868, in *Report of the Commissioner of Indian Affairs for the Year 1868*, 375. "It is not necessary that I should say anything to you in answer to the oft-repeated assertion that the efforts of the Indian peace commission have proven a failure, for you know that as far as the commission itself is concerned."

49. Kappler, *Indian Affairs*, 4:1138–1142. The treaty was with the Gros Ventres tribe on July 13, 1868, and the Blackfeet tribe on September 1, 1868. In article 3, the treaty outlined the boundaries: "commencing at a point where the parallel of forty-eight degrees North latitude intersects the dividing ridge of the main chain of the Rocky Mountains, thence in an easterly direction to the nearest source of the Teton River—thence down said river to its junction with the Marias River—thence down the Marias to its junction with the Missouri River— thence down the Missouri River to the mouth of Milk River—thence due south to the forty-ninth parallel of North latitude—thence west on said parallel to the main range of the Rocky Mountains—thence southerly along said Range to the place of beginning."

50. Shirley C. Ashby became one of the leading financiers and citizens of early-day Helena when he moved there in 1870 after his employment in the

Indian trade with I. G. Baker and Bros. of Fort Benton. He engaged in the real estate and insurance business until 1889, when he opened a store selling agricultural implements, wagons, and carriages. Alva Josiah Noyes, *In the Land of Chinook: or, the Story of Blaine County* (Berkeley: University of California Libraries, 1917); "Story as Told by Col. S. C. Ashby," SC 283, MHS (quotations).

51. "Treaty between the United States and Blackfoot Nation of Indians, November 16th 1865," handwritten copy from the files of the Overholser Archives in Fort Benton. Ashby said that another license was "issued to I. G. Baker and Co., to trade at the mouth of People's creek on the Milk River (Ft. Browning), where Chas. W. Price, could trade with the Grosventres and Assiniboines," "about a mile or two from where the town is at present." "Story as Told by Col. S. C. Ashby," SC 283, MHS.

52. Lepley, *Blackfoot Fur Trade*, 251.

53. Ibid.

54. George Stull to G. L. Anderson, Fort Benton, September 30, 1868. Fort Shaw Files, NARA.

CHAPTER 6

Epigraph: Philip Sheridan Files, LC.

1. Grant's inaugural address, March 4, 1869, in Davis Lott, ed., *The Presidents Speak: Inaugural Addresses of the Presidents of the United States, from George Washington to George W. Bush*, 4th ed. (Los Angeles: Olive Grove Publishing, 2002).

2. Ulysses S. Grant, *State of the Union Addresses* (Whitefish, MT: Kessinger Publishing, 2004), 14–15. Grant's address was delivered to Congress on December 6, 1869. Citing their reputation for "opposition to all strife, violence, and war," he said the Quakers "are generally noted for their strict integrity and fair dealings."

3. Major R. S. Lamotte to Captain J. T. McGinniss, April 18, 1869; Notation of Endorsement of April 25, 1869 re: response by McGinniss, Fort Shaw Files, NARA. LaMotte made a military gaffe when he suggested that troops should be sent from Fort Shaw. The angry response came on April 25 as a stern rebuke transmitted by the regimental adjutant, Major J. T. McGinness: "Capt. LaMotte arrogated to himself powers which do not belong to his position" for "presuming to dictate to his Commanding Officer where reinforcements shall be taken from." See Ulysses Grant McAlexander, *History of the Thirteenth Regiment United States Infantry*, ed. Frank D. Gunn (N.p.: Regimental Press, 1905), for ranks of LaMotte and McGinniss.

4. Glenn Tucker, *Hancock the Superb* (New York: Bobbs-Merrill, 1960), 246–247. In July 1864, after General George B. McClellan wrote to his wife that "Hancock was superb today," the sobriquet "Superb" stuck with him throughout the war (ibid., 89).

5. David M. Jordan, *Winfield Scott Hancock: A Soldier's Life* (Bloomfield: Indiana University Press, 1988), 179–180.

6. Albert G. Brackett Diaries, June 1 to June 28, 1869, SC 458, MHS (all subsequent Brackett quotations are from this source unless otherwise noted).

7. Ibid.

8. Story told by A. J. Noyes, Shirley Carter Ashby Papers, 1867–1889, SC 283, MHS; "General Reconnaissance in the Department of Dakota"; General Order No. 62; General Field Orders No. 2, July 5, 1869, letter, O. D. Greene, Assistant Adjutant General, NARA.

9. De Trobriand wrote to his daughter Lina regarding her new baby boy, who was to be named Regis. He said that it was all right to call him Regis de Trobriand Post, but "in such case the initials should be R. T. P., the *de* not being part of the name as Americans take the least trouble to understand." Regis de Trobriand to Lina, March 18, 1870, translated by Caroline Brammer, SC 1201, MHS.

10. Philippe Régis Denis de Keredern de Trobriand and Marie Caroline Post, *The Life and Mémoirs of Comte Régis de Trobriand, Major-General in the Army of the United States, by His Daughter Marie Caroline Post (Mrs. Charles Alfred Post)* (New York: E. P. Dutton & Company, 1910).

11. Régis de Trobriand, *Four Years with the Army of the Potomac*, trans. George K. Dauchy (Boston: Ticknor & Company, 1889). Another book on de Trobriand was published in 1941 and included some of his memoirs. See Philippe Régis Denis de Keredern de Trobriand, *Army Life in Dakota: Selections from the Journal of Philippe Régis Denis de Keredern de Trobriand* (Chicago: Lakeside Press, 1941).

12. Heitman, *Historical Register*, 1:370, s.v. de Trobriand.

13. De Trobriand and Post, *Life and Mémoirs*, 411–422. These works are held by the C. M. Russell Museum in Great Falls, Montana.

14. While at Fort Stephenson in the Dakota Territory, de Trobriand had used Indian scouts to his advantage. When he came to Montana he had some unusual ideas about including Indians in the military organization. He gave orders from Fort Shaw to the "Commanding Officer Fort Ellis," noting that ten Indian Scouts had been authorized for the post and suggesting that they should be selected from the Mountain Crows. McGinniss to Commanding Officer Fort Ellis, July 13, 1869, Fort Shaw Files, NARA; McGinniss to Brackett, July 26, 1869, Fort Shaw Files, NARA.

15. Alfred Sully to E. S. Parker, Helena, September 23, 1869, "Montana Superintendency, No. 76," in *Report of the Commissioner of Indian Affairs Made to the Secretary of the Interior for the Year 1869* (Washington, DC: Government Printing Office, 1870), 289–293. At the start of 1869 the War Department gave orders to General Alfred Sully to report for duty in the Montana Territory as a member of the Interior Department. The adjutant general of the U.S. Army, Edward D. Townsend, had written to President Grant advising that the secretary of the interior had requested that Sully "be ordered to report to him for duty connected

with the Indian Department." It was the intent to appoint Sully as superintendent of Indian Affairs for the Montana Territory. Simon, *The Papers of Ulysses S. Grant*, 17:22–23. Townsend had also advised that Sully was "now on the Board to examine Candidates for Commissions in the Infantry, in session in New York." Heitman, *Historical Register*, 1:935–936, s.v. Sully, Alfred.

16. Ray Allen Billington, foreword to Langdon Sully, *No Tears for the General: The Life of Alfred Sully, 1821–1879* (Palo Alto: American West Publishing, 1974), 9–12 (quotation); Michael L. Tate, *The Frontier Army in the Settlement of the West* (Norman: University of Oklahoma Press, 1999), 24–25; Michael Clodfelter, *The Dakota War: The United States Army versus the Sioux* (Jefferson, N.C.: McFarland & Company, 1998), 144–145.

17. Sully, *No Tears for the General*, 173–179; Alfred Sully to J. R. Doolittle, June 10, 1865, in "Condition of the Indian Tribes, Report of the Joint Special Committee Appointed under Joint Resolution of March 3, 1865," in United States, Congress, Joint Special Committee, *Joint Special Committee to Inquire into the Condition of the Indian Tribes* (Washington, DC: Government Printing Office, 1867) (quotations).

18. Alfred Sully to J. R. Doolittle, June 10, 1865, 466.

19. Ibid., 468 (quotations); Doolittle Committee, "New Directions in Government Policy," Senate Report No. 156, 39th Cong., 2nd Sess., serial 1279, 3–10.

20. Alfred Sully to Commissioner of Indian Affairs, Helena, August 3, 1869, as reproduced in *Piegan Indians, Letter from the Secretary of War in Answer to a Resolution of the House, of March 3, 1870, in Relation to the Late Expedition against the Piegan Indians, in the Territory of Montana*, 41st Cong., 2nd Sess., H. Ex. Doc. 269, 1–3 (all subsequent Sully quotations are from this source unless otherwise noted). Sully calculated that Camp Cooke had one company of infantry, Fort Shaw had three companies of infantry, and Fort Ellis had three companies of infantry, with all three companies being "very weak, averaging from twenty-five to thirty men each."

21. Ibid., 2–3.

22. Alfred Sully to E. S. Parker, September 23, 1869, in *Report of the Commissioner of Indian Affairs for the Year 1869*, 289–293.

23. Ibid. Sully also said: "There is a large number of the Blackfeet Indians belonging to the British possessions, who permanently reside there."

24. Ibid. For information on the career of Fellows David Pease, see William E. Lass, "The History and Significance of the Northwest Fur Company, 1865–1869," *North Dakota History: Journal of the Northern Plains* 61, no. 3 (Summer 1994): 21–40.

25. F. D. Pease to General Alfred Sully, Blackfeet Agency, August 10, 1869, in *Report of the Commissioner of Indian Affairs for the Year 1869*, 300–301.

26. Ibid. Pease went on to have a long career as agent for the Crows.

27. James A. Hardie to George L. Hartsuff, Chicago, January 29, 1870, in *Piegan Indians, Letter from the Secretary of War*, 27.

28. *Helena Weekly Herald*, August 19, 1869.

29. Overholser, *Fort Benton*, 72.

30. Colin G. Calloway, *Our Hearts Fell to the Ground: Plains Indian Views of How the West Was Lost* (Boston: Bedford/St. Martin's, 1966), 105–106. See Donald D. Pepion, "Marias Massacre: Killing the Heavyrunner Band of Blackfeet" (Blackfeet Community College, Browning, Montana, March 29, 1999), 7–9. See also M. I. McCreight, *Firewater and Forked Tongues: A Sioux Chief Interprets U.S. History* (Pasadena, CA: Trails End Publishing, 1947), 105–106.

31. Larpenteur, *Forty Years a Fur Trader on the Upper Missouri*, 351–354. See also Helene Clarke's version in *Bradley Manuscript*, MHS, 3:257–258, in which she says that both were probably to blame for the quarrel. Pepion, "Marias Massacre," 7–9.

32. *Helena Weekly Herald*, August 19, 1869.

33. Ibid.

34. Vaughn, *Then and Now*, 77–79. Sherman entered the United States Military Academy in 1836 when he was sixteen and graduated in 1840. Clarke had entered West Point in 1834, however, when he was seventeen and was dismissed in March 1835, which would have been before Sherman got there. Larpenteur, *Forty Years a Fur Trader on the Upper Missouri*, 346. Vaughn's recollections may have been influenced by his state of inebriation at the time: according to Charles Larpenteur, Vaughn "would take almost anything which would make drunk come" (*Forty Years a Fur Trader on the Upper Missouri*, 418). Vaughn said that in 1875, when "General Sherman passed through this section . . . on his tour of inspection" and "the story of Clark's career and of his death had been told, and the grave of his early associate shown him, he had been but a few moments on the spot when he showed signs of grief and requested to be left alone for a while. He stayed for some time and when he came away, traces of tears could be seen on the cheeks of the brave old warrior."

35. David Hilger, "Interview with Horace Clark on Sept. 27, 1924, from Notes Taken for the Purpose of Perpetuating Historical Data," Horace Clark Reminiscences, SC 540, MHS.

36. Charlotte Ouisconsin Clark Van Cleve, *Three Score Years and Ten* (Minneapolis: Harrison & Smith, 1888). 75–79.

37. President Grant appointed Wheeler on May 15, 1869, to replace Neil Howie, the U.S. marshal at the time. Wheeler was a Civil War veteran as a lieutenant colonel in the Minnesota militia, who at one time had served as private secretary to the governor of Minnesota. MC 65, MHS; *Helena Herald*, June 28, 1894.

38. Barbara Fifer, *Montana Battlefields, 1806–1877: Native Americans and the U.S. Army at War* (Helena: Farcountry Press, 2005), 34. In October Helene and the scarred Horace testified before a Helena grand jury that indicted all five of the Piegan men for murder.

39. Hamilton, *From Wilderness to Statehood*, 185–186.

40. J. T. McGinniss to A. G. Brackett, Fort Shaw, October 13, 1869, Fort Shaw Files, NARA.

41. P. H. Sheridan to E. D. Townsend, Chicago, October 21, 1869, in *Piegan Indians, Letter from the Secretary of War*, 7. Sheridan, writing to General Sherman, reported that the tribal numbers were "about fifteen hundred men, women and children, all told."

42. Grant's inaugural address, March 4, 1869, in Lott, *The Presidents Speak*, 149–156.

CHAPTER 7

Epigraph: W. T. Sherman to James A. Hardie, January 15, 1870, in *Army and Navy Journal*, February 19, 1870. The founders of the *Army and Navy Journal* were the brothers Francis and William Church of New York, both of whom had been with the *New York Sun*. On August 29, 1863, the inaugural issue carried this motto: "Established in obedience to an insistent demand for an official organ for members of the American Defense and those concerned with it."

1. E. D. Townsend to P. H. Sheridan, Washington, DC, November 4, 1869, in *Piegan Indians, Letter from the Secretary of War*, 8. Townsend served as Adjutant general for General Sherman. The letter said: "Sir: Referring to your communication of the 21st ult., relating to depredations by Piegan Indians in Montana, I have the honor to inform you that your proposed action as stated therein for the punishment of these marauders, has been approved by the General of the Army. Very respectfully yours."

2. P. H. Sheridan "Report of Lieutenant General Sheridan," November 1, 1869, Report of the Secretary of War, House of Representatives, 41st Cong., 2nd Sess., H. Ex. Doc. 1, part 2.

3. Justin Kaplan, ed., *Bartlett's Familiar Quotations*, 16th ed. (Boston: Little, Brown and Company, 1992), 516. According to *Bartlett's*, "Edward Sylvester Ellis (1840–1916) reported that after Custer's fight with Black Kettle's band of Cheyenne Indians, the Comanche Chief Toch-a-way (Turtle Dove) was presented to General Sheridan. The Indian said: 'Me Toch-a-way, me good Indian.' This prompted Sheridan's reply."

4. W. T. Sherman to P. H. Sheridan, Division of the Missouri, January 18, 1869, in Athearn, *William Tecumseh Sherman*, 275n9.

5. E. D. Townsend to P. H. Sheridan, November 4, 1869, in *Piegan Indians, Letter from the Secretary of War*; P. H. Sheridan to W. S. Hancock, November 15, 1869, in *Letter from the Secretary of War*.

6. P. H. Sheridan to W. S. Hancock, November 15, 1869, in Piegan Indians, Letter from the Secretary of War; P. H. Sheridan, "Personal Recollections by an Officer of His Command," *Army and Navy Journal*, November 27, 1869.

7. *Bradley Manuscript*, 3:262. According to Elk Horn, a Piegan who kept winter counts, the winter camps for twelve successive years, starting around 1849, ranged from the Sweetgrass Hills north toward the British boundary to places south of the Missouri. Yet the Marias was the favorite location, and over half the camps were there during those years. "Although some of the Blackfoot bands may have wintered on the Marias occasionally prior to 1850, the earliest reference I have to their wintering on that river appears in the Reports of Explorations and Surveys for a Pacific Railway covering the year 1853. James Doty visited the Blackfoot winter camps on the Milk and Marias Rivers during the winter of 1853. Gov. Stephens [*sic*], in charge of that survey reported: The winter homes of the Blackfeet, some six to seven thousand in number, are on the Teton, the Marias, and Milk Rivers. . . . It has been the habit of the fur companies to have winter posts on Milk River at the point known as Hammell's House and also at the fords of the Marias River." *Bradley Manuscript*, 3:259. Hammell's Houses on the Marias were about fifteen or twenty miles below Birch Creek, which would put them south of present-day Shelby. See also George Gibbs, *Indian Tribes of Washington Territory* (Fairfield, WA: Ye Galleon Press, 1972), 49.

8. John C. Ewers, *The Horse in Blackfoot Indian Culture* (Washington, DC: Government Printing Office, 1955). See also *Bradley Manuscript* 3:258.

9. Quoted in Lepley, *Blackfoot Fur Trade on the Upper Missouri*, 253–260.

10. *Bradley Manuscript*, 3:259–260.

11. Ewers, *The Horse in Blackfoot Indian Culture*, 124–126, 147. In addition to not knowing the exact location of the winter camps, there were also questions about how large the camps would be. See Ewers's explanation of the factors determining lodge and camp size. According to Ewers, "the several bands were spread out, at distances of several miles apart, from near the junction of Cut Bank and Two Medicine Creeks forming the Marias to the big bend of the Marias." "Yet in the spring of the year, when the Indians were eager to leave their winter camps on the Marias to obtain fresh buffalo meat, they made it as far as the Sweetgrass Hills in a day, a distance of at least 18 miles." See James Willard Schultz, *Blackfeet and Buffalo: Memories of Life among the Indians* (Norman: University of Oklahoma Press, 1962), 37. According to Shultz, "the Marias was a favorite stream with the Blackfeet for their winter encampments, for its wide and by no means deep valley was well timbered. In the shelter of the cottonwood grove the Lodges were protected from the occasional north blizzards, there was an ample supply of fuel, and there was fine grass for horses."

12. W. T. Sherman to P. H. Sheridan, November 4, 1869, *Chicago Tribune*, February 3, 1870; W. T. Sherman to P. H. Sheridan, December 30, 1869, in Sherman-Sheridan correspondence, vol. 1 of William T. Sherman Papers, Library of Congress, cited in Athearn, *William Tecumseh Sherman*, 271–278, 278n16, 278n17.

13. James A. Hardie to George L. Hartsuff, Chicago, January 29, 1870, in *Piegan Indians, Letter from the Secretary of War*, 19–34.

14. E. D. Townsend, "By Command of General Sherman," *Army and Navy Journal*, December 11, 1869.

15. James A. Hardie to George L. Hartsuff, Chicago, January 29, 1870, in *Piegan Indians, Letter from the Secretary of War*, 19–34 (quotation on 22). Hardie said that the increased activity of the army "had deepened the solicitude of the community, but the knowledge that military preparations were on foot for an expedition into the Indian region gave expectation of relief and produced tranquility."

16. P. H. Sheridan to W. S. Hancock, November 15, 1869, in *Piegan Indians, Letter from the Secretary of War*.

17. John Ponsford File, SC 659, MHS. Ponsford was twenty-two and a private in the army at the time of the massacre.

18. George W. Cullum, *Biographical Register of the Officers and Graduates of the U.S. Military Academy*, 2nd ed., 3 vols. (New York: D. Van Nostrand, 1868), 1:487; Stanley W. Paher, *Nevada Ghost Towns and Mining Camps* (Las Vegas: Nevada Publications, 1970), 79.

19. Geo. Blake to R. C. Drum, Fort Churchill, September 10, 1861, in Henry Martyn Lazelle and Leslie J. Perry, eds., *The War of the Rebellion: A Compilation of the Official Records of the Union Army*, 70 vols. in 128 (Washington, DC: Government Printing Office, 1880–1901), series 1, 50:24. Blake was the lieutenant colonel of the First Dragoons, commanding the post. Fort Churchill was the Nevada Territory's first and largest military post, garrisoning about six hundred men.

20. E. M. Baker, to Adjutant, Fort Churchill, Nev. Terr., October 20, 1861, in Lazelle and Perry, *The War of the Rebellion*, series 1, 50:667.

21. Cullum, *Biographical Register*, 1:487.

22. Gregory F. Michno and Susan J. Michno, *Forgotten Fights: Little-Known Raids and Skirmishes on the Frontier, 1823 to 1890* (Missoula, MT: Mountain Press, 2008), 251; Gregory F. Michno, *Encyclopedia of Indian Wars, Western Battles and Skirmishes, 1850–1890* (Missoula, MT: Mountain Press, 2003); Report of Brevet Major General George Crook, Headquarters Department of the Columbia, October 14, 1868, *Annual Report of the Secretary of War*.

23. Heitman, *Historical Register*, 1:184, s.v. Baker, Eugene.

24. De Trobriand to O. D. Greene, November 26, 1869, in *Piegan Indians, Letter from the Secretary of War*.

25. Winfield Hancock to Alfred Sully, telegram received at Helena, December 11, 1869, microfilm roll 833–2:0641, NARA.

26. Winfield Hancock to Alfred Sully, telegram, St. Paul, December 14, 1869, microfilm roll, 833–2, NARA; de Trobriand to J. A. Hardie, January 13, 1870, in *Piegan Indians, Letter from the Secretary of War* (quotation).

27. De Trobriand to "Dear Kin," September 30, 1870, typescript copy in De Trobriand Papers, SC 1201, MHS.

28. Winfield Hancock to Alfred Sully, telegram, St. Paul, December 14, 1869, microfilm roll 833–2:0641–0642, NARA.

29. Hebard and Brininstool, *The Bozeman Trail*.

30. Regis de Trobriand to Winfield Hancock, December 21, 1869, in *Piegan Indians, Letter from the Secretary of War*, 25.

31. James A. Hardie to George L. Hartsuff, Chicago, January 29, 1870, in *Piegan Indians, Letter from the Secretary of War*, 30–32.

32. Sharp, *Whoop-Up Country*, 38–41.

33. F. H. Eastman to W. F. Wheeler, November 27, 1869, Fort Benton, microfilm roll 833–2: 0631–0632, NARA. Eastman was sometimes referred to as "Major," a complimentary title given to principal traders at fur posts in the territory.

34. F. H. Eastman to Alfred Sully, November 28, 1869, microfilm roll 833–2, NARA.

35. F. H. Eastman to Alfred Sully, December 14, 1869, microfilm roll 833–2, NARA.

36. F. H. Eastman to Alfred Sully, April 21, 1870, microfilm roll 833–2, NARA. Due to the illegibility of the handwriting, we cannot be sure that it says 10 "gallons" of whiskey, but an amount was expressed in what looks like an abbreviation for "gallons."

37. Copy of permit at Galt Museum and Archives, Lethbridge, Alberta. A number and measure were obviously to be filled in after the words "Not to exceed," such as "X" gallons, but no number is present.

38. Hugh A. Dempsey, "Jerry Potts, Plainsman," *Montana The Magazine of Western History* 17, no. 4 (1967): 3–5, http://www.jstor.org/stable/4517194.

39. Dempsey, *Firewater*, 45–48; Dempsey, "Jerry Potts," 3–5 (quotation); H. V. A. Ferguson, as told by Winfield Scott Stocking, "Fort Benton Memories," December 1, 1906, SC 797, MHS.

40. Dempsey, "Jerry Potts," 8–10. Potts and Star ended up working together. On October 24, 1870, they were hunters at Fort Whoop-Up, the whiskey trading post started by Hamilton and Healy on the Belly River in Canada.

41. Ferguson as told by Stocking, "Fort Benton Memories." Stocking was reported as saying that "Jerry was a half-breed—Piegan and white man mixed, and about the most decent specimen of that combination I ever met with." V. A. Ferguson, a government land agent, found Stocking "still hale and hearty and the age of seventy." Eastman to Sully, April 21, 1870, microfilm roll 833–2, NARA; John G. Lepley, *Birthplace of Montana: A History of Fort Benton* (Missoula, MT: Pictorial Histories, 1999), 82, 87.

42. Sully to Commissioner of Indian Affairs [no name given], January 3, 1870, in *Piegan Indians, Letter from the Secretary of War*; Charles R. Shrader, ed., *United States Army Logistics, 1775–1992: An Anthology*, Vol. 1 (Washington, DC: Center of Military History, United States Army, 1997), 206–209. This is based on logistical estimates made during the Civil War. See Johnston and den Otter, *Lethbridge*, 32, on whiskey trading procedures and the use of bull teams.

43. Sully to Commissioner of Indian Affairs [no name given], January 3, 1870, in *Piegan Indians, Letter from the Secretary of War* Ibid., 36–37, quoted in James Hardie to George Harstuff, Chicago, January 29, 1870, in *Piegan Indians, Letter from the Secretary of War*, 22–23.

44. Ibid. Sully prevaricated, as he said: "In talking to the Indians the other day, I took it upon myself to tell them we had permission from the English government to cross the line with our troops." He also said that "it had more effect upon them and the half-breeds . . . than anything I had said."

45. Alfred Sully to James Hardie, Helena, January 13, 1870, in *Piegan Indians, Letter from the Secretary of War*, 44. Fur traders were almost certainly present as interpreters in the meetings that Sully had with the chiefs. Sully did not say so outright, but he as much as said so by his comment that "from what the whites and half-breeds tell me." After the massacre, when the bargain by Sully became well known, *Harper's* had a cartoon showing Pete Owl Child's head being offered up on a platter. "An Indian Peace-Offering," *Harper's Weekly*, April 30, 1870.

46. It appears that the trip to the Belly River would have been at least about 150 miles from Fort Shaw. This could have been done in under two weeks at the rate of twelve miles a day and at a faster pace would have taken less time.

47. *Piegan Indians, Letter from the Secretary of War*, 26, 27.

48. As quoted in Armstrong, *Warrior in Two Camps*, 147. See Robert J. Ege, *Tell Baker to Strike Them Hard!* (Bellevue, NE: Old Army Press, 1970).

49. *Piegan Indians, Letter from the Secretary of War*. This was actually the second time that Hardie had been ordered to Montana, but the first time he had actually been there. As early as April 1869, the secretary of war had ordered Hardie to go to Montana to investigate the claims made in connection with the militia effort in 1867, but these orders were rescinded when General Sherman became head of the army. Sherman to Humphreys, April 24, 1869, William T. Sherman Papers, microfilm, LC. See also Sherman to Grant, September 2, 1870, in the Sherman Papers.

50. *Piegan Indians, Letter from the Secretary of War*, 19.

51. Ibid. The suspension was to be "until your report is received, or until you return to these headquarters."

52. With those instructions, whatever they were, Hardie and de Trobriand immediately went to work. Amid his investigation and battle planning, de Trobriand had been able to write Lina only once to inform her that he had been "occupied in military matters." De Trobriand to Lina, January 10, translated by Caroline Brammer, De Trobriand Papers, SC 1201, MHS.

53. James Hardie to George Hartsuff, Chicago, January 29, 1870, in *Piegan Indians, Letter from the Secretary of War*, 19–35 (quotations on 21–22).

54. Ibid., 23.

55. Ibid. The guide reported to Hardie that the "trading post is on the Marias River, seventy-five miles from Benton, and about the same distance from

Fort Shaw—and situated above the Dry Fork, and five miles below Medicine Creek."

56. Alfred Sully to James Hardie, Helena, January 13, 1870, in *Piegan Indians, Letter from the Secretary of War*, 44.

57. Alfred Sully, "Report to the Commissioner of Indian Affairs," January 3, 1870, quoted in James Hardie to George Harstuff, Chicago, January 29, 1870, in *Piegan Indians, Letter from the Secretary of War*, 22–23.

58. James Hardie to George Harstuff, Chicago, January 29, 1870, in *Piegan Indians, Letter from the Secretary of War*, 25–27.

59. James Hardie to Alfred Sully, telegram, Fort Shaw, January 10, 1870, microfilm roll 833–2, NARA.

60. Hardie's full report was not submitted until January 29.

61. Sully to Commissioner of Indian Affairs [no name given], January 3, 1870; Sully to J. A. Hardie, January 13, 1870, both in *Piegan Indians, Letter from the Secretary of War*.

62. James Hardie to George Hartsuff, telegram, Fort Shaw, January 13, 1870, in *Piegan Indians, Letter from the Secretary of War*, 47. Hardie said that he proposed to "leave here tomorrow afternoon on return to Chicago." He hoped to reach Chicago "before the end of month—possibly by 26th."

63. Ibid.

64. P. H. Sheridan to James Hardie, Chicago, January 15, 1870, in *Army and Navy Journal*, February 19, 1870.

65. "Piegan Expedition" file, Phillip Sheridan Papers, microfilm, LC. This file of hand-copied documents is probably a retained copy of the file that was sent to the Senate and was the basis for the *Piegan Indians* report.

66. E. M. Baker to J. T. McGinniss, Fort Shaw, February 18, 1870, in *Piegan Indians, Letter from the Secretary of War*, 16–17.

67. "The Piegan Fight (Correspondence of the *New York Sun*)," *Army and Navy Journal*, March 5, 1870: during the march, "the thermometer indicated from 23 to 27 degrees," although other reports indicated that those numbers might have been below zero.

68. John Ponsford File, SC 659, MHS.

69. E. M. Baker to J. T. McGinniss, Fort Shaw, February 18, 1870 in *Piegan Indians, Letter from the Secretary of War*, 16–17; McAlexander, *History of the Thirteenth Regiment United States Infantry*, 70.

70. E. M. Baker to J. T. McGinniss, Fort Shaw, February 18, 1870, in *Piegan Indians, Letter from the Secretary of War*, 16–17; "The Piegan Fight (Correspondence of the *New York Sun*)," *Army and Navy Journal*, March 5, 1870. This report said that joining Baker were Company A of the 13th Infantry and seventy-six mounted infantrymen, detailed from the different companies of the same regiment. Given the correlation with the facts set out in Colonel Baker's report of February 18, 1870, as well as other accounts, I believe that this report and the report in "Details of the Piegan Fight (Correspondence of the *Philadelphia*

Ledger)," *Army and Navy Journal,* March 19, 1870 (stating that it the report was from Bozeman, Montana Territory, February 24) are authentic accounts of the events stated therein. The author of the earlier report is unknown, and the author of the later report, one Peter Gaynor, may have used a pseudonym.

71. Regis de Trobriand to Lina, Fort Shaw, January 17, 1870, translated by Caroline Brammer, De Trobriand Papers, SC 1201, MHS.

72. James Kipp died on July 3, 1880. Jim Arthur, ed., *Retracing Kipp Family Trails: A Collection of Stories and Pictures of the Kipp Family and the Country They Lived In, with Stories by Octavia Kipp* (Lewistown: Central Montana, 1997). See also Tavi Kipp, *History of the Kipp Family in Montana,* SC 2314, MHS; Boller, *Twilight of the Upper Missouri River Fur Trade;* Ray Mattison, "James Kipp," in Hafen, *Fur Traders, Trappers, and Mountain Men of the Upper Missouri,* 35–39; Kurz, *The Journal of Rudolph Friederich Kurz;* and Wood et al., *Fort Clark and Its Indian Neighbors.*

73. Arthur, *Retracing Kipp Family Trails.* See also Kipp, *History of the Kipp Family in Montana.*

74. Dempsey, "Jerry Potts," 6–7.

75. Blackfeet Heritage Program, *Blackfeet Heritage, 1907–1908* (Browning, MT: Blackfeet Heritage Program, 1980), s.v. Cobell, Joe. It was said later that he had been in the region since "about the time that Granville Stuart made his second pilgrimage to Montana," which would have been in the early 1860s.

76. James Hardie to George Hartsuff, Chicago January 29, 1870, in *Piegan Indians, Letter from the Secretary of War,* 30.

77. Blackfeet Heritage Program, *Blackfeet Heritage, 1907–1908,* s.v. Cobell, Mary.

78. De Trobriand to O. D. Greene, January 2, 1870, Fort Shaw Files, NARA. The sources for Horace Clarke's recollections: a sworn deposition to the Indian Claims Commission in 1920; a lengthy interview with David Hilger of the Montana Historical Society in 1924 (Horace Clark Reminiscences, SC540, MHS); and articles and interview notes by Martha Plassmann in the 1920s and 1930s. On Nathan Clarke's presence, see Wesley C. Wilson, "The U.S. Army and the Piegans—The Baker Massacre of 1870," *North Dakota History* (Bismarck, State Historical Society) 32, no. 1 (January 1965). Wilson cites Helen Fitzgerald Sanders, *A History of Montana* (Chicago: Lewis Publishing Company, 1913), 237–243; Vaughn, *Then and Now,* 49. While there is no apparent record of him, another guide may have been along on the trip. Robert Vaughn, one of the early Indian agents, believed that a man named Henry Martin was with the 2nd Cavalry as a scout in addition to Kipp and Cobell.

79. John Ponsford File, SC 659, MHS.

80. "Bear River" was another name for the Marias River. James White Calf, "My Memories of the Baker Massacre," in Adolf Hungry Wolf, *The Blackfeet Papers: Volume One: Pikunni History and Culture* (Skookumchuck, BC: Good Medicine Cultural Foundation, 2006), 52.

81. Daniel Starr quoted in William Henry White, *Custer, Cavalry & Crows: The Story of William White, as Told to Thomas Marquis* (Fort Collins: Old Army Press, 1975), 32. Starr told his story to White, who in turn relayed it to Thomas Marquis. "Throughout the January storms of northern Montana the government's fighters travelled . . . northeastward from Fort Shaw." The guide, Joseph Kipp, knew of a camp in the region on the Marias River. Starr was then about thirty-five years old and on the expedition.

82. White, *Custer, Cavalry & Crows*, 30–33. According to White, Starr was a mule packer. Tom LeForge, who was nineteen in 1870, claimed that he had the ends of the toes on his left foot sheared off by a Piegan bullet.

83. "The Piegan Fight (Correspondence of the *New York Sun*)," *Army and Navy Journal*, March 5, 1870.

84. Peter Gaynor, "Details of the Piegan Fight (Correspondence of the *Philadelphia Ledger*)," *Army and Navy Journal*, March 19, 1870. The author, "Peter Gaynor," wrote the article in the first person in the voice of one who had been there. Some evidence of a man named Gaynor showed up in 1890, when the *Brooklyn Eagle* printed information coming from a former Brooklyn policeman named Bowden who said that he had gone to Montana in the 1860s as part of the 13th Infantry along with "Thomas" Gaynor and three other Irishmen from New York. He said: "What became of the other Brooklyn men, I don't know." "Early Days in Montana," *Brooklyn Daily Eagle*, February 16, 1890.

85. E. M. Baker to J. T. McGinniss, Fort Shaw, February 18, 1870, in *Piegan Indians, Letter from the Secretary of War*, 16–17; John Ponsford File, SC 659, MHS.

86. "The Piegan Fight (Correspondence of the *New York Sun*)," *Army and Navy Journal*, March 5, 1870; Gaynor, "Details of the Piegan Fight (Correspondence of the *Philadelphia Ledger*)," *Army and Navy Journal*, March 19, 1870. All quotations except the Gaynor quotation are from the March 5 edition.

87. Plassmann Papers, MC 78, MHS; White, *Custer, Cavalry & Crows*, 27.

88. E. M. Baker to J. T. McGinniss, Fort Shaw, February 18, 1870, in *Piegan Indians, Letter from the Secretary of War*, 16–17; John Ponsford File, SC 659, MHS.

89. Regis De Trobriand to Lina, Fort Shaw, January 23, 1870, translated by Caroline Brammer, SC 1201, MHS.

90. E. M. Baker to J. T. McGinniss, Fort Shaw, February 18, 1870, in *Piegan Indians, Letter from the Secretary of War*, 16–17; John Ponsford File, SC 659, MHS.

91. Gaynor, "Details of the Piegan Fight (Correspondence of the *Philadelphia Ledger*)," *Army and Navy Journal*, March 19, 1870. "Peter Gaynor" appeared to support Baker's action. After reciting a litany of wrongs by the Indians, he stated: "Other depredations and murders they have committed, the facts of which are fresh in the memory of our citizens. The details of the same would tend to make my letter too long, and besides I opine that what I have given above will lead the *Sun*'s readers to form the same opinion of this Indian nation's hellish deeds as if I had freely narrated all their evil doings for the past four years."

92. John Ponsford File, SC 659, MHS.

93. Publication of the *Pick and Plow* ceased with the May 18, 1871, edition. No complete set of these editions appears to be available in any archive, so reprints of its articles from *Army and Navy Journal* have been used extensively.

94. Gaynor, "Details of the Piegan Fight (Correspondence of the *Philadelphia Ledger*)," *Army and Navy Journal*, March 19, 1870.

95. Typescript document of apparent letter from A. J. Noyes, Paul McCormick Papers, SC 423, MHS. Noyes commented: "Asking him why he did not tell his story to some one he said 'People would not believe what some of us has gone through so what is the use.'"

96. "Horace Clarke Testimony," in Stan Gibson and Jack Hayne, *Witnesses to Carnage: The 1870 Marias Massacre in Montana* (Calgary Alberta: Glenbow Archives), online at http://www.dickshovel.com/parts2.html. These reports were made some time after the event, but Martha Plassmann had witnessed Major Baker on a drinking spree at the Overland Hotel in Fort Benton a few years after the massacre, which confirmed her condemnation. Martha Plassmann Papers, MC 78, MHS.

97. E. M. Baker to J. T. McGinniss, Fort Shaw, February 18, 1870, in *Piegan Indians, Letter from the Secretary of War*, 16–17; John Ponsford File, SC 659, MHS.

CHAPTER 8

Epigraph: Spear Woman Affidavit, Heavy Runner Records, 1914–1921, MF 53, MHS (all subsequent Spear Woman quotations are from this source unless otherwise noted). This collection consists of Senate Bills 7523 and 1543 (1915), 417 (1917), 3775 (1920), and 287 (1921) and related correspondence and affidavits supporting the claims of Heavy Runner's heirs for compensation for losses suffered. Spear Woman married Hiram Upham, a clerk to Lieutenant William Pease, the Blackfeet agent. She came forward in 1915 to say that she was a massacre survivor.

1. James A. Hardie to George L. Hartsuff, Chicago, January 29, 1870, in *Piegan Indians, Letter from the Secretary of War*, 30.

2. De Trobriand to O. D. Greene, January 2, 1870, De Trobriand File, SC 5, MHS.

3. Horace Clarke Affidavit, Heavy Runner Records, 1914–1921, MF 53, MHS; Martha Edgerton Plassmann Papers, MC 78, MHS.

4. Vaughn, *Then and Now*, 49. According to Robert Vaughn, an early Blackfeet Indian agent in the 1850s, it was late at night when Baker's troops rode to the point "where the guides intended to take them." "On account of frost in the air and few inches of snow on the ground they had some difficulty in keeping the right course," but "finally the command arrived at the bluffs overlooking the

Marias river." Even from there, "the tepees of the enemy were hardly observable," but they did spot a camp, which appeared to them to have been set up by a band of Piegans.

5. John Ponsford File, SC 659, MHS (first quotation); Thompson quoted in Theophilus F. Rodenbough, *From Everglade to Canyon with the Second United States Cavalry: An Authentic Account of Service in Florida, Mexico, Virginia, and the Indian Country, 1836–1875* (1875) (Norman: University of Oklahoma Press, 2000), 401–404. It is not definite when exactly Baker had ceased to rely on the directions given by his guides, but Captain Lewis Thompson said that "on the night of the 22nd, Colonel Baker ordered the guides to the rear."

6. Ponsford File, Special Collections, MSU.

7. G. A. Doane, "Letter of March 21, 1874," in Rodenbough, *From Everglade to Canyon*, 552–553; "Details of the Piegan Fight (Correspondence of the *Philadelphia Ledger*)," *Army and Navy Journal*, March 19, 1870. All seemed to agree that they arrived on the bluffs overlooking Heavy Runner's camp "by 7 o'clock A. M." This newspaper report had a location and date as "Bozeman, M. T., February 18, 1870." A newspaper article confirmed that Gray Wolf and his family, "numbering in all fifteen . . . were made prisoners as quietly as possible."

8. "The Piegan Fight (Correspondence of the *New York Sun*)," *Army and Navy Journal*, March 5, 1870, datelined "Bozeman, M. T., February 13, 1870" (first two quotations); "Details of the Piegan Fight (Correspondence of the *Philadelphia Ledger*)," *Army and Navy Journal*, March 19, 1870 (third quotation).

9. "Details of the Piegan Fight (Correspondence of the *Philadelphia Ledger*)," *Army and Navy Journal*, March 19, 1870. The reports were unclear on the distance that they would cover to the large Piegan village. Some said that they "found the distance about sixteen miles."

10. "The Piegan Fight (Correspondence of the *New York Sun*)," *Army and Navy Journal*, March 5, 1870.

11. Lewis report quoted in Rodenbough, *From Everglade to Canyon*, 401–404; "The Piegan Fight (Correspondence of the *New York Sun*)," *Army and Navy Journal*, March 5, 1870.

12. G. A. Doane, "Letter of March 21, 1874," in Rodenbough, *From Everglade to Canyon*, 552–553.

13. James Hardie to George Hartsuff, telegram, Fort Shaw, Montana, January 13, 1870, reproduced in *Piegan Indians, Letter from the Secretary of War*, 47.

14. W. F. Butler, *The Great Lone Land: A Narrative of Travel and Adventure in the North-West of America* (London: Sampson Low, Marston, Low & Searle, 1873), 268–269.

15. "Details of the Piegan Fight (Correspondence of the *Philadelphia Ledger*)," *Army and Navy Journal*, March 19, 1870; Bear Head Affidavit, in Heavy Runner Records, 1914–1921, MF 53, MHS.

16. For Doane's character, see generally Kim Allen Scott, *Yellowstone Denied: The Life of Gustavus Cheyney Doane* (Norman: University of Oklahoma Press, 2007).

17. Gibson and Hayne, *Witnesses to Carnage*; Plassmann Papers, MC 78, MHS.

18. G. A. Doane, "Letter of March 21, 1874," in Rodenbough, *From Everglade to Canyon*, 552–553 (quotation); Scott, *Yellowstone Denied*; see F Company Muster Roll (December 31, 1869–February 28, 1870), Fort Ellis File, NARA; Stan Gibson Papers, Glenbow Library, Calgary, Alberta.

19. G. A. Doane, "Letter of March 21, 1874," in Rodenbough, *From Everglade to Canyon*, 552–553.

20. Mrs. Frank Monroe Affidavit, Heavy Runner Records, 1914–1921, MF 53, MHS.

21. There had been much confusion as to which trail would take the troops to Mountain Chief that morning and the evening of the day before. Paul McCormick, the civilian freighter, had listened to the conversations on the trail and knew the scouts had reported finding Mountain Chief's camp on the Marias. Paul McCormick Papers, SC 423, MHS; G. A. Doane, "Letter of March 21, 1874," in Rodenbough, *From Everglade to Canyon*, 552–553; Plassmann Papers, MC 78, MHS (quotation), cited in Gibson and Hayne, *Witnesses to Carnage*. It may not have been just Baker who used the spirits: "on good authority, both officers and men are reported to have been considerably the worse for liquor."

22. Paul McCormick Papers, SC 423, MHS.

23. Gibson and Hayne, *Witnesses to Carnage*, citing Plassmann Papers, MC 78, MHS. Another Montana investigator, Wayne Aldrich, wrote a widely disseminated newspaper article in 1923 for the Montana Newspaper Association that supports Mrs. Plassmann's accusations. According to Plassmann, Jerry Potts was the fur trader who had left to go north with whiskey traders John Healy and Alfred Hamilton out of Sun River on December 28 and was frequently with the Indians.

24. "Blackfeet Genealogy," http://www.blackfeetgenealogy.com/pafg136 .htm#12200.

25. Bear Head Affidavit, in Heavy Runner Records, 1914–1921, MF 53, MHS. The military wagons had stopped many miles short of the Marias, so these must have been the wagons of fur traders. As reported in "Details of the Piegan Fight (Correspondence of the *Philadelphia Ledger*)," *Army and Navy Journal*, March 19, 1870, three days after the massacre: "On the 26th we reached our wagon train." This was on the return journey to Fort Shaw. "The Piegan Fight (Correspondence of the *New York Sun*)," *Army and Navy Journal*, March 5, 1870, wrote: "After proceeding about fifty miles [from Fort Shaw] Colonel Baker very wisely left his wagons with their guards, and pushed ahead with all the rapidity possible."

26. G. A. Doane, "Letter of March 21, 1874," in Rodenbough, *From Everglade to Canyon*, 552–553.

27. McAlexander, *History of the Thirteenth Regiment United States Infantry*, 70.

28. Bear Head Affidavit, Heavy Runner Records, 1914–1921, MF 53, MHS.

29. G. A. Doane, "Letter of March 21, 1874," in Rodenbough, *From Everglade to Canyon*, 552–553.

30. Ibid. Some would say that there were more lodges than Doane counted. "Details of the Piegan Fight (Correspondence of the *Philadelphia Ledger*)," *Army and Navy Journal*, March 19, 1870. This newspaper report said the troops "burst like a hurricane upon the camp, which they found to consist of thirty-two lodges, eleven on the north and twenty-one on the south side of the river."

31. Doane's frequent mentions of the first sergeant were not accompanied by the man's name. The Fort Ellis Muster Roll for F Company indicates that the first sergeant was Alexander Anderson. Fort Ellis Muster Rolls, NARA.

32. G. A. Doane, "Letter of March 21, 1874," in Rodenbough, *From Everglade to Canyon*, 552–553 (quotations); "The Piegan Fight (Correspondence of the *New York Sun*)," *Army and Navy Journal*, March 5, 1870. The newspaper account confirms Doane's version but reports that Baker was giving the commands, not Doane.

33. Starr quoted in William Henry White, *Custer, Cavalry & Crows: The Story of William White, as Told to Thomas Marquis* (Fort Collins: Old Army Press, 1975), 32.

34. Ibid. The saying "Nits make lice" is also attributed to Lieutenant General Philip Sheridan.

35. Ibid. (quotations); transcription of notations on the Fort Ellis Muster Roll "Record of Events" (December 31, 1869–February 28, 1870), in Stan Gibson Papers, Glenbow Archives, Calgary, Alberta. First Lieutenant Samuel T. Hamilton signed for Company L as "commanding the company" because at the end of February Thompson was on detached duty at the headquarters of the Division of the Dakotas in St. Paul where General Hancock was commander. It can be speculated that Hancock wanted a firsthand account.

36. Bear Head Affidavit, Heavy Runner Records, 1914–1921, MF 53, MHS (quotation); "The Piegan Fight (Correspondence of the *New York Sun*)," *Army and Navy Journal*, March 5, 1870.

37. White Calf, "My Memories of the Baker Massacre," in Hungry Wolf, *The Blackfeet Papers*, 52.

38. Alfred Sully, "Report to the Commissioner of Indian Affairs," January 3, 1870, in *Piegan Indians, Letter from the Secretary of War*, 22–23. Sully's report had made no mention of giving Heavy Runner a paper or document that would protect him, but it was brief and did not go into much detail; Spear Woman Affidavit, Heavy Runner Records, 1914–1921, MF 53, MHS (quotations).

39. Good Bear Woman (also known as Mrs. No Chief) Affidavit, Heavy Runner Records, 1914–1921, MF 53, MHS.

40. Joe Kipp Affidavit, Heavy Runner Records, 1914–1921, MF 53, MHS (quotations); James White Calf, "My Memories of the Baker Massacre," in Hungry Wolf, *The Blackfeet Papers*, 52; Richard Lancaster, *Piegan: A Look from within*

at the Life, Times and Legacy of an American Indian Tribe (New York: Doubleday & Company, 1966), 122–124. White Calf was in Canada with his father at the time, but they soon returned to the United States. He lived to tell the stories he had heard to Richard Lancaster in the 1960s. James White Calf also said: "And then the soldiers went through the camp and killed everybody they could find, even the little children. There was 'big measles' (smallpox) in the camp at that time, and those too sick to move were burned to death in their lodges. Most of the soldiers were drunk." The survivors had said that "when the soldiers first showed up" Heavy Runner "went out to meet them." Eyewitnesses reported that "he was holding up a piece of paper and a peace medal that had been given to him by Commissioner Isaac Stevens." They also said that "an officer shot him down."

41. Bear Head Affidavit, Heavy Runner Records, 1914–1921, MF 53, MHS (quotation); "The Piegan Fight (Correspondence of the *New York Sun*)," *Army and Navy Journal*, March 5, 1870.

42. Black Bear Woman Affidavit, Heavy Runner Records, 1914–1921, MF 53, MHS. According to Black Bear Woman, who later became the wife of Joe Cobell, "[Baker] knew it was a friendly camp, because the soldiers had captured a young boy [Bear Head] who had been out at the horse herd. One of the Army's scouts, Joe Kipp, could speak Blackfoot, and he found out from the boy that the troops were surrounding Heavy Runner's friendly camp."

43. "Father—Spouses," from "1998 Blackfeet Genealogy, Treasures and Gifts" by the Blackfeet Tribal Business Council and Roxanne De Marce (P.O. Box 850, Browning, Montana 59417), 192. A story confirming Connelly's came from Black Bear Woman (later Mary Cobell). According to her, "Most of the warriors left camp on a hunt. They didn't worry about defending the place because Heavy Runner had a paper from the government saying that the band was friendly and at peace with the whites . . . Joe Kipp told the colonel, but that didn't make any difference—the colonel said he wanted to make sure . . . When Joe Cobell saw Heavy Runner carrying his peace paper, he shot the chief. That got the rest of the soldiers to start shooting too." According to her, "Joe said later, 'most of the warriors were away. It sure taught them a good lesson—and I got their horses!'" But another version of Cobell's story came out: he had boasted to Joe Connelly, his son-in-law, that he had shot Heavy Runner because the chief had taken some horses and would not give them back. In a 1931 interview Connelly confirmed what Black Bear Woman had said. His father-in-law had told him: "When the soldiers came in sight of the camp, an old Indian came out waving a little piece of paper to show that he was friendly. Cobell said that he knew that if that Indian got to Baker, there would be no fighting. He fired, and the Indian settled down upon the ground. Then the firing began." Connelly's assessment was that "Cobell was a wily old fellow, a sure shot. His wife and family belonged to Mountain Chief's family. I always thought he was trying to save Mountain Chief."

44. Doane, "Letter of March 21, 1874," in Rodenbough, *From Everglade to Canyon*, 552–553; "Details of the Piegan Fight (Correspondence of the *Philadelphia Ledger*)," *Army and Navy Journal*, March 19, 1870.

45. Doane, "Letter of March 21, 1874," in Rodenbough, *From Everglade to Canyon*, 552–553;

46. Ibid. Wise was demoted from sergeant to private on February 10, 1870, hardly a commendation for his efforts. Fort Ellis Muster Roll, Fort Ellis Files, NARA.

47. Doane, "Letter of March 21, 1874," in Rodenbough, *From Everglade to Canyon*, 552–553. Etheridge had enlisted at Fort Leavenworth in 1866. Like Sergeant Wise, he was demoted after the battle..

48. William Birth to Perry Hobbs, January 31, 1870, Special Collections, Yale University Library.

49. "The Piegan Fight (Correspondence of the *New York Sun*)," *Army and Navy Journal*, March 5, 1870; Doane, "Letter of March 21, 1874," in Rodenbough, *From Everglade to Canyon*, 552–553 (quotations). Doane's memory may not have been correct as to the man's name, because the available Fort Ellis Muster Rolls do not list a man named Mullis; nor does such a name appear in the Fort Ellis 1870 census or in the Fort Shaw Muster Rolls.

50. "Details of the Piegan Fight (Correspondence of the *Philadelphia Ledger*)," *Army and Navy Journal*, March 19, 1870. The number of lodges in this account (thirty-two) differs from the forty-four in Doane's later report. Baker did not give any such detail at all in his official report.

51. "The Piegan Fight (Correspondence of the *New York Sun*)," *Army and Navy Journal*, March 5, 1870.

52. Ibid.

53. Eunice A. MacDonald (Mrs. Ross J. MacDonald) to Jack Hayne, April 29, 1996, copy in Stan Gibson Papers, Glenbow Archives, Calgary, Alberta.

54. Mrs. Frank Monroe Affidavit, Heavy Runner Records, 1914–1921, MF 53, MHS.

55. Buffalo Trail Woman Affidavit, Heavy Runner Records, 1914–1921, MF 53, MHS.

56. William E. Farr, *Blackfoot Redemption: A Blood Indian's Story of Murder, Confinement, and Imperfect Justice* (Norman: University of Oklahoma Press, 2012).

57. E-mail correspondence in 2012 between Rod Hoare of England, the grandson of Henry Dew, and Kim Allen Scott, director of the Special Collections at Montana State University (copies in author's file). Dew is listed on the 1870 census for Fort Ellis and enlisted in the 2nd Cavalry, G Company, in November 1868 for five years. See Record Group 94, AGO, 2nd Cavalry Muster Rolls, Co. H (December 1869–February 1870), NARA.

58. White, *Custer, Cavalry & Crows*, 31–35; Leforge and Marquis, *Memoirs of a White Crow Indian*, 30–35 (quotations).

59. Starr quoted in White, *Custer, Cavalry & Crows*, 32. Marquis said of Starr: "He never indicated to me that he felt any pricklings of conscience on account of his action in the affair." He added: "In fact, all through that region in those times the killing of an Indian, under any circumstances and in any manner, was regarded as an act so commendable as to approach the status of a stern duty."

60. White Calf, "My Memories of the Baker Massacre," in Hungry Wolf, *The Blackfeet Papers*, 52; Lancaster, *Piegan*, 122–124. White Calf was said to be well over 100 years old when he told this story to Richard Lancaster in the 1960s. He said that he was in Canada with his father at the time of the Massacre, but they soon returned to the United States. White Calf's suggestion that Kipp led the troops to Heavy Runner's camp is inconsistent with the versions of Paul McCormick and others, who say that Kipp told Baker that he was going to the wrong camp. But different time frames were involved.

61. Buffalo Trail Woman Affidavit, Heavy Runner Records, 1914–1921, MF 53, MHS; Doane, "Letter of March 21, 1874," in Rodenbough, *From Everglade to Canyon*, 552–553.

62. E. M. Baker to J. T. McGinniss, Fort Shaw, February 18, 1870, in *Piegan Indians, Letter from the Secretary of War*, 16–17.

63. "Details of the Piegan Fight (Correspondence of the *Philadelphia Ledger*)," *Army and Navy Journal*, March 19, 1870.

64. Ibid.

65. E. M. Baker to J. T. McGinniss, Fort Shaw, February 18, 1870, in *Piegan Indians, Letter from the Secretary of War*, 16–17.

66. Doane, "Letter of March 21, 1874," in Rodenbough, *From Everglade to Canyon*, 552–553 (quotations); "Details of the Piegan Fight (Correspondence of the *Philadelphia Ledger*)," *Army and Navy Journal*, March 19, 1870.

67. "The Piegan Fight (Correspondence of the *New York Sun*)," *Army and Navy Journal*, March 5, 1870.

68. Ibid.

69. Regis de Trobriand to Lina, Fort Shaw, January 23, 1870, translated by Caroline Brammer, SC 1201, MHS.

70. "Details of the Piegan Fight (Correspondence of the *Philadelphia Ledger*)," *Army and Navy Journal*, March 19, 1870.

71. Spear Woman's story is in an account written by her great-great-granddaughter, Julie Schildt, who had the story handed down to her from her grandmother. E-mail from Jordan S. Dill to Stan Gibson, September 22, 1998, Stan Gibson Papers, Glenbow Archives, Calgary, Alberta.

CHAPTER 9

Epigraph: W. S. Hancock to R. de Trobriand, telegram, St. Paul, January 29, 1870, NARA.

1. Regis de Trobriand to O. D. Greene, telegram, January 26, 1870, De Trobriand Papers, SC 1201, MHS. De Trobriand also reported "some wounded soldiers said to be with the train."

2. Ibid.; O. D. Greene to E. M. Baker, telegram, "care Gen'l De Trobriand" ("rec'd Jan. 26"), from "St. Paul Jan'y 24, 1870."

3. P. H. Sheridan to W. T. Sherman, telegram, January 31, 1870, in *Piegan Indians, Letter from the Secretary of War.*

4. Regis de Trobriand to Eugene Baker, Fort Shaw, January 16, 1870, in *Piegan Indians, Letter from the Secretary of War*, 15–16.

5. De Trobriand File, SC 5, MHS. Also quoted in Montana Historical Society, *Not in Precious Metals Alone: A Manuscript History of Montana* (Helena: Montana Historical Society, 1976). De Trobriand also said that "Eagles Rib who escaped with three or four others from Bear Chief's camp is badly wounded by a bullet through the hips, and not likely to recover" and that "Red Horn was killed in his camp."

6. Ibid.

7. See comments on Peter Gaynor in chapter 7, notes 70 and 84.

8. "The Piegan Fight (Correspondence of the *New York Sun*)," *Army and Navy Journal*, March 5, 1870 (quotation); "Details of the Piegan Fight (Correspondence of the *Philadelphia Ledger*)," *Army and Navy Journal*, March 19, 1870.

9. James Hardie to George Hartsuff, Chicago, January 29, 1870, in *Piegan Indians, Letter from the Secretary of War*, 30–32.

10. "Details of the Piegan Fight (Correspondence of the *Philadelphia Ledger*)," *Army and Navy Journal*, March 19, 1870; W. B. Pease to Alfred Sully, February 6, 1870, in *Second Annual Report of the Board of Indian Commissioners* for *the Year 1870* (Washington, DC: Government Printing Office, 1871), 89.

11. The Piegans who were considered targets of the campaign were identified as Bear Chief, Black Weasel, Eagle's Rib, Black Bear, White Man's Dog, Pete Owl Child, Star (half Mexican and half Piegan), Crow Top, Cut Hand, Bear Chief, Under Bull, Red Horn, and Bull's Head: "Bear Chief's band." Joe Kipp, the presumed messenger sent out by General Hardie, had come back and given "the localities of Mountain Chief's, Bear Chief's, and other bands of Piegans, both those called friendly and the unfriendly." The wording was unclear as to whether Bear Chief's camp was considered friendly or unfriendly. Some even thought that Bear Chief was simply another name for Heavy Runner. Schultz, *Blackfeet and Buffalo*, 294–295. When over forty Piegan chiefs and headmen signed the 1868 treaty presented to them by Commissioner Cullen, the name "Bear Chief" was not on the treaty. The only names that matched the names of chiefs on the various reports of the massacre were Mountain Chief and Heavy Runner.

12. James Hardie to George Hartsuff, Chicago, January 29, 1870, in *Piegan Indians, Letter from the Secretary of War*, 32.

13. *Helena Daily Herald*, January 28, February 2, and April 8, 1870; *New North-West*, February 4 and 25 and March 4, 1870.

14. On January 24, the day after the massacre, even before Baker had returned from battle, a telegraphic order was sent to him at Fort Shaw detailing him for duty there "as a member of a General Court Martial to meet February first at Fort Shaw for trial of Capt. Robinson, at the same time your board for Inspection of Mounted Infantry Horses should assemble there." Fort Shaw Files, NARA; *Army and Navy Journal*, February 5, 1870. The defendant in the court-martial was Captain O. O. G. Robinson of F Company at Fort Ellis, charged with being absent without leave. *Army and Navy Journal*, February 19, 1870.

15. Winfield Hancock to Regis de Trobriand, telegram, January 29, 1870, Fort Shaw Files, NARA.

16. The number 173 was even in the reports of General Sully and Lieutenant Pease, who were then with the Indian department.

17. "The Piegan Fight (Correspondence of the *New York Sun*)," *Army and Navy Journal*, March 5, 1870.

18. Doane, "Letter of March 21, 1874," in Rodenbough, *From Everglade to Canyon*, 552–553.

19. "The Piegan Fight (Correspondence of the *New York Sun*)," *Army and Navy Journal*, March 5, 1870; "Details of the Piegan Fight (Correspondence of the *Philadelphia Ledger*)," *Army and Navy Journal*, March 19, 1870.

20. Joe Kipp Affidavit, Heavy Runner Records, 1914–1921, MF 53, MHS; Alfred B. Hamilton Affidavit, Heavy Runner Records, 1914–1921, MF 53, MHS.

21. From an article in the *Sun River Sun*, "Pop It to 'Em Boys," September 4, 1884, typescript copy in MHS collections.

22. Ponsford File, Special Collections, MSU.

23. "The Piegan Fight (Correspondence of the *New York Sun*)," *Army and Navy Journal*, March 5, 1870.

24. James Hardie to George Hartsuff, telegram, Fort Shaw, Montana, January 13, 1870, reproduced in *Piegan Indians, Letter from the Secretary of War*, 47.

25. E. S. Parker to J. D. Cox, "Report of the Commissioner of Indian Affairs," Washington, DC, October 31, 1870, in *Report of the Commissioner of Indian Affairs for the Year 1870* (Washington, DC: Government Printing Office, 1870), 1–2.

26. "Details of the Piegan Fight (Correspondence of the *Philadelphia Ledger*)," *Army and Navy Journal*, March 19, 1870.

27. Regis de Trobriand to Lina, January 30, 1870, in De Trobriand Papers, SC 1201, MHS.

28. P. H. Sheridan to Eugene Baker, telegram, January 31, 1870, Fort Shaw Files, NARA.

29. F. H. Eastman to Alfred Sully, January 31, 1870, NARA microfilm files.

30. *New North-West*, February 4, 1870.

31. Alfred Sully to Regis de Trobriand, Helena, February 1, 1870, in *Piegan Indians, Letter from the Secretary of War*, 11.

32. Regis de Trobriand to Alfred Sully, Fort Shaw, February 3, 1870, in *Piegan Indians, Letter from the Secretary of War*, 11–12.

33. W. B. Pease to Alfred Sully, February 6, 1870, cited in *Second Annual Report of the Board of Indian Commissioners for the Year 1870*, 89.

34. Ibid.

35. Quoted in *Rocky Mountain Gazette*, February 25, 1870; Regis de Trobriand to A. B. Dyer, February 3, 1870, Fort Shaw Files, NARA. In his report to Brevet Major General Dyer, army chief of ordnance in Washington, DC, de Trobriand said: "During the fall the Companies were replenished by recruits, who before practicing firing at a target must be instructed in the *Manual of Arms*, and Company drills, a course of instruction slow and much interrupted during the winter by the severity of the season. An Officer is now appointed to superintend the target practice."

36. File marked 106 I 1869, "Relative to the Piegan Indians," Stan Gibson Papers, Glenbow Archives, Calgary, Alberta.

37. P. H. Sheridan to W. T. Sherman, February 28, 1870, in *Piegan Indians, Letter from the Secretary of War*, 9, 10.

38. Winfield Hancock to Regis de Trobriand, telegram, January 29, 1870, Fort Shaw Files, NARA.

39. Vincent Collyer to Felix Brunot, Washington, DC, February 22, 1870, in Congressional Globe, 41st Cong. 2nd Sess., 1576 (1870).

40. P. H. Sheridan to W. T. Sherman, telegram, February 28, 1870, in *Piegan Indians, Letter from the Secretary of War*.

41. W. T. Sherman to P. H. Sheridan, Washington, DC, March 5, 1870, in *Piegan Indians, Letter from the Secretary of War*, 10.

42. W. T. Sherman to P. H. Sheridan, March 7, 1870, in Simon, *The Papers of Ulysses S. Grant*, 20:119–120; *Times–Picayune* (New Orleans), March 15, 1870.

43. Regis de Trobriand to Lina, Helena, March 9, 1870, in De Trobriand Papers, SC 1201, MHS.

44. George Hartsuff to Eugene Baker, telegram, March 14, 1870, Fort Shaw Files, NARA.

45. Regis de Trobriand to Lina, Fort Shaw, March 18, 1870, De Trobriand Papers, SC 1201, MHS.

46. *National Anti-Slavery Standard*, March 19, 1870.

47. "Resolution," *Bozeman Pick and Plow*, February 10, 1870, reprinted in *Army and Navy Journal*, March 26, 1870.

48. P. H. Sheridan, "Report of General Sheridan," March 18, 1870, reprinted in *Army and Navy Journal*, March 26, 1870.

49. C. L. Baker to P. H. Sheridan, Fort Ellis, March 23, 1870, telegram, in *Piegan Indians, Letter from the Secretary of War*, 73. C. L. Baker, the author of the telegram, is likely E. M. Baker, as the rank and posting match his. This could be a typographic error in the congressional report.

50. "The Slaughter of the Piegans," *New York Times*, February 24, 1870; "The Piegan Village Slaughter," *New York Times*, March 30, 1870.

CHAPTER 10

Epigraph 1: W. T. Sherman to P. H. Sheridan, March 24, 1870, in *Piegan Indians, Letter from the Secretary of War.*

Epigraph 2: Hugh A. Dempsey, "L'HEUREUX, JEAN," in *Dictionary of Canadian Biography* (Toronto: University of Toronto/Université Laval, 2003), http:// www.biographi.ca/en/bio/1 _heureux_jean_14E.html, vol. 14: s.v. L'Heureux, Jean.

1. *Second Annual Report of the Board of Indian Commissioners for the Year 1870,* 89–90.

2. W. T. Sherman to P. H. Sheridan, March 28, 1870, in Simon, *The Papers of Ulysses S. Grant,* 20:119–120n.

3. W. T. Sherman to P. H. Sheridan, Washington, DC, March 24, 1870, in *Piegan Indians, Letter from the Secretary of War,* 72.

4. "The Piegan Fight," *Army and Navy Journal,* March 26, 1870. The editorial then launched into a lengthy harangue defending the army against the attacks made in the press and elsewhere: "in so soldierly a manner was the surprise of Big Horn's camp, on Marias River, arranged, that our loss in the affair was but one killed and one wounded."

5. Turning to the issue of smallpox in Heavy Runner's camp, the *Journal* (March 26, 1870) quoted General Winfield Hancock: "It was not known, when Colonel Baker's expedition received its orders, that small-pox was in the camps." The *Army and Navy Journal* also quoted General Hancock as saying: "It was supposed the warriors belonging to these camps were all present. If they were not, as has since been alleged, it is presumed the fact was not known to Colonel Baker until the attack ended."

6. Wm. B. Pease to Alfred Sully, Fort Benton, April 7, 1870, in *Second Annual Report of the Board of Indian Commissioners for the Year 1870,* 89–90 (all subsequent Pease quotations are from this letter unless otherwise noted).

7. Regis de Trobriand to Kin [Albert Kintzing Post], Fort Shaw, April 13, 1870, De Trobriand Papers, SC 1201, MHS.

8. "The Indian Slaughter," *Helena Weekly Herald,* April 8, 1870.

9. Regis de Trobriand to Lina, Helena, June 15, 1870, De Trobriand Papers, SC 1201, MHS, where de Trobriand quotes from an unidentified Helena paper of June 15, 1870.

10. Eastman to Sully, April 21, 1870, microfilm roll 833–2, NARA (quotations); Lepley, *Birthplace of Montana,* 82, 87.

11. "Our Barbarian Brethren," *Harper's Weekly,* April 30, 1870.

12. Alfred Sully to E. S. Parker, "Letter from a Jesuit Missionary: "A Talk with the Piegans—Penitence and Humility Manifested—Other Tribes Quiet," *New York Times,* April 26, 1870. Imoda also said that he had talked to Stojas of Lame Bull's band, White Calf, Generous Woman, Cut Head, Big Talk, and one other, all chiefs of various bands, and that they all wanted peace. *Freemont Weekly Journal* (Ohio), May 6, 1870.

13. *Army and Navy Journal*, June 11, 1870.

14. Dempsey, "L'HEUREUX, JEAN," in *Dictionary of Canadian Biography*, s.v. L'Heureux, Jean.

15. Ibid. (quotation); Allen Ronaghan, ed. *Three-Persons and the Chokitapix: Jean L'Heureux's Blackfoot Geography of 1871* (Red Deer, Alberta: CAHS Press, 2011), 4–6.

16. Parker, *Report of the Commissioner of Indian Affairs for the Year 1870*, 1–2.

17. P. H. Sheridan, *Record of Engagements with Hostile Indians within the Military Division of the Missouri, from 1868 to 1882* (Chicago: Headquarters Military Division of the Missouri, 1882), 25–26. Starting his recounting of the events under the heading "1870," Sheridan gives a detailed report of the depredations in Montana. In describing the attack and battle he wrote that "the column completely surprised the camps of Bear Chief, and Big Horn, killing one hundred and seventy-three Indians, wounding twenty, capturing one hundred and forty women and children and over three hundred horses." A notable item in Sheridan's late addition to the massacre reports is that for the first time it includes a count of the number of wounded Indians.

CHAPTER 11

Epigraph 1: "The Piegan Fight (Correspondence of the *New York Sun*)," *Army and Navy Journal*, March 5, 1870.

Epigraph 2: Horace Clarke Affidavit, Heavy Runner Records, 1914–1921, MF 53, MHS.

1. Regis de Trobriand to Lina, April 13, 1870, De Trobriand Papers, SC 1201, MHS.

2. Joseph Kipp Affidavit, Heavy Runner Records, 1914–1921, MF 53, MHS. In his 1915 affidavit Kipp said: "The soldiers rounded up "some four or five hundred head of horses belonging to Chief Heavy Runner."

3. "Details of the Piegan Fight (Correspondence of the *Philadelphia Ledger*)," *Army and Navy Journal*, March 19, 1870.

4. E. M. Baker to J. T. McGinniss, Fort Shaw, February 18, 1870, in *Piegan Indians, Letter from the Secretary of War*, 16–17.

5. Alfred B. Hamilton Affidavit, Heavy Runner Records, 1914–1921, MF 53, MHS.

6. Regis de Trobriand to Winfield Hancock, "Bvt. Brig. Gen. O. D. Greene Asst Ad'gt Genl Dept of Dakota," May 2, 1870.

7. "Army Gazette," *Army and Navy Journal*, December 11, 1869; "General Order No. 79" issued on December 6, 1869, by General Sherman.

8. J. T. McGinniss, Special Order April 28, 1870, Fort Shaw file, NARA.

9. Regis de Trobriand to O. D. Greene, Assistant Adjutant General, May 3, 1870, Fort Shaw Files, NARA.

10. "The Piegan Fight (Correspondence of the *New York Sun*)," *Army and Navy Journal*, March 5, 1870.

11. William Birth to friend, Fort Shaw, January 31, 1870, Special Collections, Yale University Library.

12. The Piegan heirs of Heavy Runner sought to obtain a reimbursement of $75,000 from Congress for the horses and property taken from him during the Baker Massacre. Horace Clarke Affidavit, Senate Bill S. 7523, Heavy Runner Records, 1914–1921, MF 53, MHS. Senate Bill S. 7523 seeking authorization to pay that amount was introduced in the Senate on February 2, 1915, by Senator Harry Lane of Oregon.

13. David Hilger, "Interview with Horace Clark on Sept. 27, 1924, from Notes Taken for the Purpose of Perpetuating Historical Data," Horace Clark Reminiscences, SC 540, MHS. David Hilger's notes of his interview with Horace Clarke are telegraphic in style; most of them are paraphrased, except for directly quoted passages.

14. Horace Clarke Affidavit, Senate Bill S. 7523, in Heavy Runner Records, 1914–1921, MF 53, MHS.

15. Fort Shaw to Fort Ellis, telegram, June 26, 1870, attaching Hancock's telegram of the same date, Fort Ellis Files, NARA. The acting assistant adjutant general of the 13th Infantry sent to the "Commanding Officer, Fort Ellis" a telegram received there from O. D. Green, Hancock's adjutant.

16. J. A. Viall to John Gibbon, November 7, 1870, Fort Shaw Files, NARA. Gibbon had succeeded de Trobriand at Fort Shaw. Thompson had also garnered another endorsement to release the robes "from further detention" from U.S. marshal W. F. Wheeler on behalf of Henry Thompson "of the firm of Taylor, Thompson + Co. merchants and miners of this town." Wheeler said: "Mr. T. is one of our best citizens and any courtesy you can extend him will [be] greatly reciprocated."

17. E. D. Townsend to Winfield Hancock, Washington, DC, October 29, 1870, Fort Ellis File, NARA.

18. Letter from John Gibbon to O. D. Greene, Fort Shaw, November 16, 1870, Fort Shaw Files, NARA. On November 16 Colonel John Gibbon of the 7th Infantry, which had replaced de Trobriand and his 13th at Fort Shaw, wrote to Hancock's adjutant that in "accordance with your endorsement of the 4th on the letter of the Adjutant General of the Army regarding the release of Buffalo Robes, that there is no action on the subject called for at this Post, No robes being held at this place under the instruction of the War Dept."

19. Overholser, *Fort Benton*, 76. Overholser estimated that in the period from 1860 to 1890 "Down cargoes included 750,000 buffalo robes."

20. "How Small-Pox Spreads," *Cincinnati Enquirer*, November 11, 1871. The article continued: "At that time they were forbidden to be sold to traders, but several months ago they disappeared from those neighborhoods and found their way elsewhere."

21. Ewers, *The Blackfeet*, 256—259. See also Hugh A. Dempsey, *The Amazing Death of Calf Shirt and Other Blackfoot Stories: Three Hundred Years of Blackfoot History* (Norman: University of Oklahoma Press, 1994).

22. Andrew Graybill, *The Red and the White: A Family Saga of the American West* (New York: Liveright, 2013), 143–148.

23. Horace Clarke Affidavit, Heavy Runner Records, 1914–1921, MF 53, MHS; Graybill, *The Red and the White*, 147–148; Martha Plassmann Papers, MC 78, MHS. Martha Edgerton was born May 14, 1850, in Ohio. Her father, Sidney Edgerton, was the first appointed governor of the Territory of Montana, created on May 26, 1864. She lived in Great Falls, starting in 1881, and became the editor and owner of a newspaper, which she sold in 1896. She then went into a variety of occupations, which included writing articles for publication. Married twice, Martha Edgerton Rolfe Plassmann died on September 25, 1936, in Great Falls, at the age of eighty-six.

24. "1998 Blackfeet Genealogy."

CHAPTER 12

Epigraph: General Court Martial Orders, No. 48, Headquarters of the Army, Adjutant General's Office, Washington, DC, July 5, 1881, Baker Court Martial File, NARA.

1. Merrill G. Burlingame and K. Ross Toole, *A History of Montana* (New York: Lewis Historical, 1957), 2:114.

2. Elizabeth "Lizzie" Chester Fisk was born on February 18, 1846, in East Haddam, Connecticut, of staunch Presbyterian and Republican parents. Rex C. Myers, ed., *Lizzie: The Letters of Elizabeth Chester Fisk, 1864–1893* (Missoula, MT: Mountain Press, 1989); Elizabeth Fisk to Mother, July 24, 1871, and January 19, 1872; Elizabeth Fisk to Fannie, October 10, 1871, Elizabeth Chester Fisk file, MC 31, MHS.

3. Elizabeth Fisk to Mother, January 19, 1872, August 6, 1872, Elizabeth Chester Fisk file, MC 31, MHS; Myers, *Lizzie*, 68–69, 79–80. Mae was married in 1874 to Mr. Charles D. Hard.

4. "Typescript copy of apparent letter from A. J. Noyes," Paul McCormick Papers, SC 423, MHS. Noyes commented that Baker did not tell his story because he thought that people would not believe what he had gone through.

5. Baker military record, Stan Gibson Papers, Glenbow Archives, Calgary, Alberta; Heitman, *Historical Register*, vol. 1, s.v. Baker, Eugene; Cullum, *Biographical Register*, vol. 1, s.v. Baker, Eugene. A senator from West Virginia intervened with General Sherman, who referred the matter to General Hancock. Afterward it was apparently dropped.

6. Baker returned to duty at Fort Sanders, Wyoming, on November 1, 1876, and served there until September 1877. He became commander of Fort Fred

Steele, Wyoming, until December 1, 1876, then was on duty again at Fort Sanders until September 1877. He went to Fort Keogh, Montana, from October 1877 until August 15, 1878. During this time, Baker had some interesting assignments, first with the Hoyt-Miles visit to Yellowstone Park then with a field expedition against hostile Indians (to November 6, 1878), followed by duty with a battalion in the field (October 14 to November 6, 1878) and at Fort Keogh, Montana (November 6, 1878, to June 24, 1879), where he was a frontier duty commander of a field battalion until September 1, 1879.

7. Martha Edgerton Plassmann Papers, MC 78, MHS. Baker's unavoidable absence resulted in a minor penalty, when he was relieved from duty for three days.

8. J. R. Brooke to E. C. Gilbraith, telegram, April 23, 1881, Baker Court Martial File, NARA. The officers on the court were Colonel T. H. Ruger, 15th Infantry; Colonel J. R. Brooke, 3rd Infantry, Lieutenant Colonel A. J. Alexander, 2nd Infantry; Lieutenant Colonel E. T. Townsend, 11th Infantry, Major J. A. Brisbin, 2nd Cavalry; and Major H. L. Chipman, 3rd Infantry. The assigned judge advocate was Captain C. H. Potter of the 18th Infantry.

9. Baker Court Martial File, NARA (all subsequent court-martial quotations are from this source unless otherwise noted).

10. Signed April 18, 1881. Other statements were from General. Jno. E. Smith, 14th Infantry; Col. J. W. Forsyth, 1st Cavalry; and General Wesley Merritt, 5th Cavalry. Baker Court Martial File, NARA.

11. Gromin emphasized that the offense was "the first committed by the accused, and to have been attended by no public scandal." Baker Court Martial File, NARA.

12. The order was passed on down to the secretary of war, who determined the six-month suspension would start on July 25, 1881. Baker Court Martial File, NARA.

13. General Court Martial Orders, No. 48, Headquarters of the Army, Adjutant General's Office, Washington, DC, July 5, 1881, issued by R. C. Drum, Adjutant General, by Command of General Sherman. Baker Court Martial File, NARA.

14. Baker sick leave file from NARA records. Copy in Stan Gibson Papers, Glenbow Archives, Calgary, Alberta.

15. General Affidavit of Salome Baker, May 14, 1888, pension files, NARA. Copy in Stan Gibson Papers, Glenbow Archives, Calgary, Alberta.

16. "Captain G. A. Doane, 2nd Cavalry, Record of Service," handwritten document, No. 2211, File 3.1, Special Collections, MSU.

17. G. C. Doane to W. F. Sanders, January 7, 1891, Gustavus C. Doane Papers, 1860–1939, Collection 2211, Box 4, Vol. 3, 85–87, Merrill G. Burlingame Special Collections, MSU Libraries, Bozeman, Montana.

Bibliography

MANUSCRIPTS

Albert G. Brackett Diaries. SC 458. Montana Historical Society (MHS), Helena.

Baker Court Martial File. National Archives and Records Administration (NARA), Washington, DC.

Camp Cooke Records. Group 393. NARA.

De Trobriand Papers. SC 1201. MHS.

Elizabeth Chester Fisk file. MC 31. MHS.

"The Fort Benton Journal, 1854–1856, and the *Fort Sarpy Journal,* 1855–1856." *Contributions to the Historical Society of Montana* 10 (1940). MHS.

Fort Ellis Files. NARA.

Fort Shaw Files. NARA.

Heavy Runner Records, 1914–1921. MF53. MHS.

Horace Clark Reminiscences. SC 540. MHS.

Interior Department Territorial Papers: Montana. M-192. NARA.

John Ponsford File. SC 659. MHS.

Kipp, Tavi. *History of the Kipp Family in Montana.* SC 2314. MHS.

Martha Plassmann Papers. MC 78. MHS.

Martin Hogan Papers. D. C. Donoghue-Montgomery Collection. SC 864. MHS.

Montana Territorial Papers. MHS.

Office of Indian Affairs, Letters Received. RG 75. NARA.

Overholser Archives. Fort Benton, MT.

Paul McCormick Papers. SC 423. MHS.

Phillip Sheridan Papers. Microfilm. LC, Washington, DC.

Presidential Papers: Microfilm Editions to Ulysses S. Grant Papers. Microfilm. LC.

Records of the Montana Superintendency of Indian Affairs. M-833. NARA.

Samuel Latham Mitchell Barlow Collection. Huntington Library and Archives, San Marino, California.

Shirley Carter Ashby Papers. SC 283. MHS.

Special Collections. Yale University Library, New Haven, Connecticut.

Stan Gibson Papers. Glenbow Archives, Calgary.

State Department Territorial Papers. M-356. NARA.

Territorial Governor File. MHS.
William T. Sherman Papers. Microfilm. LC.
Willson Collection. MSU Special Collections, Bozeman.

PUBLISHED GOVERNMENT DOCUMENTS

Annual Report of the Secretary of War. 40th Cong., 1st Sess., 1868, H. Ex. Doc. 1, serial 1367.

Congressional Globe. 41st Cong., 2nd Sess. (1870).

Doolittle Committee. "New Directions in Government Policy." Senate Report No. 156, 39th Cong., 2nd Sess., serial 1279.

House Miscellaneous Documents. 39th Cong., 2nd Sess. H. Ex. Doc. 37.

"Information Furnished by Surgeon P. C. Davis and Assistant Surgeon Clarence Ewen, United States Army." *Circular No. 4.* Washington, DC: War Department, Surgeon General's Office, December 5, 1870.

Piegan Indians, Letter from the Secretary of War in Answer to a Resolution of the House, of March 3, 1870, in Relation to the Late Expedition against the Piegan Indians, in the Territory of Montana. 41st Cong., 2nd Sess., H. Ex. Doc. 269.

Report of the Commissioner of Indian Affairs for the Year 1865. Washington, DC: Government Printing Office, 1865.

Report of the Commissioner of Indian Affairs for the Year 1866. Washington, DC: Government Printing Office, 1866.

Report of the Commissioner of Indian Affairs for the Year 1867. Washington, DC: Government Printing Office, 1867.

Report of the Commissioner of Indian Affairs for the Year 1868. Washington, DC: Government Printing Office, 1868.

Report of the Commissioner of Indian Affairs Made to the Secretary of the Interior for the Year 1869. Washington, DC, Government Printing Office, 1870. http://digital.library.wisc.edu/1711.dl/History.AnnRep69.

"A Report on Barracks and Hospitals, with Descriptions of Military Posts." Washington, DC: Government Printing Office, 1870.

Report to Accompany Bill S. 519. 41st Cong., 2nd sess. Report No. 31.

Report to Accompany H. Res. 23. 42nd Cong., 2nd Sess., Report No. 82.

Report upon the Montana Indian War Claims of 1867, 41st Cong., 3rd Sess., H. Ex. Doc. No. 98.

Second Annual Report of the Board of Indian Commissioners for the Year 1870. Washington, DC: Government Printing Office, 1871.

Senate Executive Journal. 39th Cong., 2nd Sess.

Senate Executive Journal. 40th Cong., 1st Sess.

Sheridan, P. H. *Record of Engagements with Hostile Indians within the Military Division of the Missouri, from 1868 to 1882.* Chicago: Headquarters Military Division of the Missouri, 1882.

NEWSPAPERS

Army and Navy Journal
Chicago Tribune
Great Falls Tribune
Harper's Weekly
Helena Herald
Irish American
Missouri Republican
Montana Post
New York Herald
New York Times
Rochester Union and Advertiser
Ronan Pioneer
Salt Lake Tribune
Union and Dakotaian
Virginia Tri-Weekly Post
Weekly Montana Democrat

ARTICLES

Bradley Manuscript. Contributions to the Historical Society of Montana 10. Helena: Rocky Mountain Publishing, 1940.

Dempsey, Hugh A. "Jerry Potts, Plainsman." *Montana The Magazine of Western History* 17, no. 4 (1967).

Genetin-Pilawa, C. Joseph. "Ely Parker and the Contentious Peace Policy." *Western Historical Quarterly* 41, no. 2 (Summer 2010).

Gibson, Stan, and Jack Hayne. *Witnesses to Carnage: The 1870 Marias Massacre in Montana*. Calgary, Alberta: Glenbow Archives. http://www.dickshovel .com/parts2.html.

Huckabee, Rodger. "Camp Cooke: Montana Territory's Forgotten First U.S. Army Post." *Montana The Magazine of Western History* 62, no. 4 (Winter 2012).

———. "Camp Cooke: The First Army Post in Montana—Success and Failure on the Missouri." Master's thesis, Boise State University, 2010.

Kuppens, Francis Xavier. "Thomas Francis Meagher, Montana Pioneer." *Mid-America: An Historical Review* 14, no. 3 (1931–1932).

Lass, William E. "The History and Significance of the Northwest Fur Company, 1865–1869." *North Dakota History: Journal of the Northern Plains* 61, no. 3 (Summer 1994).

Meagher, Thomas Francis. "A Journey to Benton." *Montana The Magazine of Western History* 1, no. 4 (October 1951). http://www.jstor.org/stable/4515758.

Morton, W. L. "The North West Company: Pedlars Extraordinary." *Minnesota History* 40, no. 4 (Winter 1966).

Pepion, Donald D. "Marias Massacre: Killing the Heavyrunner Band of Blackfeet." Blackfeet Community College, Browning, Montana, March 29, 1999.

Walter, David A. ed. "Montana Episodes: The 1855 Blackfeet Treaty Council, a Memoir by Henry A. Kennerly." *Montana The Magazine of Western History* 32, no. 1 (Winter 1982). http://www.jstor.org/stable/4518633.

Wilson, Wesley C., "The U.S. Army and the Piegans: The Baker Massacre of 1870." *North Dakota History* 32, no. 1 (January 1965). Bismarck: State Historical Society.

Wood, W. Raymond. "James Kipp: Upper Missouri Fur Trader and Missouri River Farmer." *North Dakota History* 77, nos. 1 and 2 (2011).

BOOKS

Armstrong, William H. *Warrior in Two Camps: Ely S. Parker, Union General and Seneca Chief.* Syracuse, NY: Syracuse University Press, 1978.

Arthur, Jim, ed. *Retracing Kipp Family Trails: A Collection of Stories and Pictures of the Kipp Family and the Country They Lived In, with Stories by Octavia Kipp.* Lewistown: Central Montana, 1997.

Athearn, Robert G. *Thomas Francis Meagher: An Irish Revolutionary in America.* Boulder: University Press of Colorado, 1949.

———. *William Tecumseh Sherman and the Settlement of the West.* Norman: University of Oklahoma Press, 1956.

Barbour, Barton H. *Fort Union and the Upper Missouri Fur Trade.* Norman: University of Oklahoma Press, 2001.

Belyea, Barbara, ed. *A Year Inland: The Journal of a Hudson's Bay Company Winterer.* Waterloo, Ontario: Wilfred Laurier University Press, 2000.

Bergon, Frank, ed. *The Journals of Lewis and Clark.* New York: Viking Penguin, 1989.

Black, George. *Empire of Shadows: The Epic Story of Yellowstone.* New York: St. Martin's Press, 2012.

Blackfeet Heritage Program. *Blackfeet Heritage, 1907–1908.* Browning, MT: Blackfeet Heritage Program, 1980.

Boller, Henry A. *Twilight of the Upper Missouri River Fur Trade: The Journals of Henry A. Boller.* Ed. W. Raymond Wood. Bismarck: State Historical Society of North Dakota, 2008.

Bond, Rowland. *The Original Northwester: David Thompson and the Native Tribes of North America.* Nine Mile Falls, WA: Spokane House Enterprises, 1970.

Burlingame, Merrill G. *The Montana Frontier.* Bozeman: Big Sky Books, Montana State University, 1980.

Burlingame, Merrill, and K. Ross Toole. *A History of Montana*. 2 vols. New York: Lewis Historical Publishing Company, 1957.

Butler, W. F. *The Great Lone Land: A Narrative of Travel and Adventure in the North-West of America*. London: Sampson Low, Marston, Low & Searle, 1873.

Calloway, Colin G. *Our Hearts Fell to the Ground: Plains Indian Views of How the West Was Lost*. Boston: Bedford/St. Martin's, 1966.

Catlin, George. *Letters and Notes on the Manners, Customs and Conditions of N. American Indians* (1844). 2 vols. Reprint. New York: Dover Publications, 1973.

Chardon, Francis. *Chardon's Journal, Fort Clark, 1834–1839* (1932). Ed. Annie Heloise Abel. Lincoln: University of Nebraska Press, 1997.

Chittenden, Hiram. *The American Fur Trade of the Far West* (1935). 2 vols. Lincoln: University of Nebraska Press, 1986.

Clark Van Cleve, Charlotte Ouisconsin. *Three Score Years and Ten*. Minneapolis: Harrison & Smith, 1888.

Clodfelter, Michael. *The Dakota War: The United States Army versus the Sioux*. Jefferson, NC: McFarland & Company, 1998.

Coffman, Edward M. *The Old Army: A Portrait of the American Army in Peacetime, 1784–1898*. New York: Oxford University Press, 1986.

Crakes, Sylvester. *Five Years a Captive among the Blackfeet Indians: Or a Thrilling Narrative of the Adventures, Perils and Suffering Endured by John Dixon and His Companions*. Columbus: Osgood and Pearce Printers, 1858.

Culbertson, Thaddeus A. *Journal of an Expedition to the Mauvaises Terres and the Upper Missouri in 1850*. Ed. John Francis McDermott. Bureau of American Ethnology, Bulletin 147, Smithsonian Institution. Washington, DC: Government Printing Office, 1952.

Cullum, George. *Biographical Register of the Officers and Graduates of the U.S. Military Academy*. 2nd ed. 3 vols. New York: D. Van Nostrand, 1868.

DeConde, Alexander. *This Affair of Louisiana*. New York: Charles Scribner & Sons, 1976.

Dempsey, Hugh A. *The Amazing Death of Calf Shirt and Other Blackfoot Stories: Three Hundred Years of Blackfoot History*. Norman: University of Oklahoma Press, 1994.

———. *A Blackfoot Winter Count*. Occasional Paper No. 1. Calgary: Glenbow Foundation, 1965.

———. *Firewater: The Impact of the Whisky Trade on the Blackfoot Nations*. Calgary: Calgary Fifth House, 2002.

———. *Jerry Potts, Plainsman*. Occasional Paper No. 2. Calgary: Glenbow Foundation, 1966.

Dillon, Mark C. *The Vigilantes of Montana, 1863–1870: Gold, Guns and Gallows*. Logan: Utah State University Press, 2013.

Dolin, Eric Jay. *Fur, Fortune and Empire: The Epic History of the Fur Trade in America*. New York: W. W. Norton, 2010.

Doyle, Susan, ed. *Journeys to the Land of Gold: Emigrant Diaries from the Bozeman Trail, 1863–1886.* Helena: Montana Historical Society Press, 2000.

Dunn, Jacob Piatt. *Massacres of the Mountains: A History of the Indian Wars of the Far West, 1815–1875* (1886). Mechanicsburg, PA: Stackpole Books, 2002.

Ege, Robert J. *Tell Baker to Strike Them Hard!* Bellevue, NE: Old Army Press, 1970.

Epp, Henry, ed. *Three Hundred Prairie Years: Henry Kelsey's "Inland Country of Good Report."* Regina: Canadian Plains Research Center, 1993.

Ewers, John C. *The Blackfeet: Raiders on the Northwestern Plains.* Norman: University of Oklahoma Press, 1958.

———. *The Horse in Blackfoot Indian Culture.* Washington, DC: Government Printing Office, 1955.

Farr, William E. *Blackfoot Redemption: A Blood Indian's Story of Murder, Confinement, and Imperfect Justice.* Norman: University of Oklahoma Press, 2012.

Field, Ron. *U.S. Infantry in the Indian Wars, 1865–1891.* Oxford: Osprey Publishing, 2007.

Fifer, Barbara. *Montana Battlefields, 1806–1877: Native Americans and the U.S. Army at War.* Helena: Farcountry Press, 2005.

Ford, Wendell H., ed. *Inaugural Addresses of the Presidents of the United States.* Washington, DC: Government Printing Office, 1989.

Gibbs, George. *Indian Tribes of Washington Territory.* Fairfield, WA: Ye Galleon Press, 1972.

Gough, Stephen T. *Colter's Run.* Stevensville, MT: Stoneydale Press Publishing, 2008.

Grant, Ulysses S. *State of the Union Addresses.* Whitefish, MT: Kessinger Publishing, 2004.

Graybill, Andrew, *The Red and the White: A Family Saga of the American West.* New York: Liveright, 2013.

Greene, Jerome A. *Reconnaissance Survey of Indian–U.S. Army Battlefields of the Northern Plains.* Denver: National Park Service, Cultural Resources and National Register Program Services, Intermountain Support Office, 1998.

———. *Washita: The U.S. Army and the Southern Cheyennes, 1867–1869.* Campaigns and Commanders Series, vol. 3. Norman: University of Oklahoma Press, 2004.

Grinnell, George Bird. *Story of the Indian.* New York: Appleton Publishing, 1895.

Hafen, LeRoy R., *Broken Hand: The Life of Thomas Fizpatrick, Mountain Man, Guide and Indian Agent.* Lincoln: University of Nebraska Press, 1973.

———, ed. *Fur Traders, Trappers, and Mountain Men of the Upper Missouri.* Lincoln: University of Nebraska Press, 1995.

———, ed. *The Mountain Men and the Fur Trade of the Far West.* (1965). Vol. 2. Lincoln: University of Nebraska Press, 1995.

Hamilton, James. *From Wilderness to Statehood: A History of Montana, 1805–1900* (1907). 2nd ed. Edited by Merrill Burlingame. Portland: Binford's & Mort, 1957.

Hampton, H. Duane. *Life and Death at the Mouth of the Musselshell: Montana Territory, 1868–1872, Featuring the Diary of C. M. Lee, Gunsmith, Merchant.* Stevensville, MT: Stoneydale Press Publishing, 2011.

Hanchett, Leland J., Jr. *Montana's Benton Road.* Wolf Creek, MT: Pine Rim Publishing, 2008.

Hanson, James A. *When Skins Were Money: A History of the Fur Trade.* Chadron, NE: Museum of the Fur Trade, 2005.

Hebard, Grace Raymond, and E. A. Brininstool. *The Bozeman Traill: Historical Acounts of the Blazing of the Overland Routes into the Northwest and the Fights with Red Cloud's Warriors.* Vol. 1. Lincoln: University of Nebraska Press, 1922.

Hedren, Paul L. *Fort Laramie and the Great Sioux War.* Norman: University of Oklahoma Press, 1998.

Heitman, Francis B. *Historical Register and Dictionary of the United States Army, from Its Organization, September 29, 1789, to March 2, 1903* (1903). 2 vols. Urbana: University of Illinois Press, 1965.

Henry, Alexander. *The Journal of Alexander Henry the Younger, 1799–1814.* Ed. Barry M. Gough. 2 vols. Toronto: Champlain Society, 1992.

Hoig, Stan. *The Battle of the Washita: The Sheridan-Custer Indian Campaign of 1867–69.* Lincoln: University of Nebraska Press, 1980.

———. *The Chouteaus: First Family of the Fur Trade.* Santa Fe: University of New Mexico Press, 2008.

Hungry Wolf, Adolf. *The Blackfeet Papers: Volume One: Pikunni History and Culture.* Skookumchuck, BC: Good Medicine Cultural Foundation, 2006.

Hyde, Anne F. *Empires, Nations, and Families: A New History of the North American West, 1800–1860.* Lincoln: University of Nebraska Press, 2011.

Institute for the Development of Indian Law. *Treaties and Agreements of the Indian Tribes of the Pacific Northwest.* Washington, DC: Institute for the Development of Indian Law, 1974.

Jackson, John C. *Jemmy Jock Bird: Marginal Man on the Blackfoot Frontier.* Calgary: University of Calgary Press, 2003.

———. *Shadow on the Tetons: David E. Jackson and the Claiming of the American West.* Missoula: Mountain Press Publishing, 1993.

Jackson, John G. *The Piikani Blackfeet: A Culture under Siege.* Missoula: Mountain Press Publishing, 2000.

Johnson, Susan. *Roaring Camp: The Social World of the California Gold Rush.* New York: Norton, 2000.

Johnston, Alex, and Andy A. den Otter. *Lethbridge: A Centennial History.* Ed. Hugh A. Dempsey, Lethbridge: City of Lethbridge and Whoop-Up Country Chapter, Historical Society of Alberta, 1985.

Jordan, David M. *Winfield Scott Hancock: A Soldier's Life.* Bloomfield: Indiana University Press, 1988.

Kaplan, Justin, ed. *Bartlett's Familiar Quotations.* 16th ed. Boston: Little, Brown and Company, 1992.

Kappler, Charles J., ed. *Indian Affairs: Laws and Treaties.* 2 vols. Washington, DC: Government Printing Office, 1904. http://digital.library.okstate.edu/kappler.

Kennedy, Margaret A. *The Whiskey Trade of the Northwestern Plains: A Multidisciplinary Study.* New York: Peter Lang Publishing, 1997.

Kennedy, M. A., and B. O. K. Reeves. *An Inventory and Historical Description of Whiskey Posts in Southern Alberta.* Edmonton: Historic Sites Service, Old St. Stephen's College, 1984. Special Collections, Schwinden Library, Fort Benton, MT.

Kurz, Rudolph Friederich. *The Journal of Rudolph Friederich Kurz: An Account of His Experiences among Fur Traders and American Indians on the Mississippi and the Upper Missouri Rivers during the Years 1846 to 1852.* Trans. Myrtis Jarrell. Lincoln: University of Nebraska Press, 1970.

Lancaster, Richard. *Piegan: A Look from within at the Life, Times and Legacy of an American Indian Tribe.* New York: Doubleday & Company, 1966.

Larpenteur, Charles. *Forty Years a Fur Trader on the Upper Missouri: The Personal Narrative of Charles Larpenteur, 1833–1872.* Chicago: Lakeside Press, 1933.

Lazelle, Henry Martyn, and Leslie J. Perry, eds. *The War of the Rebellion: A Compilation of the Official Records of the Union Army.* 70 vols. in 128. Washington, DC: Government Printing Office, 1880–1901.

Leforge, Thomas, and Thomas Marquis. *Memoirs of a White Crow Indian* (1928). Lincoln: University of Nebraska Press, 1974.

Lepley, John G. *Birthplace of Montana: A History of Fort Benton.* Missoula: Pictorial Histories Publishing Company, 1999.

———. *Blackfoot Fur Trade on the Upper Missouri.* Missoula: Pictorial Histories Publishing Company, 2004.

Lott, Davis, ed. *The Presidents Speak: Inaugural Addresses of the Presidents of the United States, from George Washington to George W. Bush.* 4th ed. Los Angeles: Olive Grove Publishing, 2002.

Lowie, Robert H. *Indians of the Plains.* Bison Book edition. Lincoln: University of Nebraska Press, 1982.

MacGregor, James G. *A History of Alberta.* Edmonton: Hurtig Publishers, 1972.

MacGregor, Jas. G. *Behold the Shining Mountains.* Edmonton: Applied Art Products, 1954.

Mattes, Merrill. *Great Platte River Road: The Covered Wagon Mainline via Fort Kearny to Fort Laramie.* Lincoln: Nebraska State Historical Society, 1969.

McAlexander, Ulysses Grant. *History of the Thirteenth Regiment United States Infantry.* Ed. Frank D. Gunn. N.p.: Regimental Press, 1905.

McBride, Genevieve. *The Bird Tail.* New York: Vantage Press, 1974.

McChristian, Douglas C. *Fort Laramie: Military Bastion of the High Plains.* Norman: University of Oklahoma Press, 2008.

McCreight, M. I. *Firewater and Forded Tongues: A Sioux Chief Interprets U.S. History.* Pasadena, CA: Trails End Publishing, 1947.

Michno, Gregory F. *Encyclopedia of Indian Wars, Western Battles and Skirmishes, 1850–1890.* Missoula: Mountain Press Publishing, 2003.

Michno, Gregory F., and Susan Michno. *Forgotten Fights: Little-Known Raids and Skirmishes on the Frontier, 1823 to 1890.* Missoula: Mountain Press Publishing, 2008.

Montana Historical Society. *Not in Precious Metals Alone: A Manuscript History of Montana.* Helena: Montana Historical Society, 1976.

Morton, Arthur S. *A History of the Canadian West to 1870–71: Being a History of Rupert's Land (The Hudson's Bay Company's Territory) and of the North-West Territory (Including the Pacific Slope).* Toronto: Thomas Nelson & Sons, 1939.

Myers, Rex C., ed. *Lizzie: The Letters of Elizabeth Chester Fisk, 1864–1893.* Missoula: Mountain Press Publishing, 1989.

Nabokov, Peter, ed. *Native American Testimony* (1978). Revised ed. New York: Penguin Books, 1999.

Noyes, Alva Josiah. *In the Land of Chinook: or, the Story of Blaine County.* Berkeley: University of California Libraries, 1917.

Oglesby, Richard Edward. *Manuel Lisa and the Opening of the Missouri Fur Trade.* Norman: University of Oklahoma Press, 1963.

O'Neil, Paul. *The Rivermen.* New York: Time-Life Books, 1975.

Overholser, Joel. *Fort Benton: World's Innermost Port.* Helena: Falcon Press, 1987.

Paher, Stanley. *Nevada Ghost Towns and Mining Camps.* Las Vegas: Nevada Publications, 1970.

Palladino, Lawrence B. *Indian and White in the Northwest: A History of Catholicity in Montana, 1831 to 1891.* Lancaster, PA: Wickersham Publishing, 1922.

Perdue, Theda, and Michael D. Green, eds. *The Cherokee Removal: A Brief History with Documents.* Boston: Bedford/St. Martin's, 1955.

Phillips, Paul C. *Forty Years on the Frontier, as Seen in the Journals and Reminiscences of Granville Stuart, Gold-Miner, Trader, Merchant, Rancher and Politician.* 2 vols. Cleveland: Arthur H. Clark, 1925.

Phillips, Paul Chrisler. *The Fur Trade.* Norman: University of Oklahoma Press, 1961.

Point, Nicholas. *Wilderness Kingdom: Indian Life in the Rocky Mountains, 1840–1847: The Journals and Paintings of Nicolas Point, S.J.* Trans. and introduced by Joseph P. Donnelly. Chicago: Loyola University Press 1967.

Prucha, Francis Paul. *American Indian Treaties: The History of a Political Anomaly.* Berkeley: University of California Press, 1994.

———. *Documents of United States Indian Policy.* Lincoln: University of Nebraska Press, 2000.

Quaife, Milo M., ed. *The Journals of Captain Meriwether Lewis and Sergeant John Ordway: Kept on the Expedition of Western Exploration, 1803–1806.* Madison: State Historical Society of Wisconsin, 1965.

Reid, John Phillip. *Patterns of Vengeance: Cross-Cultural Homicide in the North American Fur Trade.* Pasadena, CA: Ninth Judicial Circuit Historical Society, 1999.

Richardson, Albert D. *Beyond the Mississippi: From the Great River to the Great Ocean: Life and Adventure on the Prairies, Mountains, and Pacific Coast, 1857–1867.* Hartford, CT: American Publishing, 1867.

Robertson, R. G. *Competitive Struggle: America's Western Fur Trading Posts, 1764–1865.* Boise: Tamarack Books, 1999.

Rodenbough, Theophilus F. *From Everglade to Canyon with the Second United States Cavalry: An Authentic Account of Service in Florida, Mexico, Virginia, and the Indian Country, 1836–1875.* (1875). Norman: University of Oklahoma Press, 2000.

Roe, Frank Gilbert. *The North American Buffalo: A Critical Study of the Species in Its Wild State.* 2nd ed. Toronto: University of Toronto Press, 1951.

Ronaghan, Allen, ed. *Three-Persons and the Chokitapix: Jean L'Heureux's Blackfoot Geography of 1871.* Red Deer, Alberta: CAHS Press, 2011.

Safford, Jeffrey. *The Mechanics of Optimism: Mining Companies, Technology, and the Hot Spring Gold Rush, Montana Territory, 1864–1868.* Boulder: University Press of Colorado, 2004.

Sanders, Helen Fitzgerald. *A History of Montana.* Chicago: Lewis Publishing Company, 1913.

Schoolcraft, Henry Rowe, ed. *Information respecting the History, Condition, and Prospects of the Indian Tribes of the United States.* Philadelphia: Lippincott, Grambo, 1851–1857.

Schultz, James Willard. *Blackfeet and Buffalo: Memories of Life among the Indians.* Norman: University of Oklahoma Press, 1962.

———. *Floating on the Missouri.* Ed. Eugene Lee Silliman. Norman: University of Oklahoma Press, 1979.

Scott, Kim Allen, ed. *Splendid on a Large Scale: The Writings of Hans Peter Gyllembourg Koch, Montana Territory, 1869–1874.* Helena: Bedrock Editions & Drumlummon, 2010.

———. *Yellowstone Denied: The Life of Gustavus Cheyney Doane.* Norman: University of Oklahoma Press, 2007.

Sharp, Paul F. *Whoop-Up Country: The Canadian–American West, 1865–1885* (1955). Helena: Historical Society of Montana, 1960.

Shrader, Charles R., ed. *United States Army Logistics, 1775–1992: An Anthology.* Vol. 1. Washington, DC: Center of Military History, United States Army, 1997.

Simon, John, ed. *The Papers of Ulysses S. Grant.* 32 vols. Carbondale: Southern Illinois University Press, 1967–2012.

Starr, Kevin, and Richard J. Orsi, eds. *Rooted in Barbarous Soil: People, Culture, and Community in Gold Rush California.* Berkeley: University of California Press, 2000.

Stevens, Hazard. *The Life of General Isaac I. Stevens.* 2 vols. Boston: Houghton Mifflin, 1901.

Sully, Langdon. *No Tears for the General: The Life of Alfred Sully, 1821–1879.* Palo Alto: American West Publishing, 1974.

Sunder, John E. *The Fur Trade on the Upper Missouri, 1840–1865.* Norman: University of Oklahoma Press, 1965.

Tate, Michael L. *The Frontier Army in the Settlement of the West.* Norman: University of Oklahoma Press, 1999.

Thwaites, Reuben Gold. *Early Western Travels, 1748–1846* (1906). Vols. 22–25. New York: AMS Press, 1966.

———, ed. *Original Journals of the Lewis and Clark Expedition, 1804–1806.* Vol. 5. New York: Antiquarian Press, 1959.

Touchie, Rodger D. *Bear Child: The Life and Times of Jerry Potts.* Victoria and Vancouver: Heritage House Publishing, 2005.

Trobriand, Philippe Régis Denis de Keredern de. *Army Life in Dakota: Selections from the Journal of Philippe Régis Denis de Keredern de Trobriand.* Chicago: Lakeside Press, 1941.

———. *Four Years with the Army of the Potomac.* Translated by George K. Dauchy. Boston: Ticknor & Company, 1889.

Trobriand, Philippe Régis Denis de Keredern de, and Marie Caroline Post. *The Life and Mémoirs of Comte Régis de Trobriand, Major-General in the Army of the United States, by His Daughter Marie Caroline Post (Mrs. Charles Alfred Post).* New York: E. P. Dutton, 1910.

Tucker, Glenn. *Hancock the Superb.* New York: Bobbs-Merrill, 1960.

Twenebroker, George Parkin de, ed. *The Hargrave Correspondence, 1821–1843* (1938). New York: Greenwood Press, 1968.

Tyrrell, J. B., ed. *David Thompson's Narrative of His Explorations in Western America, 1784–1812.* Toronto: Champlain Society, 1916. Online at https://archive .org/details/davidthompsonsna00thom.

Utley, Robert M. *Frontier Regulars: The United States Army and the Indian, 1866– 1891.* Bison Books edition. Lincoln: University of Nebraska Press, 1984.

———. *Indian Wars.* Boston: Houghton Mifflin, 2002.

Vaughn, Robert. *Then and Now; or, Thirty-Six Years in the Rockies, 1864–1900* (1900). Helena: Farcountry Press, 2001.

Walker, Dale. *The Calamity Papers: Western Myths and Cold Cases.* New York: Tom Doherty, Associates, 2004.

Warkentin, John. *The Kelsey Papers.* Regina: Canadian Plains Research Center, 1994.

Watson, Blake A. *Buying America from the Indians: Johnson v. McIntosh and the History of Native Land Rights.* Norman: University of Oklahoma Press, 2012.

Welch, James. *Fools Crow.* New York: Viking, 1986.

Welch, James, with Paul Stekler. *Killing Custer: The Battle of the Little Bighorn and the Fate of the Plains Indians.* New York: W. W. Norton, 1994.

Weygant, Charles H. *The Sacketts of America: Their Ancestors and Descendants, 1630–1907*. Newburgh, NY: published by the Author, 1907.

White, Helen McCann, ed. *Ho! For the Gold Fields: Northern Overland Wagon Trains of the 1860s*. St. Paul: Minnesota Historical Society, 1966.

White, William Henry. *Custer, Cavalry & Crows: The Story of William White, as Told to Thomas Marquis*. Fort Collins: Old Army Press, 1975.

Wischmann, Lesley. *Frontier Diplomats: The Life and Times of Alexander Culbertson and Natoyist-Sissina'*. Spokane, WA: Arthur H. Clark Company, 2000.

Wishart, David J. *The Fur Trade of the American West, 1807–1840*. Lincoln: University of Nebraska Press, 1979.

Wood, W. Raymond. *A White-Bearded Plainsman: The Memoirs of Archaeologist W. Raymond Wood*. Salt Lake City: University of Utah Press, 2011.

Wood, W. Raymond, William Hunt, and Randy Williams. *Fort Clark and Its Indian Neighbors: A Trading Post on the Upper Missouri*. Norman: University of Oklahoma Press, 2011.

Wylie, Paul R. *The Irish General: Thomas Francis Meagher*. Norman: University of Oklahoma Press, 2007.

Zimmer, William E. *Frontier Soldier: An Enlisted Man's Journal of the Sioux and Nez Perce Campaigns, 1877*. Ed. Jerome A. Greene. Helena: Montana Historical Society Press, 1998.

Acknowledgments

A nyone who knows my wife, Arlene Wylie, appreciates her energy and the strong support that she has always given me. Whether it is a book, a historical play that we have put on, or a presentation, she is always there to participate and help. It goes far beyond cheerleading. She has been a devoted researcher, proofreader, explorer, and motivator. Without her help these past several years, I could not have pushed this book to publication. I would also like to thank my daughter, Lynne Catherine, and my sons, John and Thomas for their feedback. They know that I have two badges: one says "Ask Me about the Really Swell Book" and the other says "Don't Ask Me about the Damn Book." They know which days to ask the hard questions.

Many people from the academic world have supported me during my research and writing. Kim Allen Scott has given me invaluable insights into Gustavus Cheney Doane. His book *Yellowstone Denied* is a biography of Doane, who has come out as the chief facilitator of the massacre. Heather Hultman and Gary Barnhart, who have been of great help, ably assist him in the Montana State University Special Collections. Mary Murphy of the MSU history department put me in touch with Jeff Bartos, who is working on his PhD there and greatly aided me during this past summer in putting the citations in a proper form. His many suggestions improved the book markedly. Dale Martin has given me great encouragement, as has Jeff Safford, who is now retired from the history department. No one could have been more helpful to me over the years than my friend Pierce

Mullen. He has been my guiding light for a few years now and has always offered his encouragement. I would like to give special thanks to Gordon Bakken of the California State–Fullerton history department, who, before his sad passing, provided guidance not only through his many books but through my personal contacts with him.

At the Montana Historical Society, I can't thank Brian Shovers, Martha Kohl, Zoe Ann Stoltz, and Jody Foley enough for their warm welcomes and all their help. I have been at this for a while now, and they are old friends. I would also like to thank Molly Holz for her guidance, Rich Aarstad for his great knowledge, and Lory Morrow and Becca Kohl for their help and direction in selecting photographic images.

Special thanks go to Ken Robison of the Overholser Historical Research Center in Fort Benton, Montana. He is a noted author, presenter, and researcher. He and Jack Lepley have put me on the right track several times. Doran Degenstein at the Fort Whoop-Up historical museum was of great help with his knowledge of the Piegan Indians.

I made the acquaintance of Darrell Robes Kipp of the Piegan Language Institute in Browning early on. He gave me great insights, and his death last year was a loss. Brenda and Jim Johnston of Browning were always interested in my research. Jim was a fellow townsman from White Sulphur Springs. Before he passed on we were planning some explorations together relating to the book.

I would like to thank Michelle Wright of the Library of Congress for helping me obtain copies of microfilms containing essential correspondence of President Ulysses S. Grant and Generals William Tecumseh Sherman and Philip Sheridan for my research. I would like to thank Brenda Kornick of the Russell Museum for researching the collections of the museum to find the artwork of General de Trobriand, which was done while he was at Fort Shaw.

Douglas Cass and his staff at the Glenbow Archives were extremely helpful during the four days that we spent there. Paul Harrison of the National Archives in Washington, DC, was very helpful in ordering material from there and in working with us when we searched records in the archives for five days.

This book, of course, would not be here if not for the encouragement and direction that I received from Chuck Rankin, the Editor-in-Chief of the University of Oklahoma Press, with the help of Rowan Faye Steineker in getting the illustrations in order. Mapmaker Tom Jonas did a fine job on the complicated maps, which had to be formatted to include everything that needed to be there in the vast territory. Steven Baker did a great job in getting the book put together and once again securing the services of Kathy Burford Lewis, my excellent copyeditor, and Gordon Schroeder, the outstanding indexer. I would also like to thank Paul Hedren and Bill Farr, the reviewers of my manuscript, who offered great suggestions and encouragement.

Index

References to illustrations appear in italic type.